GREAT BOOK OF
Woodworking
Projects

GREAT BOOK OF
Woodworking Projects

50 PROJECTS FOR INDOOR IMPROVEMENTS AND OUTDOOR LIVING

from the Experts at American Woodworker

FOX CHAPEL
PUBLISHING

Published by Fox Chapel Publishing Company, Inc., 1970 Broad St., East Petersburg, PA 17520, 717-560-4703, *www.FoxChapelPublishing.com*

American Woodworker, ISSN 1074-9152, USPS 738-710, is published bimonthly by Woodworking Media, LLC, 90 Sherman St., Cambridge, MA 02140, *www.AmericanWoodworker.com*.

Library of Congress Control Number:
ISBN-13: 978-1-56523-504-5
ISBN-10: 1-56523-504-5

Library of Congress Cataloging-in-Publication Data

Great book of woodworking projects : 50 projects for indoor improvements and outdoor living from the experts at American woodworker / edited by Randy Johnson.
    p. cm.
Includes index.
ISBN 978-1-56523-504-5 (alk. paper)
1. Woodwork--Amateurs' manuals. I. Johnson, Randy. II. American woodworker.
TT185.G7667 2011
684'.08--dc22
                        2010025278

To learn more about the other great books from Fox Chapel Publishing, or to find a retailer near you, call toll-free 800-457-9112 or visit us at *www.FoxChapelPublishing.com*.

Printed in China
Fourth printing

Contents

What You
Can Learn

Kitchen Improvements, page 8

Storage Projects, page 42

Outdoor Living, page 86

Furniture Projects, page 136

Quickies & Gifties, page 208

Kitchen Improvements

Although the kitchen is one of the busiest rooms in a house, it often lacks enough storage for sundry pots, pans, utensils, small appliances, and cleaning supplies—let alone food. But here is some help. This section includes kitchen improvements to help you maximize your space, plus a few stand-alone projects that make storing and serving food a pleasure. For starters, you'll find eight different ways to improve the storage areas in your kitchen, ranging from adding a handy pull-out trash drawer to building a mini-pantry for canned goods. The appliance garage is a favorite not only because it stores small appliances, but also because it hides other items, such as cutting boards, while keeping them close at hand. If you travel to holiday gatherings with your prize pies or cakes, then check out the portable food safe; it's not only handy and attractive, it's also fun to build. For a project that makes a great gift, consider the salad tongs. Spend a couple hours to make a pair—or spend a day and make several.

Toe-kick
drawer and
pull-out trash
drawer add
convenience
to the
kitchen.

by MAC WENTZ

Simple Kitchen Upgrades

THREE EASY PROJECTS THAT ADD STORAGE, CONVENIENCE, AND SMOOTHER RUNNING DRAWERS TO YOUR KITCHEN

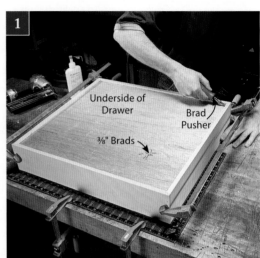

Underside of Drawer

Brad Pusher

⅜" Brads

Assemble and square the drawer box. For no-fuss squaring, try this: With clamps in place, nudge the drawer against a framing square and push a brad through the bottom near each corner. Unless your brad nailer shoots ⅜-in. brads, a brad pusher is the best tool for this.

New Drawers and Slides

If your old drawers are coming apart, here's a way to build new boxes and save the drawer faces. Rabbeted corners and a bottom that slips into dadoes make for quick, simple, sturdy construction (Photo 1).

You can reuse the old slides, or you can upgrade to ball-bearing slides. Ball-bearing slides allow full extension and provide years of smooth, quiet service. These slides are more expensive (around $12 per set of 22-in. slides), but are worth it, especially for large or heavily loaded drawers.

If you upgrade the slides, your new box may need to be slightly different in width from the old. To determine the drawer width, *carefully* measure the width of the cabinet opening and subtract 1 in. to allow for the slides. The slides shown here require at least 1 in. of clearance (½ in. per side) and no more than 1¹⁄₁₆ in. Since correcting a drawer that's too narrow is a lot easier than correcting one that's too wide, I allow 1¹⁄₁₆ in. of clearance (see "Oops!"

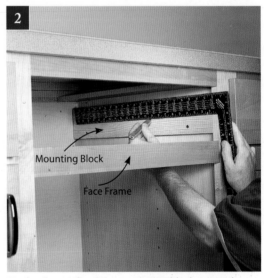

Mounting Block

Face Frame

Mark a "screw line" on a mounting block screwed to the inside of the cabinet. You'll position the slide by driving screws through the line. The location of the line isn't critical—the slides will work fine whether they're mounted high, low or in the middle of the drawer side. But the line must be square to the cabinet front.

page 14). If your cabinets have face frames, you'll need mounting blocks inside the cabinet to provide surfaces that are flush with the inside of the face frame (Photos 2 and 3).

Begin by ripping plywood into strips for the drawer box front, back and sides, but don't cut them to length just yet. Cut dadoes in the plywood strips by making overlapping passes with your tablesaw blade. You're not going for a squeaky-tight fit here; the ¼-in. plywood bottoms should slip easily into the dado.

Cut the strips to length for the drawer sides and rabbet the ends. Use the completed sides to determine the length of the front and back pieces. Cut the drawer bottoms from ¼-in. plywood, undersizing them by about ¹⁄₁₆ in.

Assemble the drawer using glue at the corner joints (Photo 1). The bottom is held by dadoes, so there's no need to glue it.

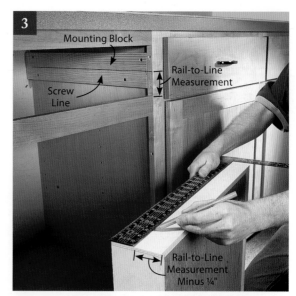

Mark screw lines on the drawer sides. First, measure from the face frame rail to the screw line on the mounting block. Then subtract ¼ in. and measure from the bottom edge of the drawer box to determine the placement of the screw lines on the drawer. That way, the drawer will have ¼-in. clearance above the rail.

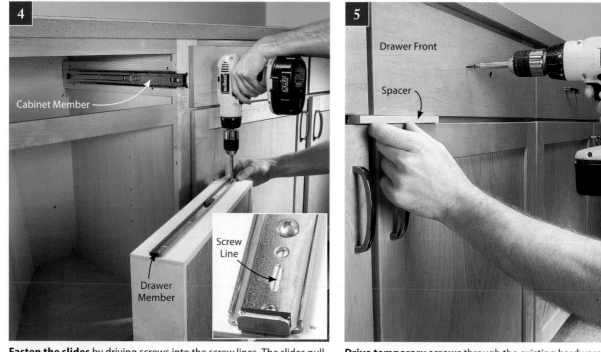

Fasten the slides by driving screws into the screw lines. The slides pull apart for easy mounting. Begin by using only the vertical slots on the drawer member and the horizontal slots on the cabinet member. This lets you adjust the drawer's fit before adding more screws.

Drive temporary screws through the existing hardware holes into the drawer box. Then pull out the drawer and attach the front with permanent screws from inside. A spacer positions the drawer front evenly.

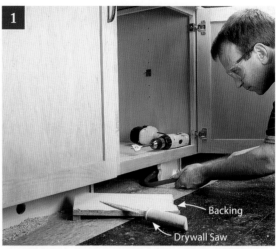

Pry off the toe-kick and remove the backing by drilling a large hole near the center, cutting the backing in half and tearing it out. Then grab a flashlight and check for blocks, protruding screws or anything else that might interfere with the drawer.

Toe-Kick Drawer

The toe space under the cabinets is a great place to add drawers. I mounted the drawer and slides in a self-contained cradle that slips easily under the cabinet (Fig. A). Because the cabinet overhangs the toe-kick by 3 or 4 in., use full-extension slides or "overtravel" slides that extend an extra inch.

The toe-kick shown here was just a strip of ¼-in. plywood backed by ⅝-in. particleboard (Photo 1). You might run into something different, like particleboard without any backing at all.

To determine the dimensions of the cradle, measure the depth and width of the space and subtract ¹⁄₁₆ in. from both to provide some adjustment room. If your floor covering is thicker than ¼ in. (ceramic tile, for example), glue plywood scraps to the underside of the cradle to raise it and prevent the drawer from scraping against the floor when extended. Size the drawer to allow for slides and the cradle's sides. For drawer construction and slide installation, see pages 11 and 12.

You'll have to make drawer fronts and attach them to the boxes using the method shown in Photo 5, page 12. Don't worry too much about an exact match of the finish with your existing cabinets. In that dark toe space, nobody will be able to tell. For hardware, consider handles instead of knobs so you can pull the drawers open with your toe.

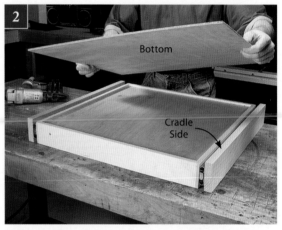

Build a cradle, simply two sides and a bottom, to hold the drawer. Attach the cradle's sides to the slides and drawer, then add the plywood bottom.

Slip the cradle under the cabinet. Then drive a pair of screws through each side and into the cabinet box as far back as you can reach.

Figure A: Toe-Kick Drawer and Cradle

A drawer mounted in a cradle forms a self-contained unit that slips under a base cabinet.

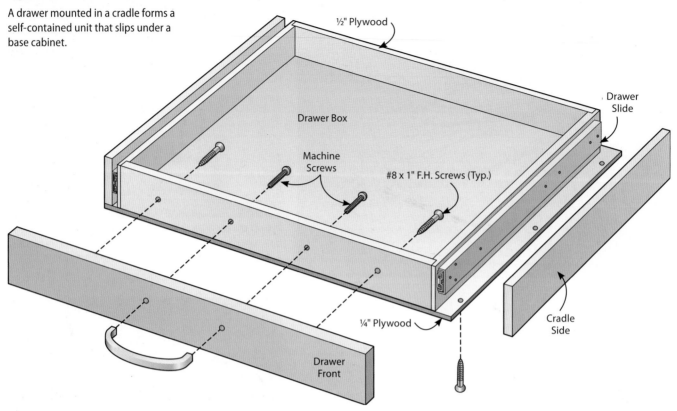

½" Plywood

Drawer Slide

Drawer Box

Machine Screws

#8 x 1" F.H. Screws (Typ.)

¼" Plywood

Cradle Side

Drawer Front

Oops!

The manufacturer of these slides says that the drawer box must be between 1-in. and 1¹⁄₁₆-in. narrower than the drawer opening. They're not kidding. I learned the hard way that a drawer that falls outside this range won't slide smoothly no matter how much grease or brute force you apply.

With such a small margin for error, occasional mistakes are inevitable. And I've found that it's better to err on the too-narrow side of that

Drawer Member

Too-Narrow Drawer

margin. If a drawer turns out a tad too wide, you have to sand down the sides or route a super-shallow dado to recess the slide. Both are a pain. But if the drawer comes out a hair too narrow, a few layers of tape applied to the back of the drawer member is all that's needed. So I'm now in the habit of making drawers 1¹⁄₁₆ in. (instead of just 1 in.) narrower than the opening. Most of the time they glide perfectly. And when they don't, I just grab the masking tape for a quick, easy fix.

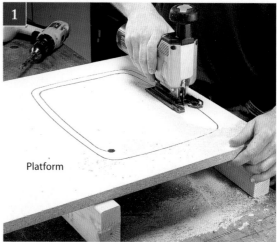

Cut out an opening for the trash bin after placing the bin upside down and tracing around the rim. To allow for the rim, cut about ½-in. inside the outline, then check the fit and enlarge the opening as needed.

Pull-Out Trash Drawer

In one cabinet, replace the shelves with a simple trash can holder mounted on drawer slides. By attaching the existing cabinet door to the front of the pull-out unit, you create a convenient trash drawer. Fig. B and the photos at right show how to build the unit.

Melamine board is a good material for this project because it's easy to clean. A 4 × 8 sheet costs about $25 at home centers. The melamine coating, however, tends to chip during cutting. This chipping is worst where the saw teeth exit the material.

You'll also need iron-on edge banding ($9 at home centers) to cover the exposed edges (Photo 2). When cutting the platform to width, subtract ¹⁄₁₆-in. to allow for the width of the edge banding.

Drawer slides rated for 75-or 100-lb. loads are fine for most drawers. But since this drawer will get more use than most, 120-lb. slides are a good idea.

If the back of your cabinet door is a flat surface, you can run strips of double-faced tape across the front, stick the door in place and fasten it with four small "L" brackets. The back of the door shown here has a recessed panel, so getting it positioned right was a trial-and-error process. Before removing the door, I cut blocks that fit between the door and the floor. Then I extended the unit, rested the door on the blocks, and attached two brackets. The resulting fit wasn't quite perfect, so I tried again before adding the remaining brackets.

Edge band the melamine and file away the excess edge banding. To avoid loosening the banding, cut only as you push the file forward, not as you pull back. If you do loosen the edge banding, just reapply with the iron.

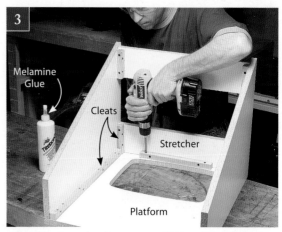

Assemble the unit with screws and ¾-in. x ¾-in. cleats. Be sure to use coarse-threaded screws; fine threads won't hold in particleboard. For extra strength, you can use glue that's made especially for melamine's slick surface.

Figure B: Pull-Out Trash Drawer

Made from melamine-coated particleboard, this trash drawer is simple enough to build and install in a day.

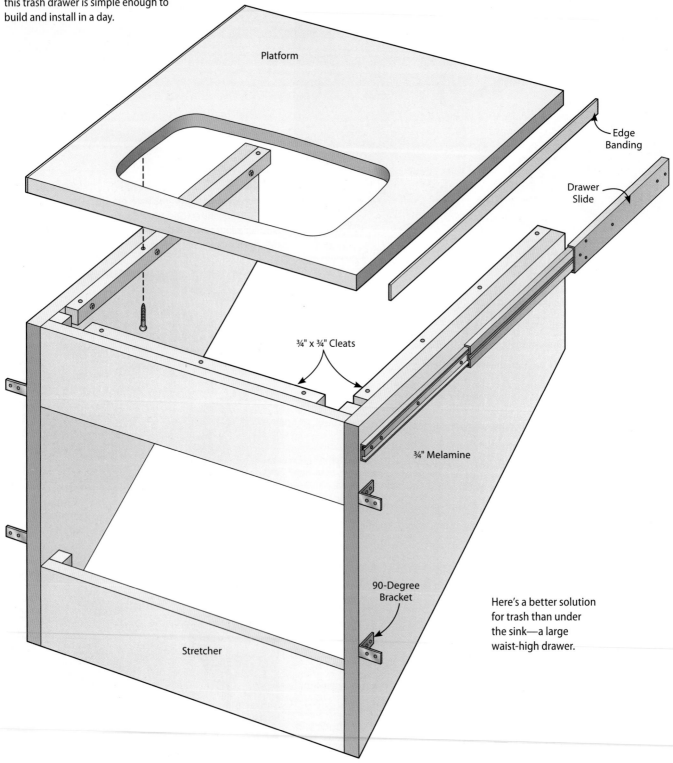

Platform

Edge Banding

Drawer Slide

¾" x ¾" Cleats

¾" Melamine

90-Degree Bracket

Stretcher

Here's a better solution for trash than under the sink—a large waist-high drawer.

Scrap-Wood Cutting Boards

I make beautiful cutting boards from gnarly offcuts. Maple, beech, cherry and birch are safe woods to use for serving food.

Hand plane boards that are too short to flatten with your jointer and planer.

Remove decayed or unstable wood using a high-speed rotary tool equipped with a round or pear-shaped bit.

Fill cavities with slow-setting epoxy and level with the board's surface. I mix in artists oil paint to add color. Here I've added ivory black, but I often mix bright colors to create a dramatic effect.

Prepare the Board

Scrap pieces usually need two or three operations: removing bark, flattening the surfaces and filling voids with epoxy. After you remove bark, clean the surface with a brass brush to get rid of grit and other loose material. Then sand.

Flatten the surfaces before you fill the voids. This takes longer than filling the voids first, because you have to remove the excess epoxy by hand. But epoxy can dull a sharp edge—why risk your jointer or planer knives when you can sand or chisel off the excess?

If the board you've chosen is more than 12" long, you can use your jointer and planer to flatten it.

If the board is too short to be milled, savor the moment; this is a great opportunity to hone your hand-planing skills (Photo 2).

If your scraps are long enough, but too wide for your jointer, flatten them using only your planer. With the knives set to make a light cut, run the board cupped-face-down until the face you're planing is flat. Then flip the board and flatten the cupped side. Use a sled if the board is twisted. Shim unsupported areas caused by the twist before planing. Once one face is planed, you won't need the sled to flatten the other face.

Use a thin-bladed spatula to work the epoxy into narrow cracks and crevices. Dab on wax to keep the epoxy from draining out the end of a check.

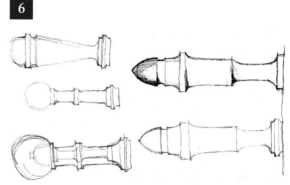

I sketch new handle designs for each cutting board. All of the boards I build are unique, so it makes sense that the handles should be, too.

It's easiest to turn two handles on the same blank, with the tenons facing one another. Then you can turn one long tenon.

Test-fit the handle to make sure it seats fully. It's okay if the tenon is a bit loose, because epoxy can fill gaps and still create a strong bond.

Use a chisel to finish shaping the handle after it's glued to the board. Saw off the waste first and complete the job by sanding.

Rub on flaxseed or walnut oil. Then sand with 400-grit wet/dry sandpaper. Wipe the board dry and let the oil cure for several days.

Clean and Fill the Cavities

Cavities in a board are a natural home for minerals, sand and dirt to settle in over the years—these contaminants will dull your chisels and carving gouges. That's why I use a high-speed rotary tool equipped with a carbide bit to remove decayed wood (Photo 3).

Use slow-setting epoxy to fill the cavities. I usually color the epoxy (Photo 4). For shallow cavities, just pour in the epoxy. If the void goes all the way through the board, seal the opening on the back side with masking tape. Use a spatula to work the epoxy into awkward cracks and small dents (Photo 5). When the epoxy is dry—but before it has fully cured—remove the excess by hand with a chisel, hand plane, or sandpaper.

Turn and Install the Handle

I never make two handles alike, so I have to come up with novel shapes every time I turn a new one (Photo 6). I use this opportunity to explore interesting resources in the environment around me. Architectural details, mechanical components and natural formations are all sources of inspiration. Sometimes, I laminate the handle blanks.

It's most efficient to turn two handles out of one long blank (Photo 7). The tenons on the ends of the handles are the only parts that must be accurately turned. I turn 1" dia. tenons for thick cutting boards (1½" and up); anything thinner gets a ¾" tenon. Always make the tenons longer than necessary and cut them to length when you fit the handle to the board.

If you orient the handles so they meet in the middle, you can turn one long tenon. But if you're used to working in one direction, from the headstock toward the tailstock, for example, it may be easier to orient the handles in the same direction.

Establish the tenon's diameter by plunging in with a parting tool at several locations along its length, using calipers to gauge the depth. Complete the tenon by removing the waste with a spindle gouge and finishing with a skew chisel.

Shape the handles' beads, coves and fillets with spindle gouges and the skew. Sand the handles while they're still on the lathe; remove them to cut them apart. Use the handles' unfinished ends as clamping surfaces when you glue them in.

Drill a hole in the board and test-fit the handle (Photo 8). Then brush epoxy into the hole and around the tenon. Install the handle and clamp it until the epoxy cures. Remove the clamps and lay the board on your bench. If it rocks because the handle's diameter is too big, plane or sand the handle flush on both sides, so the board sits flat. Then finish shaping the end of the handle (Photo 9). Sand each board with 150-, 220- and 320-grit sandpaper before you apply the finish.

Food-Safe Finishes

I prefer using flaxseed oil or walnut oil for finishing (Photo 10). Unlike the vegetable or mineral oils that are often used as food-safe finishes for wood, flaxseed and walnut oil completely cure and polymerize. They're very easy to apply, they enhance the wood's natural beauty and scratches don't show as they do on varnish and other surface-film finishes. You should be aware, though, that some people are allergic to walnuts. If this is a concern, go with flaxseed oil. Both oils are commonly available at health food stores.

Weekend Kitchen Projects

HERE ARE THREE QUICK WAYS TO IMPROVE STORAGE SPACE IN ANY KITCHEN

Keep cleaning supplies at your fingertips!
Want a **sink cabinet shelf** that's better than store-bought plastic or wire racks? Make one that mounts securely to the frame of your paneled door, has the same look as your cabinet and maximizes space because it's custom fit.

Store knives within easy reach!
This **countertop knife rack** stores a complete set of knives right where you need them. The lipped edges conceal a hole you cut in the countertop. You can easily remove the rack for cleaning.

Reach that stuff in the back!
Roll-out kitchen trays replace awkward, deep shelves. They'll fit in any cabinet, are adjustable in height and are especially handy for older or disabled people. Budget about $45 per cabinet for the hardware and wood.

Countertop Knife Rack

Store up to nine knives in a handy rack that puts sharp edges out of the reach of children. We've arranged the slots to fit a particular set of knives (Fig. A), but you can alter the pattern to suit your set. Experiment by cutting slots in a piece of cardboard. Then make the rack from any hardwood you like. After cutting, sand the rack smooth and finish it with three coats of spray polyurethane. A spray finish is easy to get into the knife slots.

Install a knife-blade shield under the counter (Fig. B and Photo 4). You may need to slightly shorten a drawer to make room for the shield. Also, make sure the shield doesn't interfere with the drawer slides.

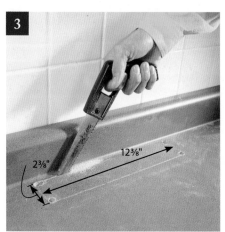

Mark the rack's outline and the knife slot locations on an oversized piece of hardwood. An oversized board provides support for your router and room to clamp a guide board.

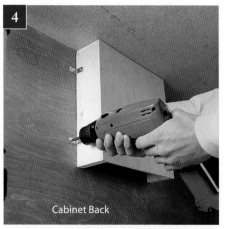

Cut the knife slots with a plunge router. Cut out the rack, round over the top edges with a router and cut rabbets around the bottom edges to form lips.

Cut an opening in your countertop with a keyhole saw. Lay out the opening far enough from the backsplash so the lips of the knife rack sit flat on the countertop. Then drill holes in the corners and saw away. (You may have enough room to use a jigsaw to make the long cut farthest from the backsplash.) Add a couple dabs of silicone caulk to the sides of the rack so it fits tight in the slightly oversized opening.

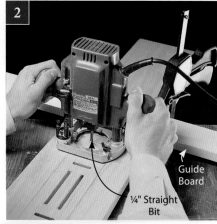

Fasten a blade shield to the back of the cabinet, underneath the knife rack. Build the shield from ¼-in. plywood and ¾-in. solid wood.

Figure A: Knife Rack Layout

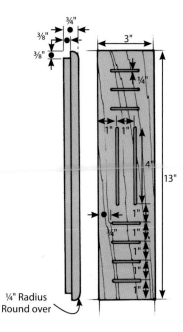

¼" Radius Round over

Figure B: Knife Blade Shield

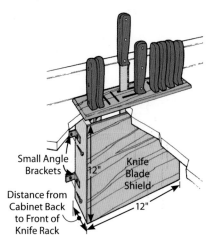

Small Angle Brackets

Knife Blade Shield

Distance from Cabinet Back to Front of Knife Rack

EDITORS: TOM CASPAR, DAVID RADTKE AND ART ROOZE • ART DIRECTION: PATRICK HUNTER, MARCIA WILLISTON AND BOB UNGAR • PHOTOGRAPHY: BILL ZUEHLKE • ILLUSTRATION: RON CHAMBERLAIN

Sink Cabinet Shelf

It's easy to customize this catchall shelf to fit your cabinet doors. Measure the opening of your cabinet (not the door!) and plug your numbers into the Cutting List below. The shelf unit clears the opening by ¼-in. on all sides.

You can mount this shelf on a cabinet door made of plywood or a door with a raised panel. Solid mounting strips get screwed into the stiles of the door, not the thinner panel.

> If you have small children, be sure that cabinets with cleaning products and other toxic substances have child-proof latches attached.

Warning: Guard must be removed for this step. Use care!

Cut two pairs of ¾-in.-wide, ¼-in.-deep dadoes in the sides: a pair for the two shelves and a pair for the mounting strips. Line up the mounting-strip dado with the shelf dado.

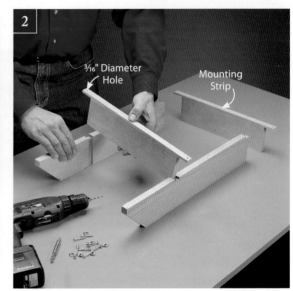

Slip the shelves into their dadoes. First drill holes for the mounting screws ⅜-in. from the end of the mounting strips. Glue the mounting strips to the shelves. Drill pilot holes in the sides and fasten the shelves with long screws. Fasten the rails to the front of the shelves with short screws and finish washers.

Clamp and screw the shelves to your door, using ¾-in. screws and finish washers. You may need to add a third hinge and a magnetic catch if the weight of the loaded shelves prevents the door from closing easily.

Cutting List

Name	Qty.	Th	W	L
Sides	2	¾"	3½"	½" less than height of cabinet opening
Shelves	2	¾"	3¼"	3" less than width of cabinet opening
Rails	2	¼"	¾"	1" more than shelves
Mounting Strips	2	¼"	¾"	2½" more than shelves

Hardware

Eight 1¼" #8 Oval-Head Wood Screws
Eight ¾" #8 Oval-Head Wood Screws
16 Finish Washers

Roll-Out Kitchen Trays

Trays on wheels put all the pots and pans in a deep cabinet within easy reach. If your doors can't open more than 90-degrees, plan on making the horizontal supports wider than shown here. There must be ¼-in. clearance between the slides and the inside faces of your doors.

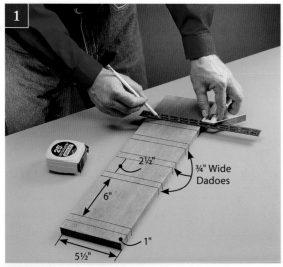

Mark the dadoes on one wide hardwood board. The four upper dadoes make the top shelf adjustable. Cut dadoes ¼-in. deep, then rip the wide board into four vertical supports. Cut horizontal supports to hold the slides.

2½"
¾" Wide Dadoes
6"
1"
5½"

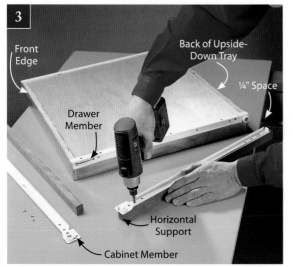

Back Vertical Support
Horizontal Support
Front Vertical Support
Face Frame
¼" Beyond Face Frame

Glue the vertical supports in place with a couple dabs of construction adhesive. Then fit the horizontal supports tightly in the dadoes, without glue. The horizontal supports must stick out at least ¼ in. beyond the face frame of your cabinet door. You'll need this clearance for the drawer side to travel freely.

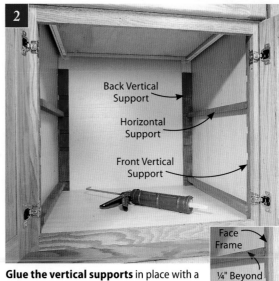

Front Edge
Back of Upside-Down Tray
¼" Space
Drawer Member
Horizontal Support
Cabinet Member

Build the plywood trays with plywood or hardwood sides. The corners may be simply butted together. Align the slide's drawer members flush with the front of the tray. Fasten the slides to the trays and the horizontal supports. Place the rear end of the cabinet member at least ¼ in. away from the end of the horizontal support.

Cutting List

Name	Qty.	Material	Th	W	L
Front vertical supports	2	Hardwood	¾"	¾"	Height of cabinet opening
Back vertical supports	2	Hardwood	¾"	1¾"	Height of cabinet opening
Horizontal supports	4	Hardwood	¾"	1"	About 1" less than cabinet depth
Tray bottom	2	Plywood	¾"	*	**
Tray sides	4	Hardwood	¾"	2¼"	To fit tray

Hardware

Two pairs of Euro-style, epoxy-coated drawer slides. They should be 2" shorter than the overall depth of your cabinet. Standard base cabinets are 24" deep. Slides are sold in increments of 2" from 12" to 24."

* Width is about 3" less than the cabinet opening. To figure the tray bottom's exact width, subtract the combined thickness of two sides plus 1" from the distance between the installed horizontal supports.

** Length is 2½" less than cabinet depth, measured from the back of the cabinet to the back of the face frame.

by RANDY JOHNSON

Portable Food Safe

THIS SAFE FEATURES TWO SLIDING DOORS AND TWO REMOVABLE TRAYS

No more smashed frosting, cracked crusts or capsized casseroles. You can take your culinary creations anywhere with this portable food safe. You can adapt the design to accommodate two pie plates, a deep casserole dish or a 9 in. by 13 in. baking pan. If you're a bread baker, size the safe for two loaf pans with a pull-out cutting board on the bottom. Whatever you're toting, it will arrive in style and in one piece!

Pine's a good choice for wood because it's easy to work and light in weight. Acrylic doors allow for peeking and the brass handle is an easy grip. Total cost: around $35. (Note: The following how-to contains specific instructions for the food safe pictured here.)

The four sides are wide so you may have to glue up some stock. Plane the material to ⅝-in. thickness and mill to width and length (Fig. A). I like to cut the parts about ¹⁄₁₆-in. long so each box joint protrudes about ¹⁄₃₂ in. It's better to sand the pins flush to the sides than the sides flush to the pins! Once the box joints are milled (Photo 1), take the two side panels and make the dadoes for the two sliding doors. The acrylic I used came a little under thickness so it worked well to make the dadoes right at ¼ in. Next make the dado for the upper sliding tray. Now is a good time to finish sand the inside surfaces.

EDITOR: DAVE MUNKITTRICK • ART DIRECTION: JOEL SPIES • ILLUSTRATION: FRANK ROHRBACH • PHOTOGRAPHY: MIKE KRIVIT PHOTOGRAPHY

Gluing and clamping all four sides at once takes four hands; here's a better way: Dry clamp the four sides, pull the top off the sides and brush glue onto the mating surfaces of the exposed pins. Replace the top and clamp (Photo 2). Make sure the top is square to the sides. When dry, flip over and repeat the gluing process with the bottom panel. When the glue is dry, you can sand the joints flush. Cut the tray bottoms from ⅛-in. hardboard. The upper tray bottom is wider than the lower tray because it needs a lip to slide in the side dado. Cut and attach the rim boards.

Your hardware store can cut the acrylic doors for you. If you choose to cut them yourself, use an 80-tooth, carbide-tipped triple chip design or a fine-tooth steel plywood blade. To remove saw marks on the edges of the acrylic, use a sanding block. The wood trim on the doors serves as a finger grip and is attached with epoxy. Scuff the acrylic with sandpaper and tape off any place you don't want smeared with epoxy. Peel off the tape when the epoxy is still semisoft.

Stain and finish to your liking. Add the handle and you're ready to go.

Routing box joints with a dovetail jig is very fast (this one is by Keller). The jig is easy to set up, reliably accurate and can also be used to make dovetails.

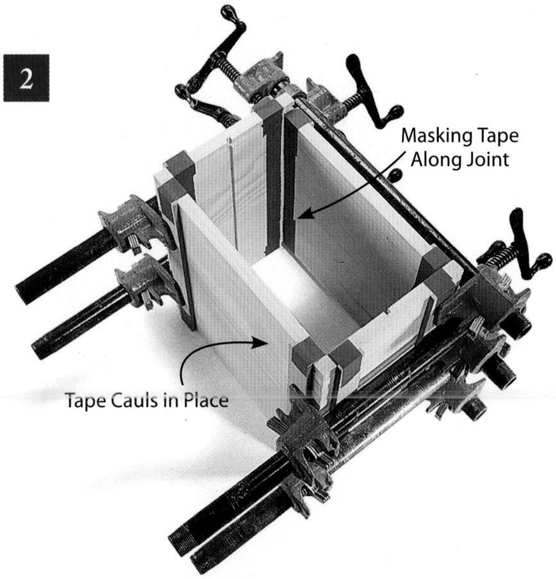

Masking Tape Along Joint

Tape Cauls in Place

Clamp up the box using cauls to clear the protruding pins. Taping the cauls in place makes the job easier. For easy cleanup, line the corners with masking tape to catch glue squeeze out.

Cutting List*

Overall Dimensions 7½" H x 11 13/16" W x 11 13/16" D

Part	Ref.	Qty.	Dimensions
Sides	A	2	⅝" x 11 13/16" x 7 9/16"**
Bottom	B	1	⅝" x 11 13/16" x 11⅞"**
Top	C	1	⅝" x 10 11/16" x 11⅞"**
Door trim/handles	D	2	5/16" x ⅝" x 10⅝"
Acrylic doors	E	2	¼" x 11⅛" x 6⅞"
Upper tray bottom	F	1	⅛" x 11" x 10⅝"
Lower tray bottom	G	1	⅛" x 10⅝" x 10⅝"
Front and back rim boards	H	4	¾" x ⅞" x 10⅝"
Side rim boards	J	4	¾" x ⅞" x 8⅝"

*Designed for two 9-in. pie plates, Corning Ware P-309 9" x 1¼." Box joint pins are 9/16" wide.

**Includes 1/16" extra (1/32" each end) for sanding pins flush after box is assembled.

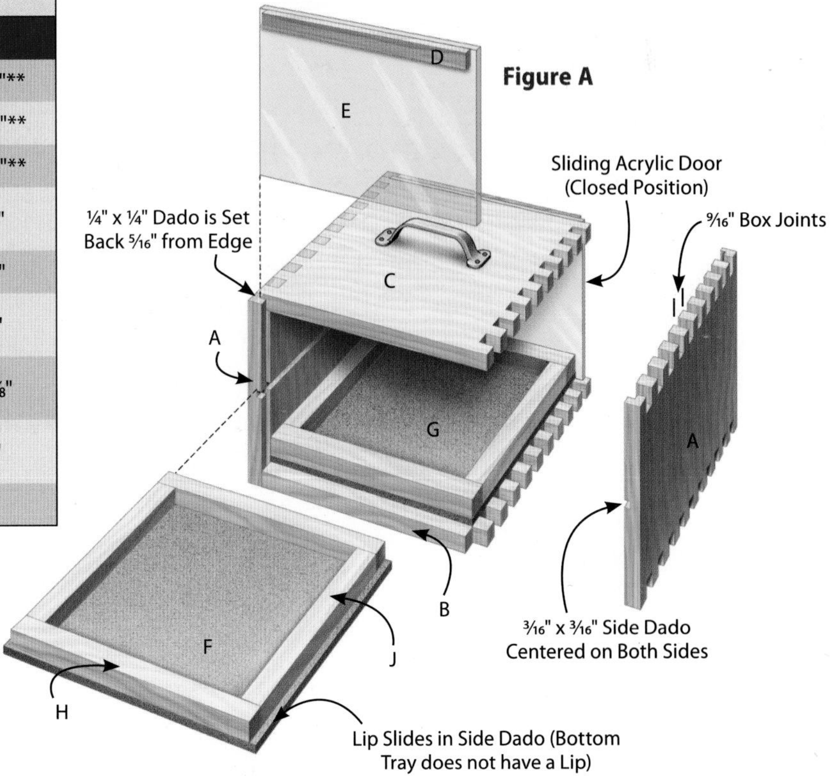

Figure A

Sliding Acrylic Door (Closed Position)

9/16" Box Joints

¼" x ¼" Dado is Set Back 5/16" from Edge

3/16" x 3/16" Side Dado Centered on Both Sides

Lip Slides in Side Dado (Bottom Tray does not have a Lip)

by TIM JOHNSON

Nesting Trays

EYE-CATCHING AND PRACTICAL, THESE HANDY CARRYALLS ARE SURE TO PLEASE

Here's your chance to cut lots of corners and still get great-looking results. These sturdy trays are easy to build, thanks to their simple box joints and template-routed curves. You don't need a super-equipped shop, just a tablesaw with a dado set, a router table and a drill press. You've probably saved enough scrap pieces from other projects to build the trays and the jigs, but even if you buy lumber and plywood, you can make this trio of trays for less than $60.

Cut the Box Joints

1. Prepare your stock, including extra pieces for test-cutting. Cut blanks for the ends (A1, B1, and C1, Fig. A, page 29) and sides (A2, B2, and C2) to length, but leave them ⅛ in. oversize in width. All the ends must be squarely cut.

2. Arrange the pieces for each box and then mark the bottom edge of every one. When you cut the box joints, these marks will correctly orient the pieces in the jig.

3. Box-joint jigs index the workpiece for cutting sockets. (Photo 1). Cutting a series of sockets creates the pins. To make the joint, one piece has pins where the mating piece has sockets.

4. Cut test box joints to dial in a precise fit. This is fussy work, because the tolerances are tiny. The pieces should slide together without binding or rattling. The best jigs have built-in adjustment systems.

5. Cut all the box joints. On the end-piece blanks, cut sockets only as far as their curved profiles dictate. The side-piece blanks are oversize, so you'll have to make an extra pass to complete the top sockets.

Rout the Ends

6. Use the end profile of the large tray (A1, Fig. C, page 29) as a pattern when you make the routing jig (Fig. B, page 29). First, transfer the curved edge profile to the jig's base. Then drill 1-in.-dia. holes with a Forstner bit to establish the ends of the handle hole. Finish rough-cutting the handle hole with a jigsaw. Then rough-cut the edge profile.

7. Smooth the edge profile using an oscillating spindle sander or a sanding drum in your drill press. Install a ¾-in.-dia. spindle or drum to smooth the handle hole.

8. Use a large end-piece blank to position the jig's fence. Each end has six pins. Fasten the fence so the top pins are flush with the base's curved profile.

9. Install the stops after centering the large end-piece blank. Mount the toggle clamps.

10. Draw edge profiles and handle holes on all the end blanks after installing them in the jig. Make spacers (W, X, Y and Z, Fig. B) to position the medium and small blanks.

11. Rough-saw all the curved profiles about ¹⁄₁₆ in. away from the pattern lines. To rough out the handle holes, drill ⅞-in.-dia. holes and use a jigsaw to saw out the waste.

12. Rout the edge profiles with a top-bearing flush-trim bit (Photo 2). Then rout the handle holes (Photo 3).

Assemble the Trays

13. Saw grooves for the plywood bottoms (A3, B3 and C3). On the side pieces, the grooves align with the top of the first pin (Fig. A). On the end pieces, they align with the top of the first socket. Because ¼-in.-thick plywood is often undersize, you can't use a dado set. Use your regular blade and make two passes. Adjust the fence between passes to widen the groove.

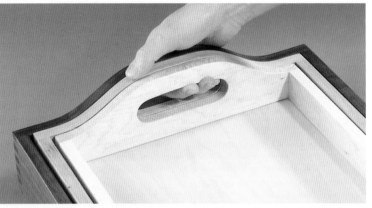

The ends of the trays match, so you can comfortably carry all three.

Box-Joint Jig

Great-looking box-joints are easy to make. I used a shop-made jig and my tablesaw, but these sturdy joints can also be cut on a router table or with a dovetailing jig.

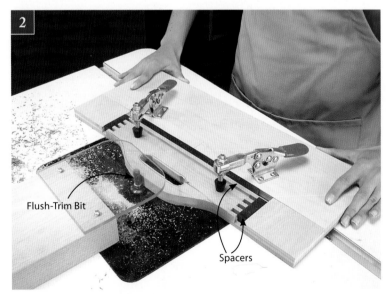

Flush-Trim Bit

Spacers

Rout the curved ends of all three boxes using the same jig (Fig. B, page 29). The large box's ends exactly fit the opening. Spacers center the ends of the medium and small boxes, so the profiles and handle holes all match.

Rout the handle holes after making sure the workpiece is securely held. With the router unplugged, center the bit inside the roughsawn opening. Hold the jig steady so the bit spins freely when you power up. Then rout counterclockwise.

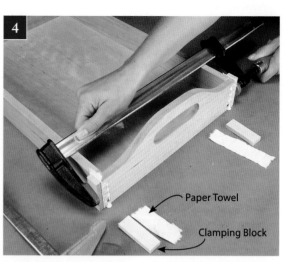

Paper Towel

Clamping Block

Protect the end grain when you glue the tray together. Paper towels absorb squeezed-out glue, so it doesn't soak deeply into the wood. Because of the towels, the clamping blocks knock off easily after the glue has dried.

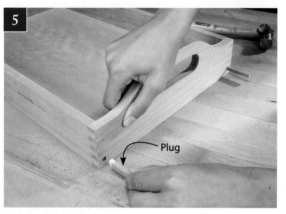

Plug

Fill holes left by the bottom grooves with end-grain plugs. Once cut and sanded flush, they'll match the end-grain pins.

Level the sides and ends with a block plane or by sanding.

14. Assemble the boxes without glue to make sure everything fits. Rip the sides to stand 1/32 in. above the ends. Disassemble the boxes for sanding.

15. Glue the boxes together. Spread a thin layer of glue on all the pins and sockets. Use a brush and glue with an extended open time. Squeeze a thin bead of glue into the grooves for the bottoms, too.

16. Clamp each box using blocks to fully seat the joints (Photo 4). Make sure the boxes are square.

17. After the glue has dried, remove the clamps and knock off the blocks. Dampen any paper that remains attached; after about a minute, it'll scrub right off. Remove any remaining glue.

18. Cut plugs (D) and fill the holes in the ends of the trays (Photo 5).

19. True up the sides and ends (Photo 6).

Spray on the Finish

20. Go over the boxes again with fine sandpaper; the grain will be raised in any area that has been wet. Slightly round all the sharp corners, especially those around the handle holes.

21. For small projects like this one, I prefer aerosol finishes. Spray on at least two light coats. Let the finish dry and sand lightly between each coat. Urethane finishes provide the best protection.

PROJECT REQUIREMENTS AT A GLANCE

Materials:

- 18 lineal ft. of ½-in.-thick x 5-in.-wide hardwood lumber
- One-quarter sheet ¼-in. hardwood plywood
- One-half sheet ½-in. Baltic birch plywood (for jigs)
- Wood glue

Tools:

Tablesaw, dado set, router table, drill press, jig saw, 3-in.-dia. and ¾-in.-dia. sanding drums, 1-in.-dia. and ⅞-in.-dia. Forstner bits, ½-in. flush-trim router bit with top-mounted bearing, block plane, assorted clamps

Cost: About $60

Cutting List

Overall Dimensions: 4¼" x 13" x 20"

Part	Name	Qty.	Dimensions
Large Tray			14¼" x 13" x 20"
A1	End	2	½" x 4¼" x 13"
A2	Side	2	½" x 2¾" x 20"
A3	Bottom*	1	¼" x 12¹¹⁄₃₂" x 19¹¹⁄₃₂"
Medium Tray			3¾" x 11¾" x 18¾"
B1	End	2	½" x 3¾" x 11¾"
B2	Side	2	½" x 2¼" x 18¾"
B3	Bottom*	1	¼" x 11³⁄₃₂" x 18³⁄₃₂"
Small Tray			3¼" x 10½" x 17½"
C1	End	2	½" x 3¼" x 10½"
C2	Side	2	½" x 1¾" x 17½"
C3	Bottom*	1	¼" x 9²⁷⁄₃₂" x 16²⁷⁄₃₂"
D	Plug	12	Cut to fit
Routing Jig			3¼" x 10½" x 17½"
W	Medium end spacer	2	½" x ⅝" x 2½"
X	Medium bottom spacer	1	½" x ½" x 11¾"
Y	Small end spacer	2	½" x 1¼" x 2½"
Z	Small bottom spacer	1	½" x 1" x 10½"

* Plywood

Figure A: Exploded View

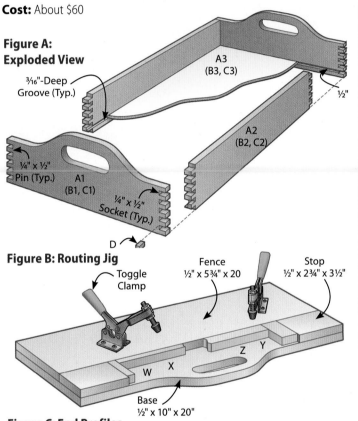

³⁄₁₆"-Deep Groove (Typ.)

A3 (B3, C3)

½"

¼" x ½" Pin (Typ.)

A1 (B1, C1)

A2 (B2, C2)

¼" x ½" Socket (Typ.)

D

Figure B: Routing Jig

Toggle Clamp

Fence ½" x 5¾" x 20

Stop ½" x 2¾" x 3½"

Z   Y

W   X

Base ½" x 10" x 20"

Figure C: End Profiles

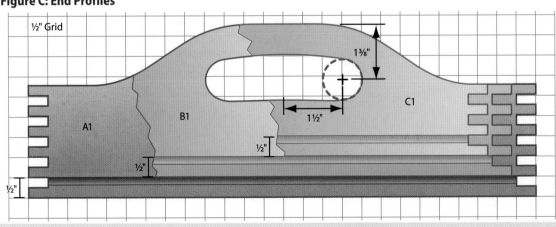

½" Grid

1⅜"

A1

B1

C1

1½"

½"

½"

½"

ART DIRECTION: JODIE DELOHERY · PHOTOGRAPHY: MIKE HABERMAN · ILLUSTRATION: DAN WESTERBERG

by RICK CHRISTOPHERSON

Appliance Garage

CLEAR OFF YOUR COUNTERTOPS! HIDE YOUR APPLIANCES BEHIND EXTRA-WIDE BI-FOLD DOORS

An appliance garage provides functional storage for the hodgepodge of appliances that clutter kitchen countertops. Close the doors, and everything is out of sight. Open the doors, and the appliances are at the ready.

Unlike most appliance garages that have a roll-top tambour door, this bifold door design provides twice the opening size, is easy enough to build in a weekend, and costs less than $100. For smooth operation, a roller bearing and routed track guide the doors.

Figure A: Appliance Garage Exploded View

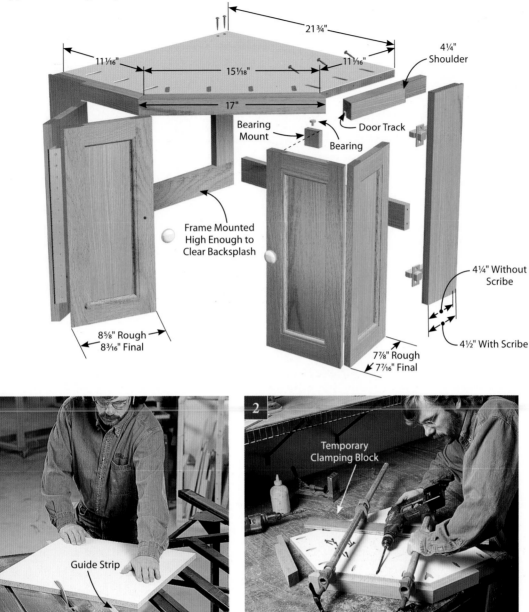

Cut the plywood top at 45 degrees using a ¾-in. strip of scrap wood as a guide in your saw's miter slot. Screw the guide strip to the underside of the plywood. *Saw guard removed for photo clarity. Use yours!*

Install the face frame to the top using pocket-hole screws. The clamps hold the frame in place while the screws are driven in.

Most factory-built corner cabinets are 24-in. on each side with a 17-in. diagonal face. Measure yours to verify the size. If your cabinets are a different size from these you can resize the dimensions following the instructions in "Resizing Your Garage," p. 32.

Cutting the Top

To cut the top of the appliance garage, start out with a 21¾-in.-square piece of plywood or melamine-coated particle board. From this you need to cut the 45-degree face using the dimensions shown in Fig. A. If you don't have a sliding table on your tablesaw, you can use the miter-slot in your saw's table as a guide (Photo 1).

After the top is cut, drill for pocket holes across the front three edges, as shown in Photo 2. These pocket holes are used to secure the face frame.

Resizing Your Garage

If your existing diagonal corner cabinet is not the same size as discussed here, you will have to modify the dimensions of the garage. The easiest method for changing the dimensions is to draw them out on a piece of plywood.

Draw the size of your existing corner cabinet on a sheet of plywood, then draw three offset lines at ¾-in., 1¾-in., and 2¼-in. setback from the first. Because the appliance garage is ¾-in. smaller than the existing cabinet, the ¾-in. offset line is the front of the face frame and doors. To determine the size of the bifold doors, measure the length of the ¾-in. offset line across the front and divide by two. This will be the width of the center doors. The outside doors are ¾-in. narrower than the center doors. (Remember to make your doors ⅜-in. oversized for trimming.) Mark the width of the outside doors on the plywood. The width of the cabinet stiles can then be measured from this plywood template, but add an extra ¼-in. to this measurement for the scribe (see "Installing the Garage" p. 35).

The 1¾-in. offset line gives you the dimensions of the template for routing the door track, and the 2¼-in. offset line gives you the dimensions for the top of the cabinet.

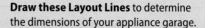

Draw these Layout Lines to determine the dimensions of your appliance garage.

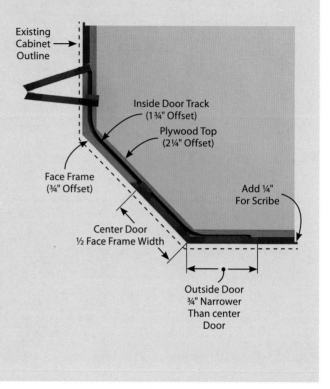

Existing Cabinet Outline

Inside Door Track (1¾" Offset)

Plywood Top (2¼" Offset)

Face Frame (¾" Offset)

Center Door ½ Face Frame Width

Add ¼" For Scribe

Outside Door ¾" Narrower Than center Door

Making the Face Frame

The face frame stock is 1½-in. thick by 2-in. wide, and has 4¼-in. shoulders on each end where the frame meets the side stiles. The material is made from two pieces of ¾-in. stock (48-in. by 2⅛-in. by ¾-in., and 39-in. by 2⅛-in. by ¾-in.) face-glued together. One piece is shorter than the other to create the shoulders. The stock is oversized to allow for trimming. Center the 39-in. piece onto the 48-in. piece and glue it so there is a 4½-in. shoulder on each end. After the glue is dry, joint one edge so the pieces are flush. Rip and joint the other edge to 2-in.

Next, trim the ends of the board so the two shoulders are 4¼ in. long. With the miter saw set to 22½ degrees, cut the face frame parts from this stock. I cut my joints slightly long at first to check the angles. When the joints are tight, I make the final cut to length without changing the saw's settings.

Installing the Face Frame

Using pocket-hole screws to secure the face frame to the top is the fastest and easiest method. After applying glue to the edges, clamp the righthand frame to the plywood, and drive in the screws. The end of the frame should be flush with the back of the plywood. The top edges should be flush as well.

Next, attach the center part of the frame. Screw a clamping block to the top of the plywood, but make sure your screws don't poke all the way through the plywood top. With this in place, clamp the middle frame the same way you did the side frame (Photo 2). Finish with the left-hand frame piece.

Routing the Door Track

To rout the door track into the bottom edge of the face frame, you need a ⁹⁄₁₆ in., top-bearing pattern bit for your plunge router. You'll also need to make a template for the router to follow.

Cut a piece of scrap plywood for the template which is 1-in. inset from the front of the face frame. Next, round the corners of the template with a 4-in. radius, using a smooth, sweeping motion with your belt sander. Position the pattern 1 in. back from the front of the face frame, and clamp it down. Add spacers under the template for clamping.

Routing from left to right (counterclockwise), make several shallow passes until the depth of the dado is about ½-in. (Photo 3). Don't let the router wander—jogs in the track will interfere with smooth door-roller operation. When completed, soften the sharp edges of the track and sand the inside of the dado.

Side Stiles and Frames

The vertical sides of the cabinet (the stiles) determine the height of the garage and support the doors. The length of the stiles should be ⅛-in. to ¼-in. shorter than the distance from your countertop to the upper cabinet.

Rip the stiles to 4½-in. wide (¼-in. wider than the face frame shoulders), and cut them to the length needed. Then rabbet the back edge ¼-in. wide by ½-in. deep to make scribing the cabinet to the wall easier.

When screwing the stiles to the face frame, angle the screws as shown in Photo 4 to draw the side joint tight. Because the doors attach to these stiles, it is very important that they are mounted square to the frame.

Using 2-in. frame stock, assemble the mounting frame (Fig. A) to the cabinet. Use pocket-hole construction to hold the frame together.

Figure B: Hinge Cup Location

Bore the Hinge-Cups in the door stiles at the position shown.

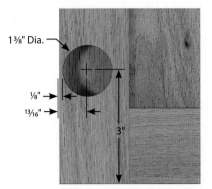

1⅜" Dia.

⅛"

13⁄16"

3"

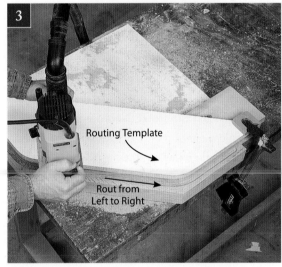

Rout the door track using a ⁹⁄₁₆-in. pattern bit and template. Make several passes to reach the final depth of ½ in. The hold-down clamps also serve as guide stops for the stopped dado.

Routing Template

Rout from Left to Right

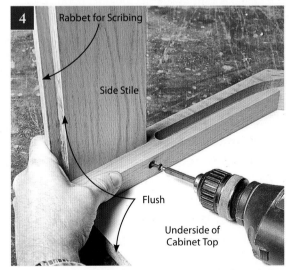

Rabbet for Scribing

Side Stile

Flush

Underside of Cabinet Top

Screw the stiles to the frame using screws tilted at a slight angle to draw the side joint tight.

Front of Door

Tape Front and
Back of Door

Install the piano hinge by taping the door joint closed.

Build up for Bearing

Door Track

Install the hinge baseplates by attaching them to the hinges and fastening them to the stiles. Rough-adjust the hinges so the doors don't bind. *Appliance garage turned upside down.*

Building the Doors

This garage has a frame-and-panel door design to complement the existing doors. It takes two doors to make up each bifold. The outside doors are 7⅞-in. wide, and the center doors are 8⅝-in. wide. These dimensions are ⅜-in. oversized and will be trimmed off when the bevel is cut. The door height should be the same as the opening size. You'll trim the doors later when you square them.

After the doors are built, lightly sand them to flush-up the edges, but don't soften any of the corners yet. Joint one edge from each door. After measuring the cabinet to determine the size of each door, bevel-rip and joint the other edges at 22½ degrees to fit the opening. After the doors are the proper width, square the tops and bottoms so each door is the same height.

Using a 1⅜-in. Forstner bit, bore ½-in.-deep holes in the two outside doors for European cup hinges, positioned as shown in Fig. B. Then install the continuous (piano) hinge to the bifold pairs. To simplify the installation of the hinge, I taped the doors together tightly (Photo 5) before screwing the piano hinges in place.

Next, plane a piece of 1½-in.-wide stock to ½-in. thickness, and cut two pieces 1½ in. by 1½ in. by ½ in. Glue and clamp these pieces to the back side of the center doors (Fig. A). Make sure they are flush to the top and the outside edge where the bearings will be mounted.

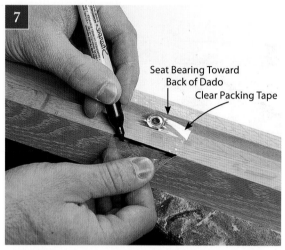

Seat Bearing Toward
Back of Dado

Clear Packing Tape

Mark the bearing locations using tape and a marker. Stick the bearing to the tape and locate it to the rear face of the dado. Mark the front edge of the face frame and transfer these locations to the door.

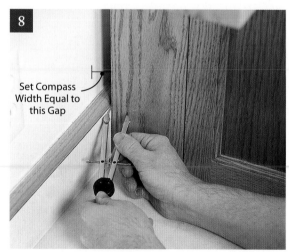

Set Compass
Width Equal to
this Gap

Rough-scribe the cabinet to the existing back splash using a compass and a coping saw. After this is cut out, re-scribe the cabinet for final fit to the wall.

Installing the Doors

I used European cup hinges for the doors because they have 3-dimensional adjustment capabilities. Cup hinges come in two parts—the hinge, and the baseplate. After predrilling the screw holes, screw the hinges to the doors. The baseplates have a small tab on the back that lines up with the edge of the face frame stiles. The easiest method for locating the baseplates is to attach them to the door hinges, place the door in position, and screw the baseplates to the cabinet (Photo 6).

With the doors mounted on the cabinet, locate the position of the track bearings. You have to determine the front-to-rear spacing to ensure the doors are flush to the face frame when closed and also the side-to-side placement so the doors don't bind when fully open. I found that a piece of clear packing tape made a good marking gauge. For the front-to-rear placement, I stuck the bearing to the back of the tape, and inserted it into the dado slot with the bearing touching the back wall of the dado. With a marker I traced the front corner of the face frame, as shown in Photo 7. To mark the side-to-side placement of the bearing, I placed the tape and bearing at the end of the track, fully opened the door, and marked where the edge of the door lined up with the tape.

Using the tape as a template, transfer these positions to the top corner of the door, and drill a hole for the bearing's screw. Because the forces on the bearing are side-to-side, you can mount it by just driving a No. 10 by 1-in. machine screw into the edge of the door.

Finishing the Garage

Sand the garage cabinet completely and soften any sharp edges. When you sand the doors, don't soften the miter joint corners unless the doors are closed. If you soften these corners separately, you will have a visible gap in the bifold. (If you use melamine, be careful not to scuff the surface—the wood stain will discolor it.)

To match the stain color with existing cabinets, take one of the original cabinet doors to a full-service paint store and have them custom-mix a stain to match.

Installing the Garage

The first step is to scribe the garage cabinet to fit the wall. I started by making a rough scribe to fit the existing back splash, as shown in Photo 8. This allowed the garage to be placed closer to the wall for a more accurate final scribe. The garage is ¼-in. oversized, so remove as much of this as needed when fitting it to the wall.

Locate the studs in the wall, and pilot-drill screw holes through the mounting frame. When you screw the cabinet to the wall, be careful not to rack the garage out of square; this will cause the doors to fit poorly. After the garage is in place, install molding to conceal the gap between the garage and the upper cabinet.

Finally, adjust the doors. There are three adjusting screws on each hinge. The front screw is used to flush the door with the face frame. The middle screw moves the door up and down, and the back screw adjusts the side-to-side placement of the door.

Now shove the toaster, the mixer, and the blender in the garage and shut the door. You've got counter space!

by DAVE RADTKE

Wooden Spring Tongs

A GREAT ALL-AROUND KITCHEN UTENSIL

Here's a great kitchen utensil you're sure to find indispensable. These wooden tongs feature a unique spring tab mechanism built into a knuckle joint. The joint allows the tongs to be folded flat for storage. When the tongs are opened up, the spring tabs contact each other so the tongs want to spring back open (Fig. A, p. 37). This is the same action found in those metal tongs used by chefs the world over. Tongs are perfect for everything from plucking corn-on-the-cob out of boiling water to fetching a trapped piece of toast from a toaster. Of course, they also shine as a salad server. It's one of those projects you'll enjoy using so much that you'll make more as gifts for friends and family. No doubt there's lots of scrap wood in your shop just looking to be fashioned into something useful. Closed grain or semi-porous woods like cherry, walnut, and maple make good tong material. The tongs are easy to make. There's a little bit of steam bending, but even that is low tech and straight forward. Feel free to experiment with the length and width of the tongs for a variety of uses.

Create the Spring Tabs

Each half of the tong starts out exactly the same. Cut the two tong blanks (Fig. A.). Next, set your table saw to rip tabs on each blank (Photo 1). Mark the outer face on each blank and rip the tabs with the outer face up.

Cut two ½-in. long spacers to fill the saw kerfs at the end of one of the tongs. Glue and clamp them to the outer tabs only (Photo 2). Let the glue cure.

Measure down one inch from the end of each blank for the starting point of the bearing angles on each tang. Use a small hand saw to cut a 60-degrees angle on the center tine of the tong with spacers. Then cut the two outer tines on the other blank (Photo 3). It's necessary to insert a spacer to cut the center tab. Take care not to push the tab up too far or it may crack.

Next, fill a tray with two inches of hot water and submerge the blanks (Photo 4). Let the blanks soak for about half an hour. Pull the blanks out of the water and separate the tabs with a spacer (Photo 5). Apply heat with a heat gun set on high for about 1½ minutes. Keep the heat gun moving on all sides of the tabs to avoid scorching and to heat the tab uniformly. Leave the spacers in place and let each piece cool to room temperature. The spring tabs are now permanently set.

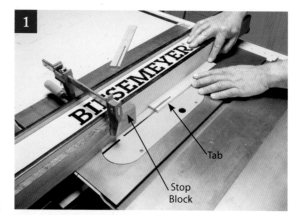

Cut saw kerfs in each blank to create the spring tabs. Set the fence to cut the outer kerf on each blank first. Then, reset the fence to cut the inner kerfs. Clamp a stop to the fence and keep the same face up for both cuts so each tab is equal in length.

Glue spacers to the outer tabs. Place small pieces of paper next to the spacers to avoid accidentally gluing them to the middle tab. Use water resistant glue.

Assemble the Knuckle Joint

Clamp the two blanks together with the bent tines facing out (Photo 6). Measure down ¼-in. from the end and then drill a ¹⁄₁₆-in. hole through all the tines. Push a ¹⁄₁₆-in. brass rod (available at hardware stores) into the hole and cut it flush with a side cutter (Photo 7).

Finish the Tongs

Shape the round beveled end of the tongs with a belt or disc sander (Photo 8). Finish sand the tongs' surfaces to 220-grit. Brush a liberal coating of walnut oil (available at health food stores) onto the tongs. Let it soak for 10-minutes or so and wipe them dry. Walnut oil is a completely non-toxic drying oil.

Unlike metal tongs, wooden tongs should never soak in hot soapy water or be put through a dishwasher. Just rinse with warm water and wipe them dry. Recoat with oil whenever they start to look "dry."

Figure A: Exploded View

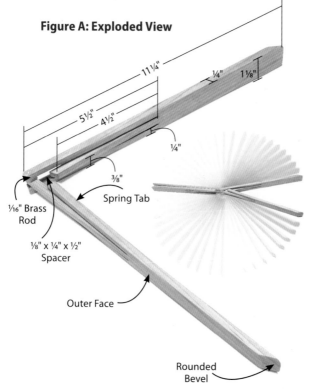

11¼"
5½"
4½"
¼"
1⅛"
¼"
⅜"
Spring Tab
¹⁄₁₆" Brass Rod
⅛" x ¼" x ½" Spacer
Outer Face
Rounded Bevel

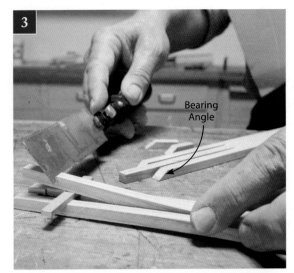

Cut 60-degree bearing angles for the spring tabs with a fine crosscut saw. Cut the middle tab on the tong with spacers and the two outer tabs on the other tong. Use a piece of scrap to lift the middle tab for cutting.

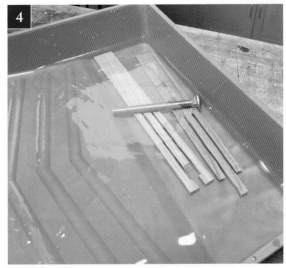

Soak the blanks in hot water for about 30 minutes. Place a weight on the wood to keep it submerged.

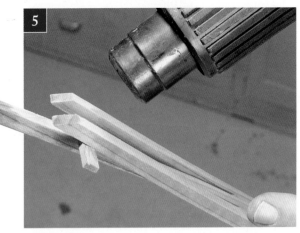

Set the spring in the tabs by inserting a ⅛-in. spacer between them and applying heat. Use a heat gun on high and keep rotating the tong to prevent scorching.

Clamp the end of the tongs together with the bent tabs facing out. Drill a ¹⁄₁₆-in. dia. hole through the tabs to create a pivot point for the knuckle joint connecting the tongs.

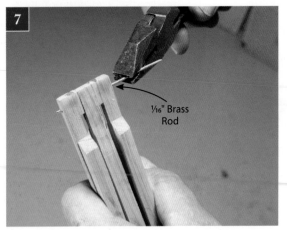

Push a brass rod into the hole to hinge the knuckle joint. Cut the excess rod to length with a wire cutter. File the ends flush. This will flare the ends of the rod and lock it in place.

Open the tongs so the spring tabs are engaged. Then push the tong halves together. Shape the outside faces on a belt sander. Gently rock the tongs as you sand to produce a slightly rounded bevel on the ends.

by ERIC SMITH AND DAVID RADTKE

2 Kitchen Storage Projects

SQUEEZE MORE SPACE FROM YOUR CABINETS WITH CUSTOMIZED ROLL-OUTS

Under-Sink Storage

To begin, measure the areas of open space around the plumbing. You may only be able to put a single pull-out on one side, or you may have to shorten them or build them around pipes coming up through the base.

Materials

To make the trays shown here, you'll need a half sheet of ¾-in. hardwood plywood, 2-ft. × 2-ft. of ½-in. plywood, 17 lineal ft. of 1- in. × 4-in. maple, 2 lineal ft. of 1-in. × 6-in. maple, four pairs of 20-in. full-extension ball-bearing slides, a box of 1⅝-in. screws, wood glue and construction adhesive.

Bottom Pull-Outs

Measure the frame opening and cut the base (A) ¼ in. narrower (Fig. A, page 40). Make the drawers 1 in. narrower than the opening between the partitions. Cut and assemble the base assembly (A, B) and drawer parts (C, D, E). Sand and apply two coats of finish to the base and drawers.

Set the drawer slides on ¾-in. spacers flush with the front edge of the partition (B). Screw them to the partitions; then pull out the drawer members. Set the drawer members on the same ¾-in. spacers to create the proper bottom clearance for the tray, and screw them to the sides of the trays flush to the fronts. Screw the base assembly to the bottom of the cabinet (Photo 1). Slide in the drawers.

Side-Mounted Pull-Outs

Make the side support cleats (K) so they sit flush or slightly proud of the face frame. Check for hinges that might get in the way of the pull-out tray. Assemble the trays with glue and screws. Apply finish.

Attach the slides and mount them in the cabinet (Photos 2 and 3). Scuff the cabinet side with sandpaper and use construction adhesive and screws to hold the cleats. Cabinet sides are often finished, so screws alone may not hold well.

Build and install a base assembly for the bottom pull-outs. Center the base assembly in the cabinet just behind the hinges. Align the front edge with the face frame and screw it to the bottom of the cabinet.

Cutting List

Part	Name	Qty.	Dimensions
A	Plywood base	1	¾" x 32¾" x 20"
B	Base partition	3	¾" x 3½" x 20"
C	Plywood tray bottom	2	¾" x 12¾" x 18½"
D	Tray side	4	¾" x 3½" x 18½"
E	Tray front and back	4	¾" x 3½" x 14¼"
F	Upper tray bottom	2	½" x 5½" x 18½"
G	Plywood upper tray side	2	¾" x 5" x 18½"
H	Plywood upper tray side	2	¾" x 3" x 18½"
J	Upper tray front, back	4	¾" x 5½" x 5½"
K	Side cleat, double layer	4	½" x 5½" x 20"

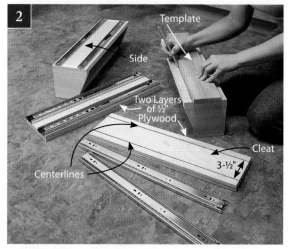

Install the slides on the side pull-out trays. Center a 3½-in. template on the cleat and the tall side of each tray and trace the edges. Center the mounting holes of the slides on these lines.

Figure A: Under-Sink Storage Exploded View

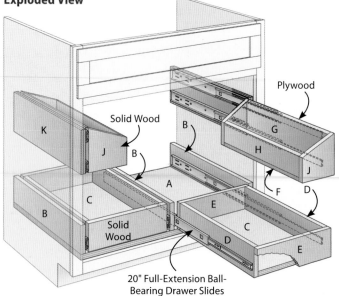

Attach the support cleats to the side of the cabinet using screws and construction adhesive. Use a temporary plywood spacer to hold each cleat in position.

Mini-Pantry

These pull-outs bring boxes, jars and cans within easy reach. To build this mini-pantry, you'll need two sheets of ¾-in. hardwood plywood (I used Baltic birch for its attractive edge) and two pairs of 20-in. full-extension ball-bearing slides.

Start by building a box to fit inside the cabinet. Measure the frame opening and subtract ¼ in. to get the box's outside dimensions. I made this pantry for a 24-in. base cabinet, so change the cutting list to fit your base. Also keep in mind that most ¾-in. plywood actually measures ²³⁄₃₂ in.

Cut the box parts (A, B, C) and assemble them with glue and screws (Fig. B, below right). Find the drawers' width by subtracting 1 in. from the openings in the box.

Cut all the pieces for the drawers (D, E, F, G). Soften the edges of the drawer sides (D) and drawer face (G) using a ¼-in. round-over bit. Assemble the drawer parts (D, E, F) with screws and glue. Position the center shelf (F) at the height you prefer. Attach the sides (D) with finish nails and glue.

Set the drawer slides on the bottom of the box. Align the slides with the front edge and attach. Remove the drawer member and screw it to the drawer side ¼ in. above the bottom.

Install the box (see photo, below). Install the drawers. Center the drawer faces (G) on the drawers and screw them from the inside. Drill 1½-in.-dia. holes for finger pulls or attach shallow pulls. Apply two coats of finish.

Cutting List
Overall Dimensions: 20¼" H x 20¾" W x 22" D

Part	Name	Qty.	Dimensions
A	Base and top	2	¾" x 20½" x 20¾"
B	Sides and center	3	¾" x 20½" x 18¹³⁄₁₆"
C	Back	1	¾" x 20¾" x 20¼"
D	Shelf side	8	¾" x 1¾" x 20¼"
E	Drawer front and back	4	¾" x 6⅞" x 18½"
F	Drawer top, bottom, shelf	6	¾" x 6⅞" x 18¾"
G	Drawer face	2	¾" x 9¾" x 19¾"

Build a box for the drawers to fit inside the base cabinet. Remove the cabinet doors and slide the box into the cabinet. Screw the box securely to the bottom of the cabinet.

Figure B: Mini-Pantry Exploded View

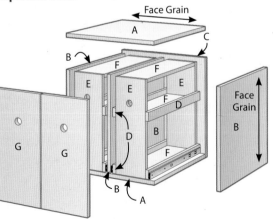

Storage Projects

Storage is always at a premium in our homes. While we use and store some things frequently, others get occasional use before they are packed away out of sight. In addition, our favorite items are often displayed prominently in our homes. The projects in this section meet all of those storage needs. There's a traditional walnut wall shelf that can be used to display pictures, awards, DVDs, or other collectables. It includes some great woodworking techniques, and illustrates how to make several styles of molding. If you're looking for something more contemporary, consider the cantilever display shelves or the free-form wall shelf. Both require only a couple of boards and a weekend or so to build. If you need a bookshelf, you'll find two to pick from. The first is a tall one that's perfect for a child's room. Its two-part design makes it portable, but also means that you may have to part with it when the kids leave home. But that's OK, because then you can turn their room into your den. Add some class to that den with the second bookcase, which is Stickley in style and built out of quartersawn white oak.

by JON STUMBRAS

Walnut Wall Shelves

VERSATILE GO-ANYWHERE SHELVES TO HOLD BOOKS, DISCS, KITCHENWARE, OR ANYTHING YOU WANT!

Never enough shelf space where you want it? This little shelf is a great way to add extra storage in just about any room.

It's compact—only 22¾-in. wide by 31¼-in. tall by 9¼-in. deep. Yet it's tall enough to accommodate three shelves of paperbacks. Hang it in your bedroom, bathroom or kitchen. This cabinet will add a touch of comfortable elegance in any room.

Details Made Easy

We've packed a ton of great details into this cabinet, and some great techniques into this project. We'll show you how to cut cove molding on your tablesaw and how a special beading bit makes quick work of the shiplapped back. Your router and router table can handle all the other moldings.

All the parts for this cabinet are made from ¾-in.-thick lumber, which keeps the materials list simple. An intermediate-level woodworker can plan on two or three weekends to complete this cabinet. And when you're done, a hidden cleat easily and invisibly secures the case to the wall.

Small Changes Make a Big Difference

In a small case, changing dimensions by even a fraction can make a world of difference in the final appearance. The top of this case is 11/16-in. thick and overhangs the side by ¼-in. more at the sides than the front. The bottom is 9/16-in. thick, the shelves are ⅝-in. thick and the face frames are ½-in. thick. These carefully chosen dimensions give this cabinet a comfortable and balanced look.

Traditional Design, Modern Tools

You'll need a surface planer, jointer, router, router table, tablesaw, dado blade and biscuit joiner for the construction. To make the moldings, seven router bits are needed, three round-over bits, a beading bit, a chamfer bit, an ogee bit and a rabbeting bit. You may have several of these already, but if you buy all the bits new, the cost will be approximately $170. We used 25 bd. ft. of 4/4 rough walnut for our cabinet at a cost of $125.

Build the Cabinet in Stages

1. Begin by selecting the wood for each part (the sides require the widest boards). Straight-grained wood looks best for face frames. Match the face-frame stiles to the case sides and they'll look like one piece when assembled.

2. Cut all the parts to rough size by adding ½ in. to the final length and width (see Cutting List, page 50) and plane the parts to their final thickness.

3. Next, rabbet the case sides (C1) with a dado blade in your tablesaw (Photo 1). Two passes are needed to make the 1-in.-wide by ⅜-in.-deep dado on the back inside edge of each side.

4. Now cut the case sides, the top and the bottom (C2) to final width and length.

5. Drill the shelf-pin holes next (Photo 2) using a drilling template (Fig. A) and a 5mm self-centering drill bit. It's a lot easier to do this now because there's not a lot of room inside the finished cabinet.

6. You can now join the top and bottom to the case sides. Two #20-size biscuits will fit neatly in the panels (Fig. B). Glue up the case, carefully checking the diagonal measurements to guarantee squareness. Note that the case bottom is set ½-in. up from the bottom ends of the case sides (Fig. B). This way the case bottom and the bottom face-frame rail will be flush on the inside of the cabinet.

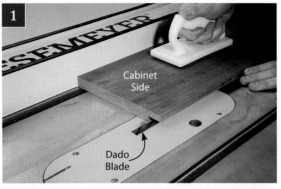

Cut rabbets along the inside edge of the cabinet sides with a dado blade. The cabinet back fits into this rabbet.

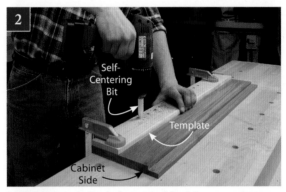

Drill shelf-pin holes before assembling the case, using a template and 5mm self-centering drill bit. The template guarantees evenly spaced holes and the self-centering bit has a built-in stop to keep you from drilling through the side.

7. Make the face frame next. It's difficult to cut accurate biscuit joints in ½-in.-thick material (see "Oops!," page 46), so we built a simple clamping jig with toggle clamps for better results (Photo 3). This jig makes it easy to cut the partial biscuit joint (Detail 1) for the bottom face-frame rail (F3), which is only 1¼-in. wide. To cut the biscuit slots in the stiles (F1), modify your first jig, or make a second jig to hold the stiles parallel rather than perpendicular to your biscuit joiner.

Glue up the face frame, making sure it is square. When dry, trim the protruding biscuits at the bottom and glue the face frame to the case (Photo 5). The total width for the face frames is ¹⁄₁₆-in. wider than the overall case dimension. This allows for some wiggle room when gluing the face frame to the case in the event the face frame or case are not perfectly square. The face frame is easily cleaned up with a hand plane, hand scraper, or a flush-trim bit in a router.

Figure. A: Drilling Template for Shelf Pin Holes

Make this template out of ½-in. material.

Figure. B: Exploded View

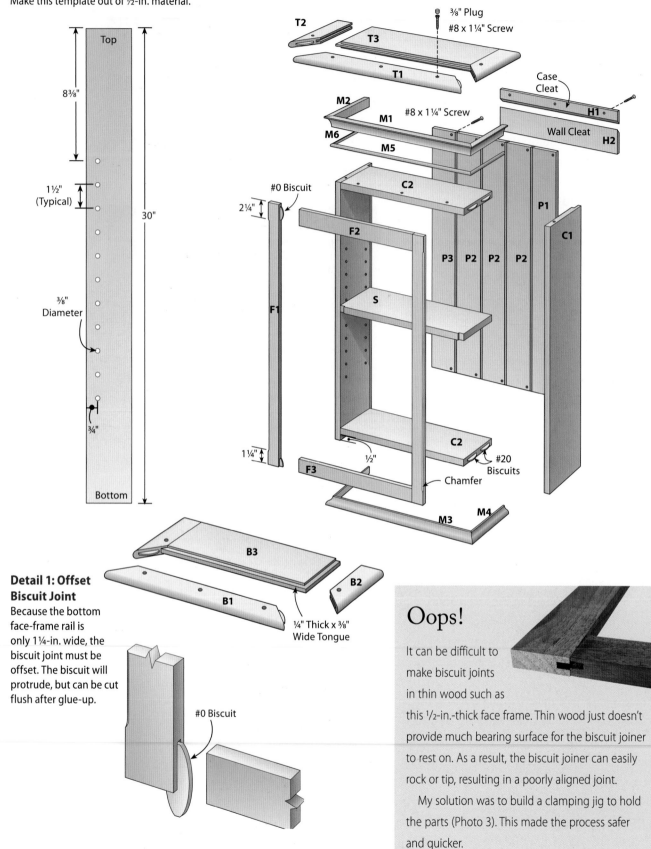

Top

8⅜"

1½"
(Typical)

30"

⅜"
Diameter

¾"

Bottom

T2

T3

⅜" Plug
#8 x 1¼" Screw

T1

M2

M1

#8 x 1¼" Screw

M6

M5

C2

Case
Cleat

H1

Wall Cleat

H2

P1

#0 Biscuit

2¼"

F2

C1

F1

S

P3 P2 P2 P2

C2

1¼"

½"

#20
Biscuits

F3

Chamfer

M3 M4

Detail 1: Offset Biscuit Joint

Because the bottom face-frame rail is only 1¼-in. wide, the biscuit joint must be offset. The biscuit will protrude, but can be cut flush after glue-up.

B3

B2

B1

¼" Thick x ⅜"
Wide Tongue

#0 Biscuit

Oops!

It can be difficult to make biscuit joints in thin wood such as this ½-in.-thick face frame. Thin wood just doesn't provide much bearing surface for the biscuit joiner to rest on. As a result, the biscuit joiner can easily rock or tip, resulting in a poorly aligned joint.

My solution was to build a clamping jig to hold the parts (Photo 3). This made the process safer and quicker.

8. Next, rout the stopped chamfer along the edge of the face frame (Fig. B).

Add the Decorative Top and Bottom

The top and bottom bullnose moldings (T1, T2, B1, and B2) are made using two round-over router bits (Photo 5). For the top bullnose moldings, use a ⁵⁄₁₆-in. round-over bit. For the bottom moldings, use a ¼-in. round-over bit. The bullnoses will have a slightly flat spot in the center but a little sanding makes them perfect. Cut the ¼-in. groove (Figs. C and G) in the bullnose parts with a dado blade in your tablesaw. Finally, miter these parts and cut to final length; then biscuit and glue them together. A stepped clamping block is used to clamp this molding together to make a three-sided frame. The frame is then screwed to the case top (Fig. A). The screw heads are hidden with wood plugs.

Next, make the top and bottom panels (T3 and B3) that fit into the grooves of the bullnose trim. To create the ¼-in.-thick by ⅜-in.-wide tongue on three sides of these parts (Fig. A), use a rabbeting router bit or your dado blade. The panels are ¹⁄₁₆-in. undersized in length to make them easy to slide in. Gluing just the front edge allows the solid-wood panels to move in their frames with seasonal humidity changes (Photo 8).

Make the Moldings

Make the cove molding on your tablesaw. For this cove molding (M1 and M2), set the auxiliary fence at 30 degrees to the blade (Photo 9). A bit of practice is in order here, so start with a scrap 4-in.-wide board for a test run. The wider blank will keep your fingers away from the blade and is less likely to tip toward the blade. Raise the blade in small increments for each cut until you reach the desired depth. When you've mastered a practice piece you're ready for the real thing. After forming the cove, cut the molding to final width (Fig. D). Hand sand or use a curved scraper to remove the saw marks from the inside of the cove.

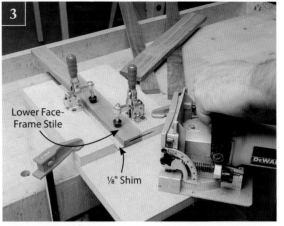

Cut biscuit joints in the face frames. Using this simple jig allows you to safely and quickly cut accurate slots in the thin, narrow parts. The bottom face-frame rail is too narrow to hold a whole biscuit so the slot is offset. The biscuit will protrude but can be trimmed after the gluing and will be hidden by the bullnose cabinet bottom.

Clamp and glue the face frame to the case. The face frame is ¹⁄₁₆-in. wider than the case to allow some wiggle room during glue up in the event that the case or face frame is a little out of square.

Rout a bullnose profile for the decorative top and bottom moldings with a round-over bit. First rout one side, flip the wood over and rout again. Presto, a bullnose!

Figure C: Bullnose Molding for Decorative Top (parts T1 and T2)

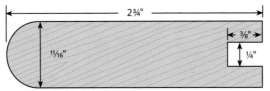

Figure D: Cove Molding (parts M1 and M2)

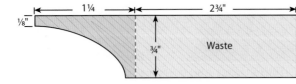

Figure E: Bead Molding (parts M5 and M6)

Figure F: Ogee Molding (parts M3 and M4)

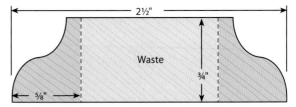

Figure G: Bullnose Molding for Decorative Bottom (parts B1 and B2)

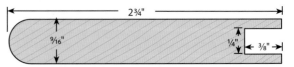

Figure H: Back Panels (parts P2) Get Routed as Shown Here

Right panel (part P1) has a rabbet and bead on one edge only. Left panel (part P3) has a rabbet on one edge only.

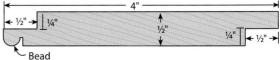

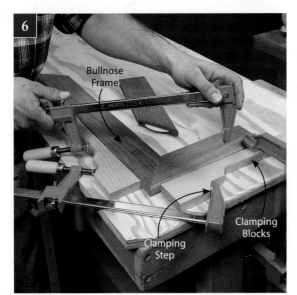

Glue and clamp the bullnose frames one corner at a time. The stepped clamping blocks shown here help pull the miters tight. Make the blocks the same thickness as your parts. First clamp the bullnose frames and clamping blocks to your bench. Then add clamps to the steps on the clamping blocks to pull the joint tight.

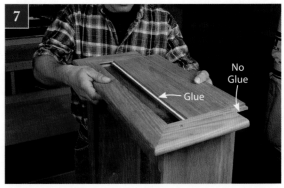

Insert the top panel into the bullnose frame. Glue only the leading edge so the panel can expand and contract with changes in humidity. Wood plugs hide the screws that attach the bullnose frame to the case.

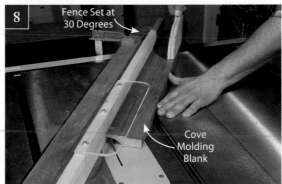

Cut the cove molding with several passes on your tablesaw using an auxiliary fence set at 30 degrees. The auxiliary fence covers half of the blade, producing only the half arc needed for this cove.

The ogee molding (M3 and M4) is next. Rout the profile with the ogee bit on both sides of a 2½-in. board (Fig. F), then rip the board on the tablesaw to create two separate moldings (Photo 9). One 25-in.-long board will yield moldings for all three sides.

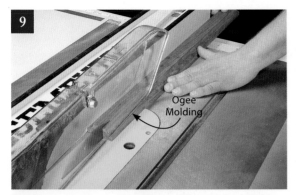

Rip the cove, ogee and beaded moldings to final width on your tablesaw. The cove molding gets ripped once to remove the waste portion while the boards for the ogee and beaded moldings get ripped twice.

Attach the cove molding with pin nails or small brads. For additional strength, the molding is glued to the case and at the miters.

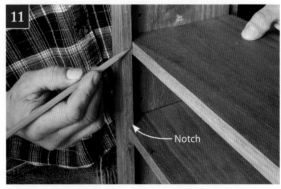

Mark each shelf for a notch before installing the back. Marking right off the cabinet is more accurate than taking a measurement. The notch permits the shelf to slightly overlap the face frame, creating a small, decorative detail.

The bead molding (Fig. E, M5 and M6) is made with two passes of a ³⁄₁₆-in. round-over bit in your router table. Also, just like the ogee, rout both sides of a wider board for safety and ease of routing.

Using a pneumatic pin nailer makes quick work of applying molding (Photo 10). If you hand nail, it's a good idea to drill small pilot holes to prevent the wood from splitting. These small holes are easily filled and hidden with a little putty or wax pencil.

Custom Fit the Shelves

Mark the shelf notches directly from the case (Photo 11). In theory, this notch should be ¾-in. long by ¼-in. wide, but if your face frame was glued slightly to one side, there will be minor differences in the sizes of the notches from one side of the shelves to the other. Measuring directly from the case will give a custom fit and avoid errors that can occur when making inside measurements with a tape measure or from assuming both sides are the same.

Traditional Shiplapped Back

Rout the beaded shiplapped back panels (Figs. B and H) for your cabinet with a beading bit (Photo 12). The interlocking rabbets allow for expansion and the screws at the top and bottom of each section hold the panels securely in place (Fig. B). Back panels P1 and P3 fit into the rabbets along the case sides. Gluing along these case sides and just around the corners provides additional strength and stability to the case (Photo 13).

Simple and Classic Finish

To make finishing easier, remove the three center back panels (P2) that are just attached with screws. We sanded our cabinet to 220 grit and applied a walnut stain to even out minor color variations in the walnut. Then we applied a wiping oil finish to give the case a soft glow. An oil finish does not provide much protection against moisture, so if you plan to use your cabinet in the kitchen or bathroom, use a varnish instead.

Hang the Case on the Wall

Attach the case cleat (H1) to the back of the cabinet with screws (Fig. B). Make sure the screws go into the case top (C2). Mount the complementary cleat (H2) to your wall using screws and wall anchors and then hang the case (Photo 14). The beveled cleats interlock and hide neatly within the back side of the case, making them invisible from the outside.

Cutting List

Overall Dimensions: 31¼" H x 22¾" W x 9¼" D

Part	Name	Qty.	Dimensions
Case			
C1	Sides	2	¾" x 7½" x 30"
C2	Top & Bottom	2	¾" x 6½" x 18"
Face Frame			
F1	Stiles	2	½" x 1½" x 30"
F2	Top rail	1	½" x 2¼" x 16⁹⁄₁₆"
F3	Bottom rail	1	½" x 1¼" x 16⁹⁄₁₆"
TOP			
T1	Bullnose front	1	¹¹⁄₁₆" x 2¾" x 22¾"
T2	Bullnose sides	2	¹¹⁄₁₆" x 2¾" x 9¼"
T3	Panel	1	¹¹⁄₁₆" x 6⅞" x 17¹⁵⁄₁₆"
			Include ⅜" wide tongue on three sides
Bottom			
B1	Bullnose front	1	⁹⁄₁₆" x 2¾" x 21½"
B2	Bullnose sides	2	⁹⁄₁₆" x 2¾" x 9"
B3	Panel	1	⁹⁄₁₆" x 6⅝" x 16¹¹⁄₁₆"
			include ⅜" wide tongue on three sides
Moldings			
	Cove Molding		
M1	Front	1	¾" x 1¼" x 21"
M2	Sides	2	¾" x 1¼" x 8¾"
	Ogee Molding		
M3	Front	1	¾" x ⅝" x 20¾"
M4	Sides	2	¾" x ⅝" x 8⅝"
	Bead Molding		
M5	Front	1	⅜" x ⅜" x 20¼"
M6	Sides	2	⅜" x ⅜" x 8⅜"
Shelves			
S	Shelves	2	⅝" x 6⅝" x 17⅞"
			¼" x ¾" notch on each front end
Panel Back			
P1	Right panel	1	½" x 4¼" x 30"
			rabbet and bead on one edge only
P2	Center panels	3	½" x 4" x 30"
P3	Left panel	1	½" x 4¼" x 30"
			rabbet on one edge only, no bead
Hanging Cleat			
H1	Case cleat	1	½" x 1½" x 18¾"
			45-degree angle on bottom edge
H2	Wall cleat	1	½" x 3" x 18½"
			45-degree angle on top edge
Hardware			
	Shelf pins	8	5mm shelf pins
	Wood screws	23	#8 x 1¼" steel wood screws
	Biscuits	12	#20 biscuits
	Biscuits	4	#0 biscuits
	Wall anchors		appropriate to wall type
	Wall screws		appropriate to wall type

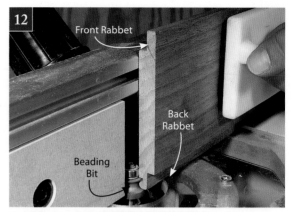

Rout the beaded profile for the back. A specialty beading bit makes quick work of this traditional molding. Opposite rabbets on each piece create the overlapping shiplapped joinery for the back panels.

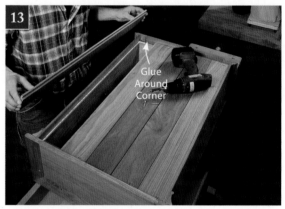

Screw the back panels in place. Gluing the outer two panels along the case sides and 1 in. around the corner adds rigidity to the case. The center three panels, attached with screws, are free to move with seasonal changes in humidity.

Hang the cabinet on the wall using a two-part beveled cleat. One part is screwed to the case and one part is screwed to the wall. Attach the wall cleat to at least one stud and add a couple of wall anchors for extra strength. The cabinet hangs flush against the wall with both cleats hidden from view.

by JOHN NESSET

Free-Form Wall Shelves

Here's a versatile shelf that allows for a creative, one-of-a-kind edge treatment. Hung on the wall without any visible means of support, these shelves are real eye catchers.

Choose boards that are at least 1¼-in. thick and no more than about 7-in. wide. Wood with wane, bark pockets or end checks is a perfect candidate. (You guessed it—this is a great way to use reject boards that are just too pretty to throw away or burn.)

First, true up the top and back edge with a hand plane or jointer. The back edge of the board is planed a degree or two less than perpendicular to keep objects from rolling off the shelf. Next, position the keyhole hangers out towards the ends of the shelves. Try to space the hangers every 16-in. so the shelves can be mounted directly to wall studs. The keyholes are mounted either horizontally or vertically and placed near the top edge to provide a bearing surface below the attachment point. Mark the profile of the hangers with a sharp knife and carefully chisel out the mortises to the exact depth of the hangers. Next, drill a recess at the bottom of each mortise

(approx. ⁵⁄₁₆-in. deep) to allow the wall-mounted screws to securely engage the hangers.

Now you're ready to shape the rest of the shelf. The gently curved and beveled ends can be cut on a bandsaw. Don't think too hard about how each piece should look. I've had good results simply letting the grain figure determine the shape of the shelf. Just remove the loose or broken stuff and smooth out any rough edges with a carver's gouge.

Finish with a couple coats of oil, hang it up and you've got a conversation piece that will wow your houseguests.

Figure A: Wall Mount

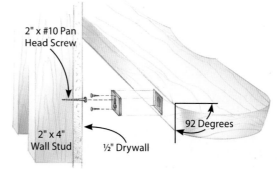

2" x #10 Pan Head Screw

2" x 4" Wall Stud

½" Drywall

92 Degrees

by DAVE MUNKITTRICK

Cantilevered Display Shelves

STRONG, GLUELESS JOINTS SUPPORT THESE ELEGANT, CANTILEVERED SHELVES

Whatever you collect—rocks, porcelain, folk art or photos of your Schnauzer—it'll get the attention it deserves when displayed on these shelves. The simple design is wide open at the front and sides so nothing interferes with what's on display. The stepped-back shelves allow ambient light to flood each shelf.

All the curves and tapers make the shelves look tricky to build. But, the joinery is simplified by making all the cuts on square stock before any of the curves and tapers are added. Most of the shaping is done on the bandsaw and tablesaw, followed by a little handwork with a plane or power sander.

The shelves are locked into the supports with bridle joints. The bridle joints consist of dadoes that wrap around three sides of the support. Notches are cut into the back of each shelf to fit the dadoes (Fig. B). The result is a strong, glueless joint that supports the shelf at the back.

You'll need a planer, bandsaw, router, drill, belt sander or hand plane and a dado set for your tablesaw. Materials will run anywhere from $25 in pine to $125 in finer hardwoods, such as the figured maple we used here. You'll need about 7 bd. ft. of 4/4 stock for the shelves (this may be the perfect opportunity to use that beautiful board you've been saving for years!) and about 5 bd. ft. of 8/4 stock for the supports.

Start your shelves by cutting your stock according to the Cutting List on page 55. Machine the supports first (Photos 1 through 4) then fit and shape your shelves (Photos 5 through 11). Sand the completed shelves to about 220 grit.

For an easy-to-apply, durable finish we used a wipe-on polyurethane. It goes on like any oil finish but dries fast and hard. For extra protection, apply a coat of paste wax after the oil dries.

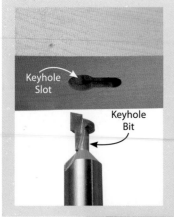

Keyhole slots are a great way to hang shelves like this on a wall. They're strong, easy to make and the clean lines of the shelves are not disrupted by visible fasteners. Best of all, they don't require buying or fitting any hardware. But, you'll need a specially designed keyhole router bit to cut the slots.

Keyhole slots are designed to fit over the head of a screw that's been fastened to the wall. The slot captures the screw head, holding the object securely to the wall.

Keyhole Slot

Keyhole Bit

ART DIRECTION: PATRICK HUNTER • PHOTOGRAPHY: MIKE HABERMANN, UNLESS OTHERWISE INDICATED • ILLUSTRATION: DON RAYMOND AND FRANK ROHRBACH

These shelves are:
sturdy, lightweight, easily knocked-down for shipping, fun to make, and easy to mass produce.

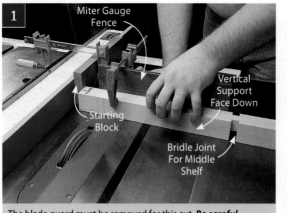

The blade guard must be removed for this cut. *Be careful.*

Cut the deep dado on the front side of the support using a long miter gauge fence and a starting block. This is the first step in creating the bridle joint that locks the shelf onto the supports.

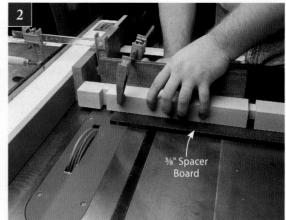

Cut the two shallow dadoes on the sides of the supports after slipping a ⅜-in. spacer board under the workpiece. You must cut all the dadoes for each shelf before moving on to the next. That way you keep the same fence and blade setting for each cut, which guarantees perfect alignment of the dadoes on all three sides of the support.

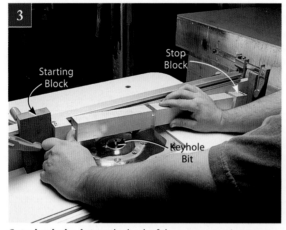

Cut a keyhole slot on the back of the supports using your router table and a keyhole bit. Brace the top of the support against a starting block and lower the vertical support onto the keyhole bit until it rests flat on your router table. Slide the support forward against the stop block to finish the cut.

Cut the tapers on the supports with a shop-made jig (Fig. A), or on a bandsaw.
  Taper the sides first.
• Set a 5/16-in. gap between the two halves of the taper jig for the first side cut.
• Set the gap at ⅝ in. for the second side cut.
• Move the fence ¼-in. further away from the blade, set the gap at ¾ in. and cut the front taper.
• Mark each setting on the jig for future reference.

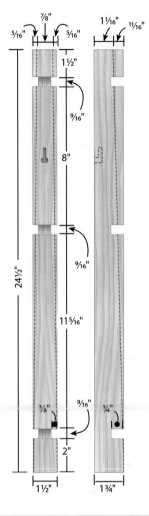

Figure C: Vertical Supports

Figure A: Taper Jig

If you plan on making more than one set of shelves, this jig is well worth the little bit of time it takes to construct. Rip a 7-in. x 30-in. piece of ¾-in. MDF into 3-in. and 4-in. pieces. Cut a cradle in the 4-in. piece the same length as the support (28½ in.). This allows you to set the amount of taper by simply measuring the gap between the two halves of the jig. Use ¼-in. plywood to make the hinge and slide. Add a knob and a threaded insert to secure the slide.

Figure B: Exploded View

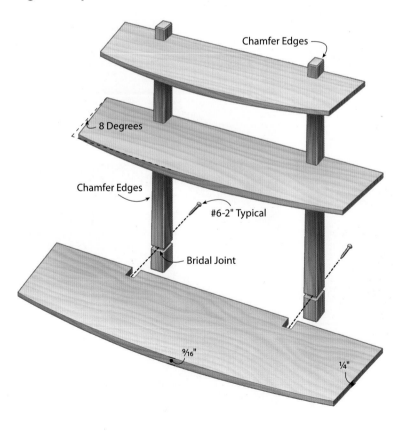

Cutting List
Overall Dimensions: 24½" H x 36" W x 8" D

Part	Name	Qty.	Dimensions	Material
A	Vertical supports	2	1½" x 1¾" x 24½"	8/4 hard or soft maple
B	Bottom shelf	1	9/16" x 8" x 36"	4/4 figured soft maple
C	Middle shelf	1	9/16" x 6¼" x 31¾"	4/4 figured soft maple
D	Upper shelf	1	9/16" x 4½" x 28¼"	4/4 figured soft maple

Tip

Mark the top, bottom and face of each support. It's easy to get disoriented machining the stock when it's square (see "Oops!," page 56).

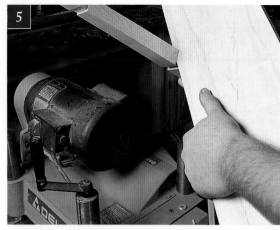

Plane the shelf stock to fit the dadoes in the supports. Use some scrap to determine the proper planer setting. Try for a slightly tight fit to allow for sanding.

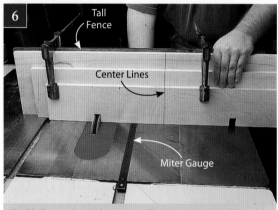

The blade guard must be removed for this cut. *Be careful.*

Cut the notches in all the shelves at once. First, make test cuts on scrap to determine the proper width and height settings for the dado blade. Mark the center of each shelf and lay out the notches on the small shelf. Align the shelves in a stack held together with double-faced tape. Clamp the stack to a tall fence fastened to your miter gauge and make your first cut. Reposition the stack, clamp and make the second cut.

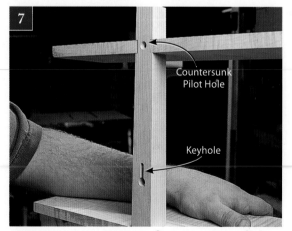

Drill and countersink pilot holes for the screws after dry fitting the shelves.

Oops!

Oh man, what a moron! I cut the keyhole slots at the *bottom* of the supports instead of the top. Now what do I do?

The slots are normally cut when the supports are still square, but now they're tapered. If I cut new slots with the tapered sides I'll end up with angled slots. Fortunately, the solution was sitting right in my scrap bin. I fished out a cut-off leftover from tapering the supports and taped it back in place. That gave me the square edge I needed to reference against the fence. Then I cut the slots where they belong, at the top. Maybe I'm not such a moron after all!

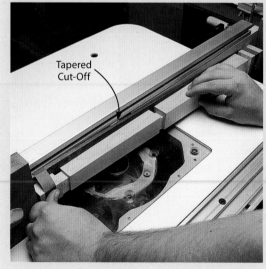

Taper the ends of each shelf on the bandsaw. You want to remove a ¼-in.-thick wedge that ends about 1½ in. from the notch. Use a block of wood as a guide to keep the shelf perpendicular to the table. Stick the block to the shelf with double-faced tape.

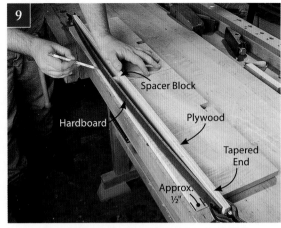

Lay out the curve on the front edge of each shelf. Clamp a ¼-in. hardboard strip on the ends of a 40-in.-long piece of wood or plywood and add a ¾-in. spacer block in the middle. Taper the ends of the plywood to create a fair curve. Cut the curve on the bandsaw.

Tip

Installation

Keyhole hangers are about as strong a wall-mounting system as you can get. But getting two screws spaced perfectly on your wall, without leaving multiple puncture wounds, can drive a grown man to tears. After the scars of my first attempt healed (on my ego as well as the wall), I came up with a solution. Take two of those little plastic pushpins for bulletin boards and slide them into the keyholes. Hold them in place with a little tape. Set a small level on the shelf. Position the shelf on the wall, check for level, and push. Voila! The pins mark the exact spot. Hanging the shelves just became a no-brainer.

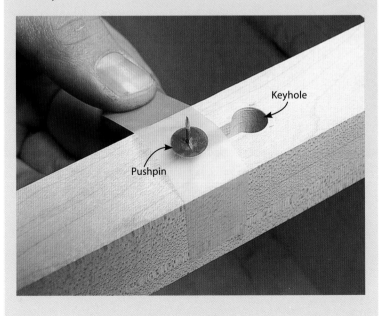

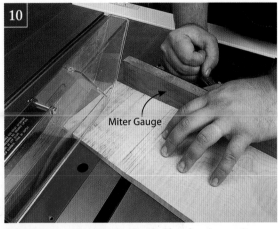

Cut an 8-degree angle on the shelf ends using a miter gauge on the tablesaw.

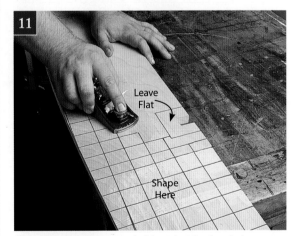

Shape the bottom taper (grid area) with a hand plane or power sander. The object is to create an even ¼-in. thickness across the ends and a sweeping curve on the front of the shelf (Fig. B). Take care not to remove any material around the notch or you'll ruin the fit of the shelf to the support.

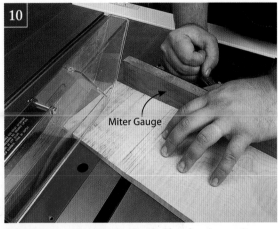

by DAVE MUNKITTRICK

Mission Plant Stand

HERE'S A GREAT PROJECT FOR DISPLAYING HOUSEPLANTS AND ADDING A LITTLE CHARM TO ANY CORNER OF YOUR HOUSE

The tripod leg design of this stand is rock-steady, even on a tiled or uneven floor. The wide bottom shelf can hold a large potted plant and anchors the stand both visually and physically. The open top shelf can handle a variety of plant or pot shapes and sizes.

This stand is made with riftsawn white oak. The oak fits the stand's quasi-Mission style and the straight riftsawn grain emphasizes the vertical thrust of the long tapered legs.

Don't let the angles scare you; this stand is easy to build. First glue up blanks for the top and bottom shelf (A and B, Fig. A). Take care to keep the joint flush during glueup. Use a belt or orbital sander to sand the blanks smooth. Cut the leg blanks (C) to size, but leave them rectangular for now. Next, head to the tablesaw and cut the angled dados on the leg blanks (Photos 1 and 2).

Note: The photos show a right-tilt saw. For a left-tilt saw, the fence positions are just the opposite. Install a crosscut blade and cut the 8-degree bevel on the bottom of each leg. Taper the legs on the bandsaw (Photo 3). Then, head to the router table and rout a 22½-degree chamfer around the two long inside edges and the top of each leg. You'll need to use the fence for this step instead of the bit's bearing, because of the dados in the legs.

Finally, lay out and cut the two shelves (Photo 4).

Assemble the stand and pre-drill shank and pilot holes for the screws. Secure with panhead screws and finish with polyurethane varnish to protect the stand from overzealous watering.

Figure A: Exploded View

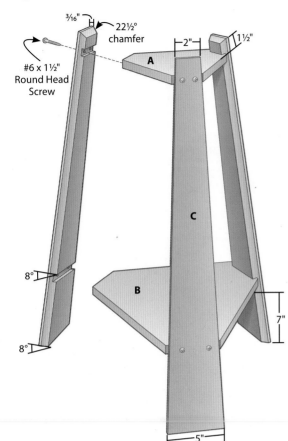

3/16"

#6 x 1½" Round Head Screw

22½° chamfer

2"

A

1½"

C

B

8°

8°

8°

7"

5"

Figure B: Shelf Dimensions

2¼" 4⅞"

12" 8¼"

2¼"

7½" 2¼"

4¾" 8¼"

21¼" 14⁹⁄₁₆"

60°

11¾" 4¾"

4¾"

Cutting List
Overall Dimensions: 56" L x 17" W x 33½" T

Part	Name	Qty.	Dimensions
A	Top Shelf	1	8¼" x 12"
B	Bottom Shelf	1	14⁹⁄₁₆" x 21¼"
C	Legs	3	5" x 30¾"

Cut the bottom dado with the blade tilted at 8-degrees and the fence set at 7-in.

Move the fence over to the left side of the blade to cut the top dado. Set the fence 1½-in. from the blade for this cut.

Tapering Jig

Taper the legs on a bandsaw. If you use a tapering jig, remember to double the angle when you cut the second taper. If you saw the tapers freehand, clean the edges with a hand plane or on the jointer.

Small Corner

Cut the triangular shelves using a miter gauge set to 60-degrees. Nip off the two small corners on a miter saw.

by TOM CASPAR

Two-Part Bookcase

HERE'S A BIG BOOKCASE THAT YOU CAN BUILD IN A SMALL SHOP

Building a tall bookcase can stretch the limits of a small shop. We all know that big boards can be a bear to handle and glue up, so I've taken an old Scandinavian design and sliced it up into bite-size pieces. My solution is to break the bookcase into two interlocking sections that require only short and narrow stuff. Not to mention, that's the only way I could get it out of my shop and up the basement stairs!

Biscuits join the shelves and sides. It's a snap to put together wide boards at right angles with a plate joiner. But biscuits alone aren't enough to make a stiff case, so I've added backboards that lock the whole bookcase into a rigid unit.

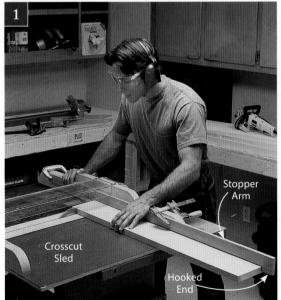

Trim long and wide boards on your tablesaw with a crosscut sled. A sled is easier to use and more accurate than a standard miter gauge. Clamp a hooked stick onto the fence to act as a stopper arm. This ensures that all your boards come out the same length.

Side View of Bookcase

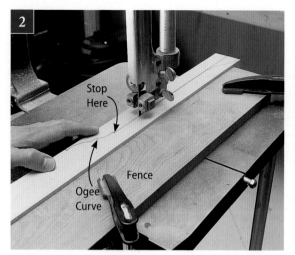

Rip the stepped board (c) on the bandsaw. A simple fence helps you make a straight cut. Stop the cut at the top of the ogee curve and withdraw the board. Remove the fence and cut out the ogee.

Glue the upper case sides from 1-in.-thick rough boards that are planed to ⅞-in. thick. This leaves some untouched low spots, but that's OK. Align the outside boards so their bottoms are even.

Materials and Tools

Rather than splurge on the best quality lumber simply to make shelves, you can save money on this project by using a lower grade of hardwood, No. 1 Common. You'll find many good boards that are too short or narrow to make the best grade but are perfect for this bookcase. I used No. 1 Common birch because it's inexpensive (about $1.75 per bd. ft.), a light color (the case looks less massive)and stiff enough to support heavy books. You'll need about 75 bd. ft. for a total cost of $130.

As an alternative you can use ¾-in.-thick boards from a home center. Pick straight ones, glue them together and plane them to ⅝ in. I built a prototype bookcase this way and it worked just fine. To tell the truth, I preferred its slim look to one made of thicker wood. However, I found that ⅝-in. thick shelves bend under a lot of weight, so they wouldn't be suitable for a set of encyclopedias.

You'll need the three basic machines for processing solid wood to make this bookcase from rough lumber: a tablesaw, a jointer, and a planer. (If you build with pre-planed, ¾-in. boards that have one straight edge, you can get by without a jointer.) A crosscut sled for your tablesaw isn't required but it sure makes life easier. In addition, you'll need a router, plate joiner, bandsaw, or jigsaw, an accurate framing square and eight pipe clamps to hold the case together during glue up.

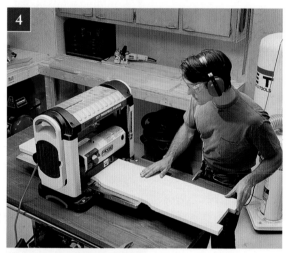

Plane the glued-up case sides until there are no low spots left. All the parts of this bookcase should be the same thickness, which can be anywhere from ¾ in. to a minimum of ⅝ in.

Any white or yellow glue works fine for the biscuit joints, because both glues contain the water needed to swell the biscuits. Use a special yellow glue with a long open time if you're going to glue up the cases by yourself and don't like working like a speed demon!

Tip

Do you have a portable planer?
Great, because we've kept every part less than 12-in. wide. That means you can flatten the sides and shelves with your planer.

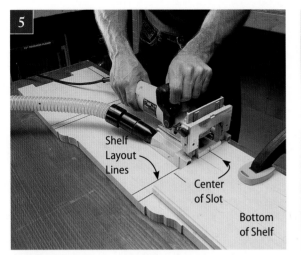

Cut biscuit slots in the ends of the shelves. You can't go wrong if you clamp each shelf in position, right above the double lines. Set the shelf in from the back edge by the thickness of one backboard.

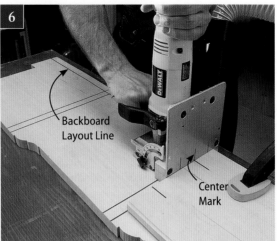

Cut more biscuit slots in the case side. Stand the plate joiner up on end and butt it against the end of the shelf. Align the center mark on the bottom of the machine with the pencil mark on the bottom of the shelf.

Tip

Do you buy lumber at a home center?

Go ahead and buy pre-thicknessed ¾-in. boards. Our plans work fine with this time-saving wood or with No. 1 Common rough lumber.

Figure A: Biscuit Placement

#20 biscuits are plenty strong to hold a shelf's weight. They won't shear off under a load because the grain of a biscuit runs diagonally.

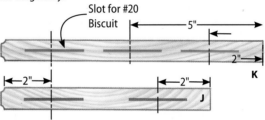

Preparing Rough Lumber

For the sides and backboards, select boards that don't have a pronounced twist. Twisted wood isn't worth the hassle. Rough cut your boards 1 in. over final length and ¼ in. over final width. Set your jointer to remove 1/32 in. Run one face over the jointer only a couple of times. It's OK if this doesn't clean up the whole board.

Run the other face of the boards through a portable planer until most of the rough spots are gone and the boards are all about ⅞-in. thick. Don't sweat it if they end up a bit thinner. Then joint one edge, rip the boards 1/32-in. over final width and joint the second edge. Pay attention to boards B and F—they've got to be exactly the same width. Square one end and trim the boards to exact length using a crosscut sled and a stopper arm (Photo 1).

Gluing the Sides

The upper and lower sides are composed of three boards that form a tongue and notch (Fig. F).There's no trick to getting the sides to nest together perfectly. It's simply a matter of being careful at glue up.

Start with the upper sides. Lay out the ogee curves on boards C and the cutouts on the top end of boards B (Figs. C and D). Cut out the curves on the bandsaw (Photo 2).

Dry clamp boards A, B, and C together. Boards A and B are flush at the top. Boards A and C are flush at the bottom. Check both ends with a straightedge, then draw an alignment mark across all three boards (Photo 3).

Glue the upper sides together. Getting a perfect alignment end-to-end drove me nuts until I adopted the method of rubbing the boards together first, before clamping. Glue the lower sides the same way. Here all three boards are flush at the bottom.

Figure C:

Detail of Top Cutout

It's easier to cut this with a jigsaw than a bandsaw because it's hard to balance the board on a bandsaw's table.

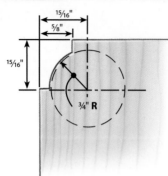

Figure D:

Details of Ogee Curve and Shelf Molding

This is a 50-percent reduction. Make a copy, double its size on a photocopy machine, paste it onto an index card, and cut it out.

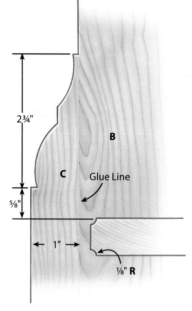

Figure E:

Detail of Bottom Cutout

Scribe the back of your bookcase to fit around your baseboard molding. The back of the bookcase should fit tight against the wall so the bookcase can be firmly anchored.

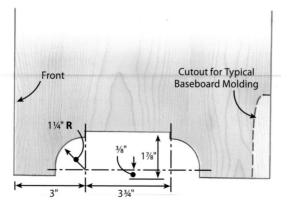

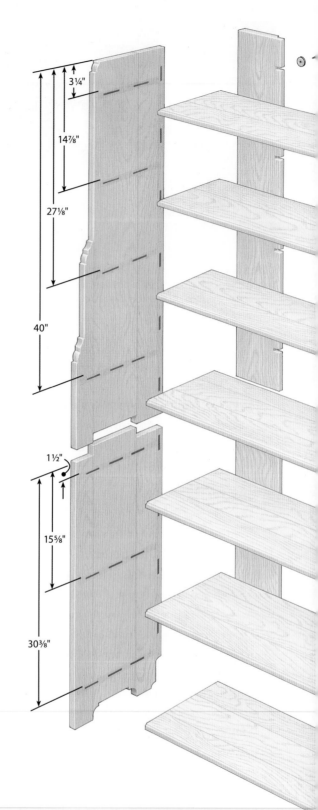

Figure B: Exploded View of Tall Bookcase

Safety Note: Anchor this bookcase to the wall with screws through the backboards so it can't accidentally tip over.

Figure F:

Connection between Top and Bottom
The top half of the bookcase fits snugly onto the bottom half. The lower backboards (H) prevent the top half from shifting side-to-side, and the notched sides lock in the top, front-to-back.

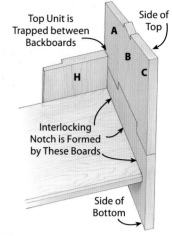

Top Unit is Trapped between Backboards

Side of Top

Interlocking Notch is Formed by These Boards

Side of Bottom

Figure G:

Detail of Shelf Slots
Screwing the backboards to the shelves stiffens the bookcase, but an allowance must be made for the backboards to shrink and swell in width with the seasons. That's why the screw passes through a slot rather than a hole. The backboard is dadoed so the head of the screw doesn't stick out.

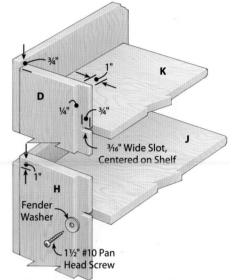

³⁄₄"
1"
K
D
¼"
¾"
J
³⁄₁₆" Wide Slot, Centered on Shelf
1"
H
Fender Washer
1½" #10 Pan Head Screw

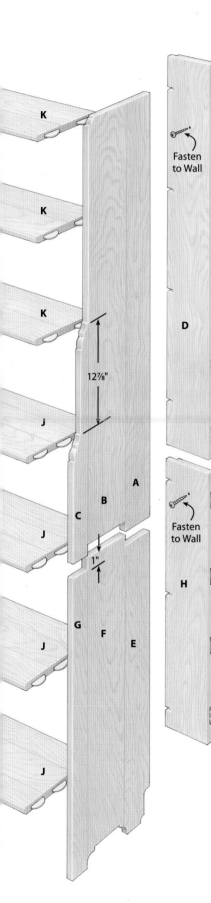

K
K
K
12⅞"
J
Fasten to Wall
D
A
B
C
J
Fasten to Wall
H
Screws Fasten Backboard to Shelves
1"
G
F
E
J
J

Cutting List
Overall Dimensions: 88" H x 36" W x 11" D

Part	Name	Qty.	Dimensions	Comments
Upper Unit				
A	Rear Board	2	⅞" x 3½" x 52¼"	Glue together, thickness to ¾" and trim bottom end so overall length is 52."
B	Middle Board	2	⅞" x 5½" x 51"	
C	Front Board	2	⅞" x 2" x 28½"	
D	Back	2	¾" x 5½" x 50"	
Lower Unit				
E	Rear Board	2	⅞" x 3½" x 36"	Glue together, thickness to ¾" and trim middle board to fit notch in upper unit.
F	Middle Board	2	⅞" x 5½" x 37¼"	
G	Front Board	2	⅞" x 2" x 36"	
H	Back	2	¾" x 5½" x 32½"	
Shelves				
J	Wide Shelves	4	¾" x 1" x 34½"	Glue up from ⅞" boards, thickness to ¾" and trim to length.
K	Narrow Shelves	3	¾" x 8" x 34½"	

Glue the backboard onto the case side. Make sure it's square along the entire length. Check opposite each clamp as you tighten it down. Shift the head of the clamp in or out to change the angle of the backboard.

Oops!

Nuts! We forgot to remove some squeezed-out glue before it dried! Finish won't stick to it, so the glue has to be removed before we can move on. Fortunately, yellow glue can be softened with hot water and scraped off with a sharp chisel days after it has dried. Hot water turns the clear glue back to its original yellow color, so it's easy to see what must be removed. After scraping, wash the area with a rag dampened with hot water, let the wood dry and sand off the raised grain.

Tip

Working in a small space?

No problem. We've designed this bookcase from short and narrow pieces. Two stacking halves make it easier to assemble (fewer clamps!) and easier to move.

Milling the Sides and Shelves

Plane both faces of the sides and backboards so they're ¾-in. thick (Photo 4). Congratulations if you've removed *all* the low spots, but don't hang your head if you haven't. You can plane all the boards thinner, down to ⅝ in., if that's what it takes. Remove all the mill marks by sanding with 100- and 120-grit paper.

Here's how to use the crosscut sled to trim the top and lower sides until they mate: First, saw off ¼ in. from the bottom of both upper sides. This guarantees the bottoms are square and straight, leaving a 1-in.-deep notch. Then, trim the tongues of the lower sides until they fit the notches. Because the middle boards (B and F) are exactly the same width, everything should fit tight as a glove.

Finish the lower sides by sawing the cutout at the bottom (Fig. E). It's easier to use a jigsaw than be a hero and try to balance the board on the small table of a bandsaw. Make a pattern of your baseboard molding and cut out the back corner of the side so it will fit tight up against the wall.

Lay out the positions of the shelves on both the upper and lower sides (Fig. B). The shelves will be set in from the back of the sides by the thickness of the backboards. Draw this backboard layout line on the sides, too (Photo 6).

Glue up the shelves, thickness and sand them; then, rout the molding on their front edges (Fig. D). Trim them to length with the crosscut sled. Finally, lay out center marks for the biscuits on the *bottom* faces.

Now for the easy joinery. Cut biscuit slots in the sides and shelves at the same time (Photos 5 and 6). Use a framing square to make sure the shelves are clamped in the right place.

Mark the position of the shelves on the backboards with light pencil lines. These reference lines help you glue up the entire case square. Clamp each shelf in place, without glue, and adjust it until it's square to the case side.

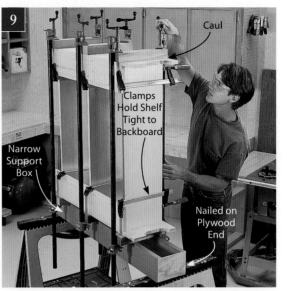

Glue the lower unit together with cauls and pipe clamps. The thick cauls distribute clamping pressure over the entire width of the side. Use short clamps to pull the shelves tight against the backboards. Align the shelves with the reference lines. Then tighten the pipe clamps.

Fitting the Backboards

If it weren't for the backboards, this bookcase wouldn't last a week. These hard-working boards help lock the upper and lower sections together, but more importantly they stiffen the case (Figs. F and G). Cut the backboards to length, place them in position on the case sides and lay out the slots for the screws (Fig. G). Cut the slots on the tablesaw. Stand the backboards on edge against a miter gauge and make two overlapping cuts with a standard saw blade. Then cut the dadoes for the screwheads.

Cut biscuit slots to join the backboards and case sides. These biscuits align the backboard flush with the side, but do not add strength. Glue the backboards to the sides (Photo 7).

Final Assembly

The backboards also help you square up the whole book-case when you glue the sides and shelves together. Thank goodness! You can get into lots of trouble by gluing things out of square, but this system is slick. Dry clamp each shelf in place with the biscuits loose in the slots and mark the shelf's position on the backboard (Photo 8). Make the pencil lines very light because you won't be able to

get into the corners with an eraser after the glue up. That's the one downside of this easy method.

Take your time and walk through a dry run of the glue up before you attempt the real thing (Photo 9). Here's the best way to do the glue up, alone, without going crazy: Support one side with a narrow (7-in.), wooden box that leaves room for the clamp heads. Insert one shelf at a time, align it with the reference lines on the backboard and clamp it in place. Once all the shelves are upright, place the other case side on the ends of the shelves, clamp the shelves tight to the backboard and finally add the pipe clamps.

Finishing and Installation

After gluing both cases, sand them with 150-grit paper. Avoid dyeing or staining birch, because it has a tendency to unevenly soak up color and become blotchy. Even an oil finish can look bad, so stick with shellac, brushed-on varnish, or lacquer.

This tall bookcase stands quite well on its own, but for safety, fasten it to the wall through the backboards. Then there'll be no chance for it to tip if a pet or rambunctious kid tries to climb the shelves!

by LAURIE MCKICHAN

Stickley Bookcase

HOW TO BUILD A STRONG BOOKCASE WITHOUT A BACK

Begin by routing double mortises in the legs. I'm using a Leigh FMT Pro, a jig which has templates of various sizes to guide the router. Many types of shop-made jigs can make these joints, too.

Rout similar mortises in the ends of the rails. This jig holds work both horizontally and vertically.

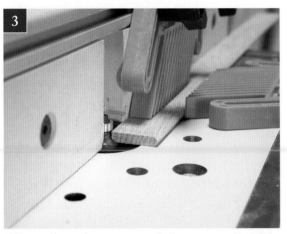

Mill some long, thin pieces to make loose tenons. Round the edges of these pieces to fit the mortises.

Cut the tenon stock into short pieces and glue them into the rails.

When I'm designing furniture, I often turn to the Arts and Crafts era for inspiration. I love this style. It's simple, but elegant. When a client commissioned me to build a small bookcase, I knew exactly what to start with: a photograph of a piece built by L. & J. G. Stickley around 1904.

This Stickley bookcase was perfect for my clients' modern condo. They wanted a bookcase with an open back, so it could be accessed from both sides and used as a room divider. I changed the Stickley piece's dimensions and design a bit, but kept the distinctive look of its side panels.

As it turned out, my clients moved just as I was completing their bookcase. They didn't need a divider in their new living room, but they did need a piece to fit behind their sofa. The bookcase was a natural. It's proven to be a very versatile design!

Materials and tools

I built this bookcase from quartersawn white oak, the same kind of wood that was used to build most Arts and Crafts furniture. This wood's most prominent feature is its ray fleck, but some quartersawn boards have much better-looking figure than others. Before I got started, I set aside the best boards for the side panels and the top.

The double tenons I used on this bookcase can be tricky to machine. I've found that the easiest method is to make them as loose pieces, like dowels or biscuits. This requires a lot of accurately machined mortises, made with a plunge router. You can make your own jigs to guide the router, but I used the Leigh FMT, which is designed for this kind of work.

Make the joints

Begin by making the legs (B). Cut them to final size and mark the best sides to face front and out. Rout all the mortises in the legs (Photo 1 and Fig D).

Strong Joints Reduce Racking

Although this bookcase is relatively small, it's pretty heavy when it's loaded up. To handle that load, and to withstand being picked up and shoved around, it needs to be strong. Most bookcases have backs, which help stiffen what's essentially a box with an open front. My bookcase doesn't have a back, so I had to design joints that were very strong, without resorting to increasing the width of the rails. That would have spoiled the look of the bookcase.

Instead, I made the rails quite thick (1¼"), and used mortise and tenon joints. Most of these joints have double tenons—two tenons side by side—rather than one large tenon. This strengthens the joints by doubling the area of their gluing surfaces. I made sure that the mortises in the legs didn't intersect each other, which could weaken the legs. Instead, the mortises are staggered.

I also added one unusual element to strengthen the case: a piece I call an "anti-racking" rail. There's one on each side of the bookcase, just under the top. They reinforce the joint between the upper rails and the sides, to prevent the case from twisting, or "racking."

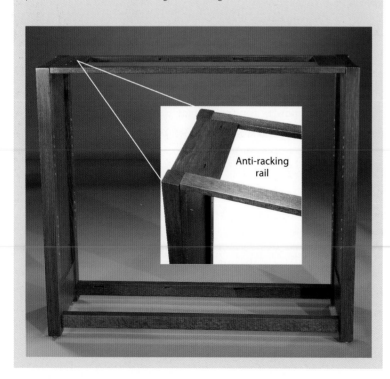

Anti-racking rail

Mill all the rails (C, D, E, F, and K). Be sure to trim all of the side rails (E and F) and the anti-racking rails (K) to the same length. Rout mortises in their ends, to match the mortises in the legs (Photo 2).

Make loose tenons (M, N, P, and Q) to fit the mortises. They're all the same thickness, but have different widths. Make each batch of tenons from one piece that's at least 12" long (shorter pieces aren't safe to mill).

Note that the tenons for the front and back upper rails are ⅛" narrower than their corresponding mortises. This important detail requires a little explanation. These mortises are horizontal, rather than vertical. The tenons are narrower than the mortises so you can adjust the position of the rails side to side later on, to accommodate the length of the anti-racking rails (K). If the tenons were exactly the same width as the mortises, you'd have to mill the joints very precisely so that all the parts would fit together. While that's not out of the question, my approach–leaving some room for adjustment–is much easier.

Round the edges of the tenon stock on the router table (Photo 3). Cut the stock into short pieces and glue the tenons into the rails (Photo 4). On the front and back upper rails (the ones with the narrower tenons), glue the tenons in the middle of the mortises.

Build the sides

Mill the side panels (G), but leave them 1" extra long. Assemble the sides, without glue, and measure the distance between the rails (Photo 5). Cut the panels to this exact length (it's best to take off a little at a time, until they fit perfectly). Disassemble the sides.

Cut three biscuit slots in the ends of the panels and in the upper and lower side rails (Photo 6 and Fig. A). Pre-finish the edges of the side rails that have the biscuit slots. The panels will contract when the weather is dry; pre-finishing prevents this shrinkage from revealing unfinished wood.

Glue the sides together, all in one shot. I use slow-acting wood glue for complicated assemblies like this. Its open time is longer than the open time of most yellow glues, so I don't have to rush as fast. Start by gluing the side panels to the rails—the joints that have three biscuits. Apply glue

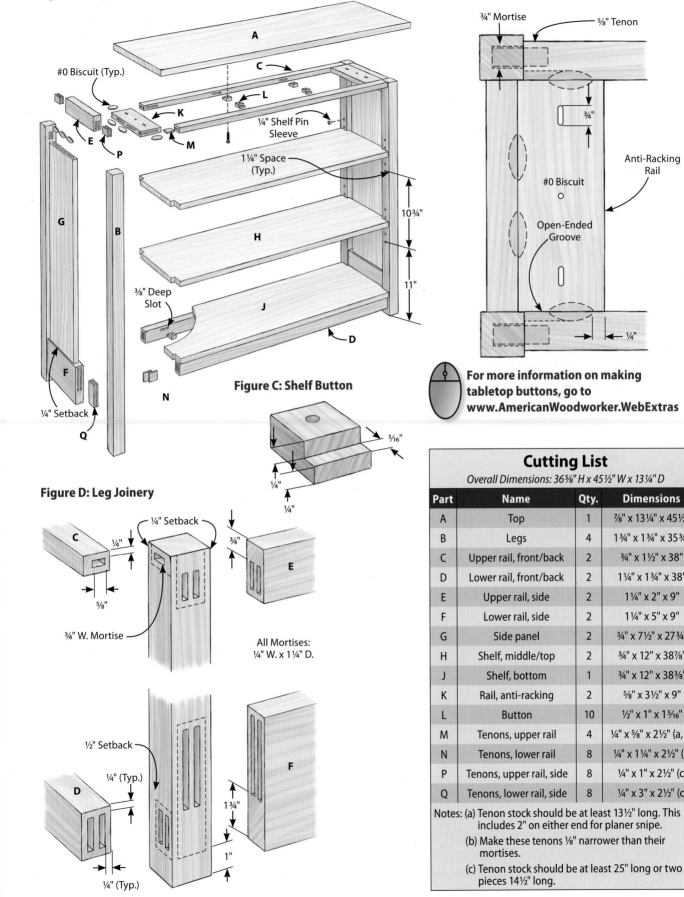

Figure A: Exploded View

#0 Biscuit (Typ.)

¼" Shelf Pin Sleeve

1¼" Space (Typ.)

10¾"

11"

⅜" Deep Slot

¼" Setback

A
C
K
L
M
E
P
G
B
H
J
F
N
Q
D

Figure B: Upper Rail Joinery

¾" Mortise

⅝" Tenon

¾"

Anti-Racking Rail

#0 Biscuit

Open-Ended Groove

¼"

For more information on making tabletop buttons, go to www.AmericanWoodworker.WebExtras

Figure C: Shelf Button

5/16"

¼"

¼"

Figure D: Leg Joinery

C
¼"
¼"
5/8"
¾" W. Mortise

¼" Setback

¾"
E

All Mortises:
¼" W. x 1¼" D.

½" Setback

¼" (Typ.)

D

¼" (Typ.)

F
1¾"
1"

Cutting List

Overall Dimensions: 36⅝" H x 45½" W x 13¼" D

Part	Name	Qty.	Dimensions
A	Top	1	⅞" x 13¼" x 45½"
B	Legs	4	1¾" x 1¾" x 35¾"
C	Upper rail, front/back	2	¾" x 1½" x 38"
D	Lower rail, front/back	2	1¼" x 1¾" x 38"
E	Upper rail, side	2	1¼" x 2" x 9"
F	Lower rail, side	2	1¼" x 5" x 9"
G	Side panel	2	¾" x 7½" x 27¾"
H	Shelf, middle/top	2	¾" x 12" x 38⅞"
J	Shelf, bottom	1	¾" x 12" x 38⅜"
K	Rail, anti-racking	2	⅝" x 3½" x 9"
L	Button	10	½" x 1" x 1 5/16"
M	Tenons, upper rail	4	¼" x ⅝" x 2½" (a, b)
N	Tenons, lower rail	8	¼" x 1¼" x 2½" (c)
P	Tenons, upper rail, side	8	¼" x 1" x 2½" (c)
Q	Tenons, lower rail, side	8	¼" x 3" x 2½" (c)

Notes: (a) Tenon stock should be at least 13½" long. This includes 2" on either end for planer snipe.

(b) Make these tenons ⅛" narrower than their mortises.

(c) Tenon stock should be at least 25" long or two pieces 14½" long.

Assemble the bookcase's side, without glue. Measure the distance between the rails. Cut the side panels to this length.

Cut biscuit slots in the ends of the side panels. Glue the sides together.

Plane the top of each side so the rails and legs are flush. Cut biscuit slots on the inside face of the top rails.

Open-Ended Groove

Left Rail

Right Rail

Make two "anti-racking" rails, and clamp them together. Cut a series of biscuit slots in their ends, to make one long groove. When you separate the pieces, the groove will run out the side of each piece (see inset, top left).

only to the center slots, and leave the outer ones dry. This will allow the panel to shrink and swell without being restrained by glue.

After the sides are glued, plane or sand the top rails and legs so they're even, if necessary. Cut a pair of biscuit slots on the inside edges of the top rails (Photo 7).

Assemble the case

Drill holes and slots in the anti-racking rails for fastening the top (Fig. B). The ends of the rails have biscuit slots that are a bit unusual. These slots are more like grooves—they stop shy of one edge, and run all the way out of the other edge. This design will allow you to slide the piece over a biscuit, as you'll see later. The easiest way to make these long slots is to clamp the two anti-racking rails together (Photo 8), and make a number of regular plunge cuts at each end.

Cut single biscuit slots in the upper front and back rails to receive the anti-racking rails. Glue biscuits in these slots, and carefully remove any glue squeeze-out.

One more thing before getting ready to glue: Rout slots on the inside faces of all four front and back rails to receive the wood buttons (L) that will fasten the top and lower shelf (Fig. A). Make the buttons from a long piece of stock (Fig. C).

You're ready for the big glue-up. First, place biscuits—without glue—into the ends of the anti-racking rails, and clamp these rails between the upper rails (Photo 9). Position the anti-racking rails so they project about ¼" beyond the ends of the upper rails. Use a framing square to align the ends of the upper rails.

Glue the case (Photo 10). Again, with so many pieces to handle, using glue with a longer open time

Cut biscuit slots in the upper rails to receive the anti-racking rails. Clamp the parts together using biscuits, but no glue. Align the ends of the upper rails with each other.

Glue the case together. Slide out the anti-racking rails before the glue dries.

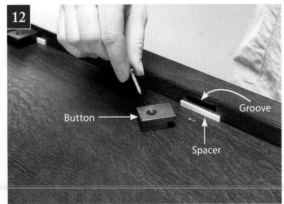

Spread glue on the ends and inner edge of the anti-racking rails, and slide them back in place. Clamp the rails to the sides.

Fasten the lower shelf and top. I like using shop-made wooden buttons, which fit into grooves in the rails. Buttons add a classy look—although you have to get on your hands and knees to see them!

will really help. Before the glue dries, loosen the clamps that hold the anti-racking rails and slide these rails back an inch or so, to ensure that they aren't inadvertently glued in place. When the glue dries, remove the anti-racking rails. Spread glue on the ends and sides of these rails, slide them back in place (Photo 11), and clamp them to the sides.

Finishing up

Glue up the shelves (H & J) and top (A), and cut them to final size. Notch the shelves so there's a ¹⁄₁₆" gap between the shelves and the end panels (so you can drop the shelves in place), and a similar gap between the shelves and the legs (so the shelves have room to expand in width). Make a plywood template

for spacing the shelf pins and drill their holes. I use brass sleeves (see Sources) to line the shelf pin holes; the sleeves add a nice decorative touch to the bookcase. Install the sleeves after the piece is finished.

I use a three-step finish on white oak. First, I apply a yellow dye. Next, I wipe on one or two coats of Bartley's Jet Mahogany gel stain, followed by three applications of Bartley's gel varnish.

After the finish is dry, fasten the lower shelf and the top to the case (Photo 12). Center the top on the case. Using a spacer, leave a ⅛" gap between the button and the rails, to allow the shelf and top to expand when the humidity is high. In addition to the buttons, secure the top with screws that go through the anti-racking rails.

ART DIRECTION: VERN JOHNSON • PHOTOGRAPHY: BILL ZUEHLKE • ILLUSTRATION: FRANK ROHRBACH

by TIM JOHNSON

Two-Drawer Coffee Table

PASS-THROUGH DRAWERS OFFER TWO-SIDED CONVENIENCE

A coffee table isn't just for coffee. It displays interesting reading and serves the Saturday night pizza. It hosts Scrabble games, labors under kids' crafts, and gives you a place to rest your feet. It's a real workhorse that has to be well built and versatile.

Our table is rock-solid, featuring mortise-and-tenon joints, splines, and dovetailed drawers. It's also easy to build, because simple, shop-made jigs ensure perfect-fitting joints. Its two drawers act like four, because they open from both sides. A standard dovetail jig is all you need to make them. Rare-earth magnets work like magic as two-way drawer stops.

This table requires only 25 bd. ft. of 4/4 stock and 9 lineal ft. of rough-cut 2-in.-square stock. If you don't have a jointer and planer, buy turning squares and rip them down to make the legs. Buy ¾-in.-thick boards for everything else but the drawer sides. Get ½-in.-thick boards for them and a 2 ft. by 4 ft. piece of ¼-in. plywood for the drawer bottoms. We built our table from cherry, and used birch for internal parts and drawer sides. Our cost, including one-half sheet of ¾-in. birch plywood for the jigs and clamping cauls, came to about $250.

The only must-have power tools for this project are a tablesaw and a plunge router equipped with an edge guide. You'll also need a drill, a coping saw, a sharp ¼-in. chisel, glue and the usual assortment of clamps, including four 4-ft. pipe clamps.

Start at the Top

I always make the top of a table right off the bat, for two reasons. First, it's the most important part, visually, so it deserves the best-looking boards. Make the aprons, rails, and drawer fronts from the leftovers.

Second, you can start finishing the top early, so the finish will have plenty of time to cure. This is especially important if you plan to build up layers of finish for long-lasting protection. Be sure to apply equal layers to both sides of the top, to keep it stable.

I like to use hide glue when I work with cherry, because of its dark color. Its long open time also makes it easy to fine-tune the joints between the top boards (Photo 1). Wait 24 hours before you remove the clamps. Hide glue takes a long time to dry.

Cut the top (A) to size, smooth it and soften all the edges. I use a router with a ⅛-in. round-over bit for this, but sandpaper and a block will work. If you have children, you may also want to round the four corners for safety.

Use Your Best Boards for the Top. Choose 'em and use 'em right away, so you don't get caught short later. Cauls above and below keep the boards aligned and flat during glue-up. Use a non-marring mallet to make minor adjustments.

Oops!

Shoot! I wish I'd paid attention while I was laying out the legs. The left one looks weird because its figure pattern runs against the taper. What's more, matching the figure and taper on one face isn't enough—legs are usually tapered on two faces. From now on, I'll be sure to look for taper-friendly figure patterns on two adjacent faces of my leg blanks.

Size Up the Legs

The four legs (B) are mortised, dadoed and tapered (Fig. A, Detail 1), but they're not identical. Be sure to make two opposing pairs, one left- and one right-sided. Mark your blanks carefully, so you don't mess up! You'll need all three jigs (Figs. B, D and E) to complete the legs; I find it easiest to make them as I go.

Plunge-Rout the Mortises

Use one of the leg blanks for sizing when you build the mortising jig (Fig. B). Make sure the leg fits snugly between the rails of the jig and is perfectly flush with them at the top.

Plunge-rout mortises for the aprons (Photo 2 and Fig. A, Detail 1), after marking the start/ stop points (Fig. C). All four mortises are cut with the edge guide at the same setting. Create the groove for the haunched tenons (Fig. F) by routing the first couple passes full length. Then use the start/stop marks to finish plunging the individual mortises.

Next, plunge side-by-side mortises for the lower rails (Fig. A, Detail 1). Both of them are cut from the same edge guide setting. After cutting the first mortise, flip the leg end-for-end to cut the second. Each mortise has its own pair of start/ stop marks.

By flipping the leg, the side-by-side mortises will be perfectly centered and their outer shoulders will be identical.

After routing, square the ends of the mortises (Photo 3).

Cut Dadoes and Tapers

The top rail joins the leg in a lapped joint (Fig. H). The leg has a centered through-dado on its top end. To cut this dado safely on the tablesaw, clamp the leg in the tenoning jig (Fig. D) and make two passes (Photo 4). Be sure to dado the face with the side-by-side mortises.

Building the tapering jig (Fig. E), takes longer than using it to taper the legs! Orient the leg so you can clamp it flat on the jig for both tapering cuts (Photo 5).

Figure A: Exploded View

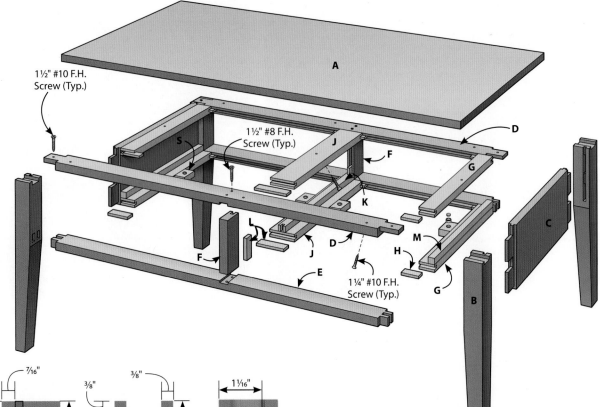

1½" #10 F.H. Screw (Typ.)

1½" #8 F.H. Screw (Typ.)

1¼" #10 F.H. Screw (Typ.)

A

S

J

F

D

G

K

L

F

J

D

M

H

G

E

C

B

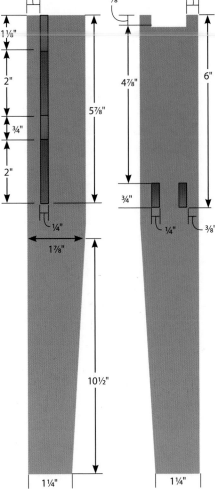

7/16"

3/8"

3/8"

1 1/16"

1⅛"

2"

5⅞"

¾"

2"

4⅞"

6"

¾"

¼"

13/16"

¼"

1⅛"

¼"

¼"

3/8"

1⅞"

10½"

1¼"

1¼"

Detail 1: Leg Joinery

The two outer faces of each leg are left untouched. All the action is on the inner faces. One of them has a long haunched mortise. The other has two mortises side-by-side and a through-dado at the top. Both inner faces are tapered. First, plunge-rout the mortises. Then cut the dadoes in the tops. Save the tapering for last.

Detail 2: Drawer Construction

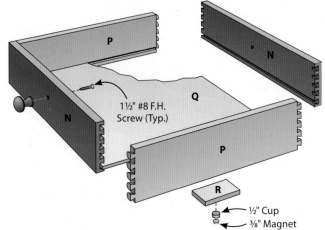

P

N

Q

N

1½" #8 F.H. Screw (Typ.)

P

R

½" Cup

3/8" Magnet

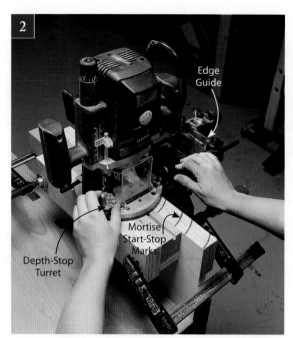

Plunge-rout mortises, using the router's depth-stop turret to increase the depth of each pass. If you have a variable-speed router, you'll get a smoother cut if you slow it down by about a third. Start/stop marks let you cut the mortises without stop blocks (Fig. C)

Square the ends of the mortises, using a block clamped on the layout line to guide the chisel.

Figure B: Jig for Plunge-Routing Mortises

This jig provides a stable surface for routing both left- and right-sided mortises (for the aprons) as well as side-by-side mortises (for the front rails). The leg tops align with one end of the short rail or the other, depending on which mortise is to be cut. The router's edge guide always rides against the long rail.

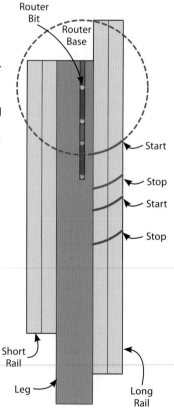

Figure C: Mortise Start/Stop Marks

Indicate each mortise on the jig, using the front edge of the router base. Orient the leg so its mortise will be adjacent to the long rail and its top end flush with the short rail. With the router unplugged, position the bit at the back and front edge of each mortise and mark both locations on the jig. You'll make four marks for each mortising operation. Use the long rail of the jig to mark the long mortises for both left- and right-hand legs and the short rail for the side-by-side mortises. Ultimately, your jig will have 12 marks.

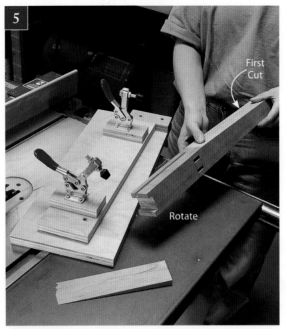

Center a wide dado in the top of each leg, using a shop-made tenoning jig (Fig. D). Make two passes, one on each opposing face, so the shoulders are the same thickness.

Taper the two mortised faces. Clamp the leg with one mortised face toward the blade and the other face down on the tapering jig (Fig. E). After cutting the first taper, rotate the leg clockwise to cut the second taper.

Figure D: Tenoning Jig

This jig rides against the rip fence and allows you to safely make accurate cuts with the workpiece standing on its end. Fasten the stop block with screws only, so it's easy to replace.

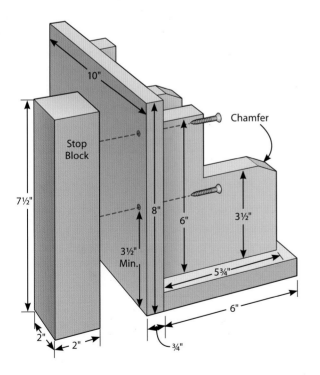

Figure E: Tapering Jig

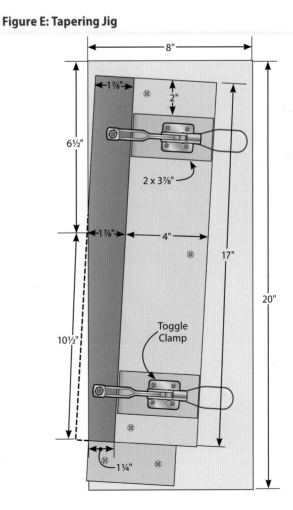

Cut shoulders in the aprons with the blade set to leave ¼-in. remaining in the center. You can use both the miter gauge and rip fence for this operation because you're not making a through cut.

Cut apron tenon cheeks using the tenoning jig. Set the blade height to score the tenon shoulder. Then adjust the tenon's thickness with the rip fence. Make two passes, one on each side of the apron.

Make the Aprons

When you machine the apron blanks (C), make an extra one. Use it for testing when you set the blade and fence on your tablesaw. Cut the tenon shoulders first, using the miter gauge and rip fence (Photo 6). Be careful when you set the blade height. A cut that's too deep will weaken the tenon.

This cut establishes the tenon's length. Be sure to include the width of the saw kerf when you set the rip fence (with a standard ⅛-in. kerf blade, setting the fence at ⅞-in. results in a 1-in.-long tenon).

Next, set the blade and fence for cutting the tenon cheeks, using a test piece with correct shoulder cuts. Test the fit, using one of the mortised legs.

In this operation, the fence setting is most important because it determines the thickness of the tenon (Photo 7). The blade height isn't as critical. Being a bit too deep won't weaken the tenon.

After the cheeks are cut, saw individual tenons from the full-length blanks (Photo 8 and Fig. F). Cut the ends straight, so they fit the mortises. The haunches don't have to be precisely cut, as long as they're short enough to allow the joint to close.

Glue the Legs and Aprons Together

Finish-sand the legs and aprons. Then soften the outside bottom edge of both aprons with the ⅛-in. round-over bit. Soften the edges of the legs too, except for the ones on the face with the side-by-side mortises, where the front rails will be attached.

Glue and clamp each side assembly (Photo 9). Be sure the top of the apron is flush with the tops of the legs. Remove squeezed-out glue, before it hardens, with a damp cloth.

Make the Rails Together

Machine the rail blanks (D and E), along with extra blanks for the drawer dividers (F) and to use for test cuts. Although the upper and lower rail joints are different (Fig. H) and the lower rails end up being shorter, the four rail blanks must be identical, and cut square on both ends.

Finish sawing the tenons with a coping saw or on the bandsaw. Be careful with your layout to make sure the haunches are properly located.

Figure F: Haunched Apron Tenons
A haunched mortise-and-tenon joint is a super-strong version of a tongue-and-groove. Haunches, like the tongue, provide full-width support for the apron. Tenons make a stronger joint than short tongues. They also have much larger gluing surfaces. On this wide apron, two tenons are stronger than one long one. The shoulder at the bottom hides the mortise.

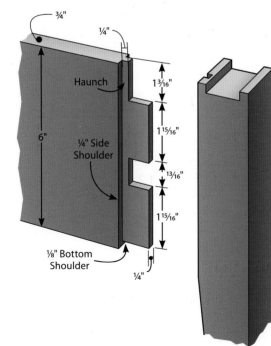

Glue the side assemblies. Brush hide glue on the walls of the mortises and on the tenon cheeks. Use blocks to distribute the pressure when you clamp things together.

First, cut dadoes for the drawer dividers across the inside faces of all four rails (Fig. G). These dadoes must be carefully sized to fit the dividers and precisely centered on the rails. Equip your miter gauge with a fence and stop block to make these cuts.

After cutting the dadoes, separate the rails into pairs and cut the tenon shoulders (Photo 10). Make a third shoulder cut on the inside faces (the ones with the dadoes for the dividers) of the two upper rails (Photo 11).

Next, remove the waste from the tenon sides. Clamp a test piece on the tenoning jig, with its face against the stop block. Raise the blade, set the fence, and cut the outer side of the tenon. Then rotate the test piece 180 degrees and cut the other side.

Test the tenon's fit in the leg-top dadoes. Adjust the fence, if necessary, and finish cutting the tenons on all four rails.

Cut the rails' tenon shoulders simultaneously. Gang them together in pairs, one upper and one lower, and make sure they're precisely mated when you make the cuts.

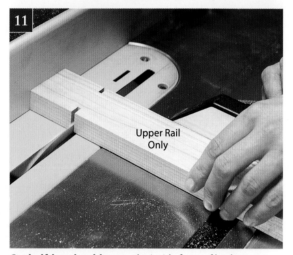

Upper Rail
Only

Cut half-lap shoulders on the inside faces of both upper rails. Use the same setup you just used to cut the tenon shoulders.

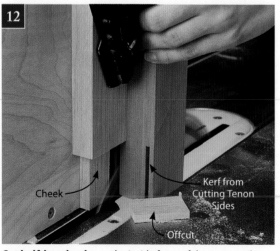

Cheek

Kerf from
Cutting Tenon
Sides

Offcut

Cut half-lap cheeks on the inside faces of the upper rails, using the tenoning jig. Orient the rail so the offcut falls out of harm's way.

Finish the Rail Joints Separately

Re-mount the upper rails in the tenoning jig and cut their half-lap tenon cheeks (Photo 12).

Shorten the lower rails so the tenons extend only ¾ in. Then mark these tenons so you can cut them into the side-by-side tenons (Photo 13). Cut their inner shoulders using the tenoning jig, rotating the rail between cuts. Remove the waste between the tenons with additional passes over the saw blade.

Dado the Rails and Drawer Dividers

Cut shallow ¼-in.-wide dadoes in the back of all four rails (Fig. G). These dadoes will be used to align and attach the drawer supports, so they must be accurately centered. Cut them on the tablesaw, using your regular ripping blade. Set the fence and make a pass dead center. Then reset the fence ¹⁄₁₆-in. off-center and make two more passes, first one face, then the other, against the rip fence.

Dado the back edges of the drawer dividers, too. Rather than dadoing each short divider, it's safest to dado a long blank and cut the dividers from it.

After drilling countersunk pilot holes for screws in the rails, dry-assemble the base on a flat surface. Clamp it together and test the drawer openings with a gauge block (Photo 14).

Glue the Base Together

Hide glue is a good choice for this job. Its long open time gives you the opportunity to check the drawer openings and measure diagonals to make sure everything is square before you drive the screws (Photo 15). Be sure to work on a flat surface.

Cut the drawer supports (G and J) to length and dado their ends to match the dadoes on the rails, using the tenoning jig. Then make the splines (H and L). Apply glue, slide the supports in place and insert the spline. Make sure the support stays flush with both rails when you add the clamps (Photo 16).

The ends of the center drawer guide (K) are also dadoed. Splines keep it flush with the dividers (Photo 17). Glue the outer drawer guides (M) flush with the inner leg faces. Install the upper center drawer support last.

Mark the inside shoulders of the two lower-rail tenons right from the mortises on the leg, after shortening the rail's long tenon.

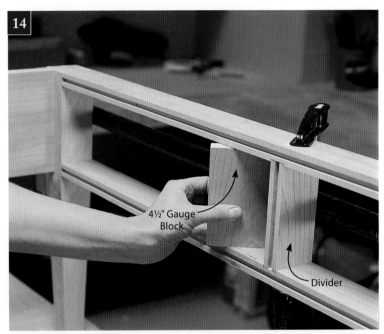

4½" Gauge Block

Divider

Fit the drawer dividers while the base is clamped together in a dry assembly. A shop-made gauge block that measures the width of the drawer opening lets you know when the dividers are the right length.

Figure G: Rail Dadoes

Figure H: Rail Tenons
The upper rails end in half-lapped open tenons that are glued and screwed in the dado on the top of the legs. The lower rails are double-tenoned to fit the side-by-side mortises in the legs. The tenon shoulders of both rails are identical, to ensure a square assembly.

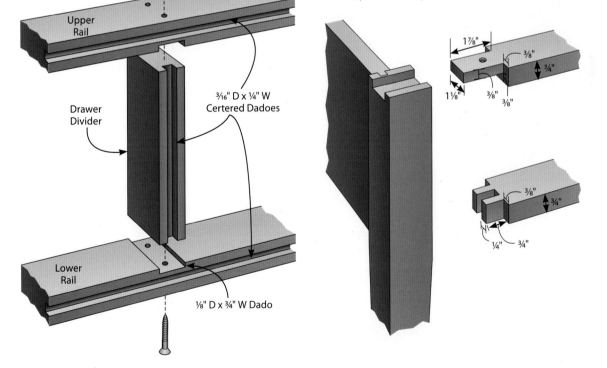

Upper Rail

Drawer Divider

³⁄₁₆" D x ¼" W Centered Dadoes

Lower Rail

⅛" D x ¾" W Dado

1⅞"   ³⁄₈"   ¾"
1⅛"   ³⁄₈"   ³⁄₈"

³⁄₈"   ¾"
¼"   ¾"

Screw the upper rails to the legs when you glue up the base. These open joints benefit from the mechanical assistance of screws.

Wooden splines align the runners and rails perfectly, just like a tongue-and-groove joint.

Drill countersunk pilot holes through all three upper supports for fastening the top with screws, dead center (Fig. A). Then drill slightly larger diameter holes in the upper rails so the top has freedom to move with changes in humidity.

Make and Install the Drawers

We used a dovetail jig and standard bit to make our drawers (Photo 18). Their finished length is ⅜-in. shorter than the pass-through openings, so they'll sit 3/16-in. back from both fronts. This reveal matches the ones between the legs and aprons. The length of your drawer sides (P) may vary from ours, depending on the length of the dovetail your jig makes.

For a good fit, the drawers should be up to 1/16-in. narrower, but only 1/32-in. shorter than the front openings. Center the dadoes for the drawer bottoms (Q) in the lowest dovetail socket of the drawer fronts and on the corresponding tails of the sides. Then they'll be hidden when the drawer is assembled.

Rare-earth magnets act as two-way drawer stops. Mount them in pairs (one on the drawer bottom, the other on the frame), on both sides of each drawer. They're self-aligning, so they've got to be precisely located, end-to-end and side-to-side.

Install each magnet in a block (R and S). Mount the blocks temporarily until you get them in just the right spots. Then glue them in place.

The rare-earth magnets we've chosen are strong enough to work great even when the drawer is loaded down with ten pounds of magazines. However, you should keep magnetic media, including credit cards and videocassette tapes out of the drawers. The magnets will damage them.

Finals

If applying a finish always seems like a chore, cherry is a great wood to work with. Even the simplest wipe-on oil finish will make it look great. For durability, choose one with urethane resins. A brushed-on polyurethane varnish will stand up even longer.

Rare-earth magnets work like magic to stop the drawers

Cutting List

Overall Dimensions: 17¾" x 22" x 46"

Part	Name	Pieces	Dimensions	Comments
A	Top	1	¾" x 22" x 46"	
	Base dimensions		17" x 20" x 39"	
B	Legs	4	1⅞" x 1⅞" x 17"	
C	Aprons	2	¾" x 6" x 18¼"	Includes 1" tenons on both ends
D	Upper rails	2	¾" x 1⅞" x 39"	
E	Lower rail	2	¾" x 1⅞" x 36¾"	Start with 39"-long blank
F	Drawer dividers	2	¾" x 1⅞" x 4¾"	Mill as long blank with Rails (D and E)
G	Outter drawer supports	4	¾" x 1½" x 16¼"	
H	Outer splines	8	¼" x ⅜" x 1¼"	
J	Center drawer supports	2	¾" x 2⅛" x 16¼"	
K	Center drawer guide	1	¾" x 1" x 16¼"	
L	Center splines	6	¼" x ⅜" x 2¾"	
M	Outer drawer guides	2	¾" x ¹³⁄₁₆" x 16¼"	Glue ¹³⁄₁₆" side on Drawer Support
	Drawers	2	4½"* x 17¼"* x 19⅝"	* Exact sizes of drawer front openings
N	Drawer fronts	4	¾" x 4⁷⁄₁₆" x 17⁷⁄₃₂"	
P	Drawer sides	4	½" x 4⁷⁄₁₆" x 18¾"*	* Sized for ⁵⁄₁₆"-long dovetails at each end
Q	Drawer bottoms	2	¼" x 16⅝" x 18½"	Plywood; fit in ³⁄₁₆"-deep dadoes
R	Drawer magnet blocks	4	¼" x 1½" x 3"	
S	Rail magnet blocks	4	¾" x 1⅜" x 2"	

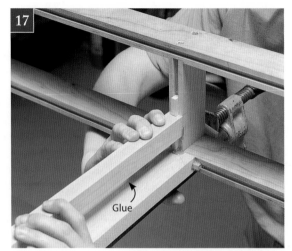

Slip the center drawer guide over the splines, and glue it to the dividers and the lower rail.

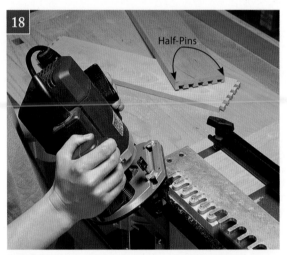

Dovetail the drawers, using a standard jig. They're sized so you'll end up with half-pins at the top and bottom of the drawer fronts.

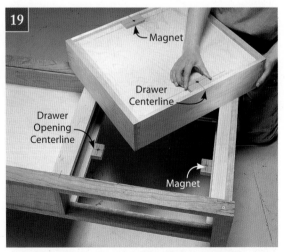

Carefully positioned rare-earth magnets stop the drawers dead center, so you can shut them from either side.

Outdoor Living

What better way to relax than in a chair you built yourself? There are five chairs in this section, from an Adirondack loveseat for two to an artsy mahogany Rietveld-style chair. Of course you'll also find the ever-favorite single Adirondack chair as well as a patio chair that's classy enough to go poolside. For the gardener, there's a cedar trellis for vining flowers and vegetables. Outdoor living also requires a place to store things such as yard games, cooking items, cushions, or gardening supplies. The cypress chest provides handy storage for almost anything. You can even line it with insulating foam and turn it into a cooler big enough for a family reunion or neighborhood party. All of the outdoor projects in this section are made of weather-resistant wood. Without finishes, however, these woods will eventually turn gray. If you're OK with gray, then skipping the finishing is an option. If not, read the section on outdoor finishes, which presents options for preserving the beauty of the wood and protecting it against the damaging effects of weather and the sun.

EDITOR: DAVE MUNKITTRICK • ART DIRECTION: JON SNYDER • PHOTOGRAPHY: BILL RAY AND MIKE HABERMANN • ILLUSTRATION: FRANK ROHRBACH

Adirondack Chair

A TIMELESS CLASSIC, BUILT TO LAST

Visit the Adirondack Mountains and you're likely to come across a familiar style of outdoor furniture named after the region. The Adirondack chair has a low seat, wide arms and a tall, sloping back. It's perfect for reading, visiting with friends or just idling away the hours.

The typical Adirondack is built from pine and protected by a layer or two of paint. Joinery is simple; butt joints and nails do the trick. But yearly painting is necessary to keep the pine from rotting, and joint failure where the arms join the front legs is common. The nails in the arms do not hold well in the end grain of the legs. When you combine that problem with dragging the chair by the arms for passing lawn mowers and the like, it's no wonder this joint is prone to failure.

Our improved Adirondack chair eliminates all these maintenance headaches.

■ **No paint or varnish!**
Mahogany never needs finishing and weathers to a beautiful silver-gray color.

■ **No loose joints!**
Sliding dovetails and mortise-and-tenon joints keep this chair rock solid through many seasons.

■ **No nails or exposed screw heads!**
Plugged stainless steel screws mean you'll never have to get the hammer and nail set out before you can sit in the chair.

The result is a comfortable, low-maintenance chair that lasts.

You'll need about 16 bd. ft. of 4/4 and 12 bd. ft. of 5/4 mahogany. Expect to spend about $90 on materials for one chair. You'll also need a tablesaw, a bandsaw or jigsaw, a plunge router, a drill press and waterproof glue or epoxy.

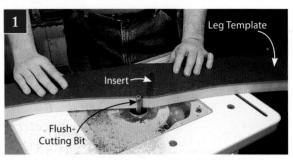

Rout the shape of the legs, arms and back slats using a hardboard template as a guide for the bearing of a flush-cutting bit. Fasten the template to the stock with double-faced tape. Make an insert to fill the gap created by the dovetail sockets in the arm and back leg templates.

Oops!

Oh, no! I forgot to put the insert into the dovetail slot before routing the shape! This made a big gouge in the back leg and I was almost done shaping too!

To fix this loused-up leg, I first made a cut parallel to the grain to remove the gouge (see photo). Then I cut a strip from a similar board so the grain ran in the same direction as the grain on the leg. I glued the block in place, sanded it flush and tried it again—this time *with* the insert.

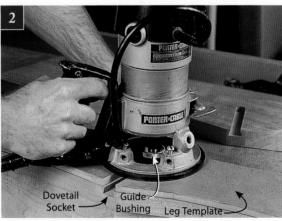

Rout the dovetail sockets in the back legs and arms using a dovetail bit and guide bushing. Set the bit to the depth of the socket, plus the thickness of the template. Then rout the socket by following the notch in the template.

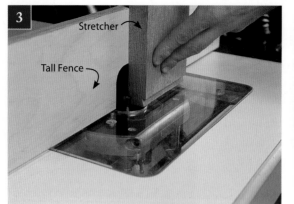

Rout the dovetail in the stretcher with the same dovetail bit you used to cut the slots. A tall fence on the router table helps steady the piece as it's machined.

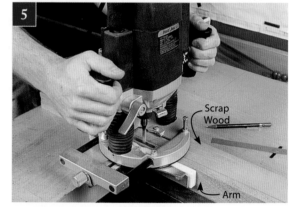

Round the ends of the dovetails so they fit the slots in the legs and arms. Make scoring cuts with a handsaw. Then pare to shape with a chisel.

Figure A: Exploded View

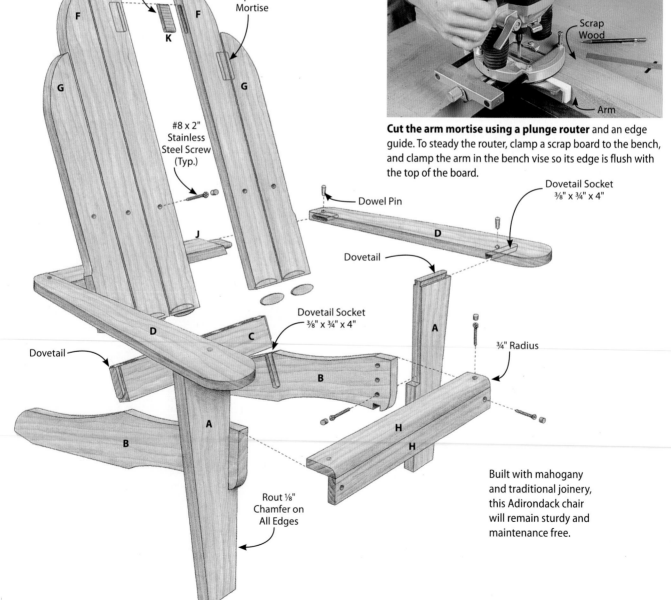

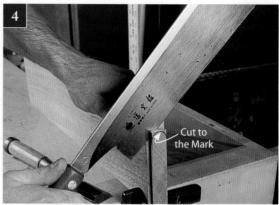

Cut the arm mortise using a plunge router and an edge guide. To steady the router, clamp a scrap board to the bench, and clamp the arm in the bench vise so its edge is flush with the top of the board.

Built with mahogany and traditional joinery, this Adirondack chair will remain sturdy and maintenance free.

Support the backs of the arms with two sticks. Bandsaw notches in the top and bottom of the sticks to help hold the back of the arms level with the fronts during assembly.

Mark for screw holes in the back slat by holding an adjustable square against the back rail. Run the line from the side of the slat to the front, then transfer the mark to the remaining slats.

Making the Templates

Template routing allows you to shape a number of curved or irregular-shaped parts quickly and precisely.

Bandsaw your templates from ¼-in. hardboard to the exact shape of the legs, arms and back slats shown in Figs. B and C on pages 92 and 93. Fair and smooth the edges with a rasp or some sandpaper wrapped around a curved block.

To determine the size of the dovetail notches in the arm and leg templates, measure the difference between the outside diameter of your guide bushing and the diameter of the bit (we used a ⅝-in. guide bushing and a ½-in.-dia. dovetail bit). Add this measurement (⅛ in., in our case) to the width and length of the ¾ in. × 4-in. finished socket (see Arm and Back Leg, Fig. C). Cut the template notches on the bandsaw and clean them up with a rasp.

The Back Slat Templates
Make two templates for the back slats: see Fig. B.

The Back Leg Template
Take the back leg pattern in Fig. B to a copy center and follow the directions for enlargement. In case you don't have access to a copier, we've added a grid diagram so you can lay out a template by hand.

The Front Leg Template
To create the notch on the front leg template (Fig. C), raise the blade on your tablesaw to full height and saw most of the waste. Finish up the cut on the bandsaw. Bandsaw the taper on the front leg. Then clean up the saw marks with a rasp or file.

The Arm Template
Use the illustration in Fig. C as your guide.

Shaping the Parts

Use the template to trace the shape of your workpieces onto the wood. Bandsaw the stock slightly oversize. Now attach the template to the workpiece with small squares of double-faced tape, and rout the work by riding the template against the bearing of a flush-cutting bit (Photo 1). When you've finished routing, pop off the template with a putty knife.

Cutting the Joints

Rout the ⅜-in.-deep dovetail sockets in the arms and back legs (Photo 2).

Cut the dovetails in the stretcher (C) and the front legs on the router table, with the same dovetail bit used to rout the sockets (Photo 3). Round the end of each dovetail (Photo 4).

Rout the back rail (J) tenons in the same manner as the dovetails using a 1¼-in.-long straight cutter in place of the dovetail bit. Round the corners of the tenon with a rasp.

Mortise the arms using a plunge router equipped with an edge guide and a ¼-in. spiral up-cutting bit (Photo 5). Rout slots for the crossgrain splines (K) that join the back slats in the same manner.

Make the splines (K) by rounding the edges of a ¼ in. x 3 in. × 12 in. board with a rasp so they fit the mortises in the back slats. Cut four ⅞-in. splines on the tablesaw.

Use a biscuit joiner to cut the slots in the bottom of the back slats and the stretcher. You could also groove the parts on the tablesaw and join the back slats to the stretcher with a ¼-in.-thick spline.

Great Book of Woodworking Projects | 91

Glue the back slats to the stretcher. Use a pipe clamp to hold the back assembly in position and join the slats to the stretcher. Use ⅛-in.-thick scrap spacers to create the correct gap between the slats.

Figure B: Templates for Back Slats

The back slats require two templates: one for the center slat (E) and another for the tall and short slats (F and G). Start with a single 8⅜ in. x 26 in. piece of template stock. Draw a 6-in. radius at the top with a compass. Rip the 4-in. center slat template from the right side. Rip the outside slat template to 4 in., but stop about 6 in. from the bottom. Finish the ¼-in. jog on the bandsaw. Bandsaw the top curves and rasp smooth.

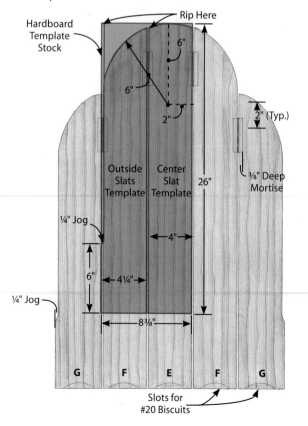

Assembling the Chair

For the ultimate in weather resistance we used epoxy to glue up the chair. Other waterproof glues, such as Titebond II, will also work fine.

The chair goes together in stages. First, join the back legs to the stretcher. Then, join the arms to the front legs. Add the back rail to the arm/front leg assembly. Use scrap sticks to support the arms while you screw the back legs to the front legs (Photo 6). Pull the arms tight to the back rail with a pipe clamp. Drill and peg the four arm joints.

With the back rail in position, hold a back slat against the rail and mark it for the counterbored screw hole (Photo 7).

Epoxy the splines into the back slats using ⅛-in.-thick scrap spacers to create the correct gap between the slats. (Go easy with the epoxy. Squeeze-out between the slats is hard to remove.) Clamp the back slats together with a single pipe clamp. Epoxy the biscuits in the stretcher. Then set the entire back slat assembly onto the stretcher (Photo 8). Once the slats are positioned in the stretcher, screw them to the back rail.

Installing the seat slats is simple: drill and counterbore all the holes in the slats, then position them using ⅛-in. spacers as before, and drive the screws home.

Finally, cut the plugs for the screw holes on the drill press with a plug cutter. To visually blend in the plugs, orient the face grain of the plugs with the grain of the chair and pare them flush to the surface with a chisel.

Finishing and Care

Mahogany weathers to a beautiful silver/gray patina so there's no need to finish this Adirondack chair. To prevent end grain checks where the chair will come in contact with the ground, apply thinned epoxy. Thinning the epoxy 50 percent with acetone allows the mixture to soak more deeply into the pores.

This Adirondack will provide you with years and years of outdoor lounging pleasure without ever having to lift a finger, except to move the chair to follow the shade over the course of a lazy afternoon.

Figure C: Chair Parts

How to Enlarge this Pattern

Use a copier to enlarge the back leg pattern at right by 200 percent. Enlarge it again by 200 percent, then enlarge this copy by 183 percent for a full-size template. You may have to tweak the last enlargement to get an exact copy. Cut out the outline with scissors and trace it onto a ¼-in. hardboard template blank.

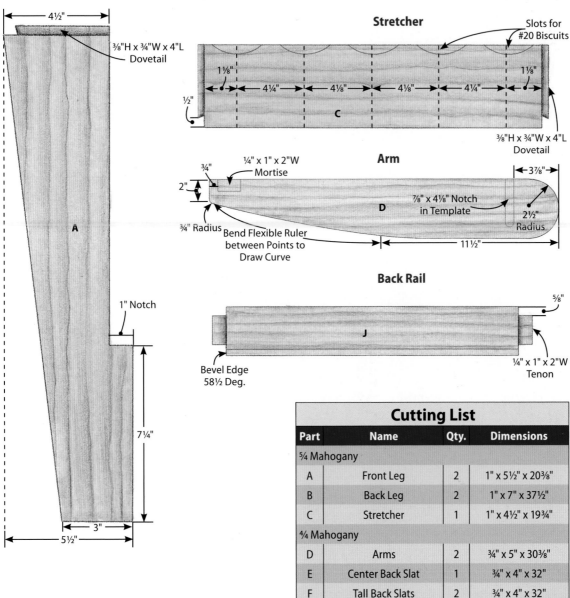

Back Leg

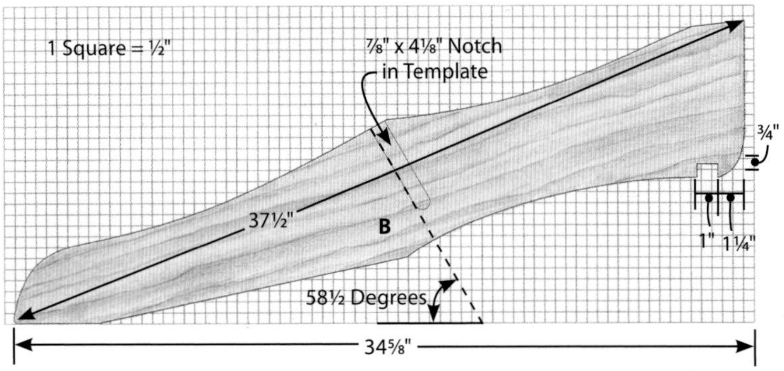
1 Square = ½"
⅞" x 4⅛" Notch in Template
37½"
B
¾"
1" 1¼"
58½ Degrees
34⅝"

Front Leg

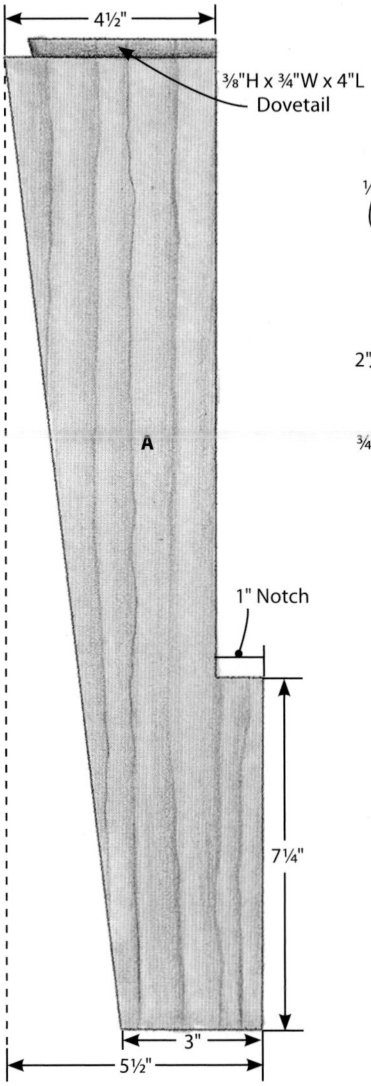
4½"
⅜"H x ¾"W x 4"L Dovetail
A
1" Notch
7¼"
3"
5½"

Stretcher

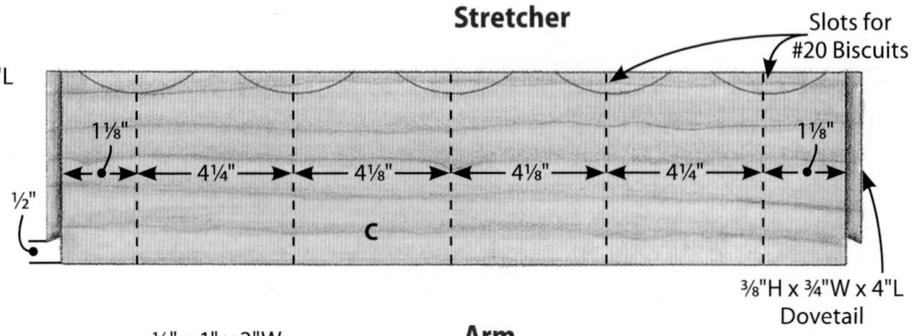
Slots for #20 Biscuits
1⅛"
4¼"
4⅛"
4⅛"
4¼"
1⅛"
½"
C
⅜"H x ¾"W x 4"L Dovetail

Arm

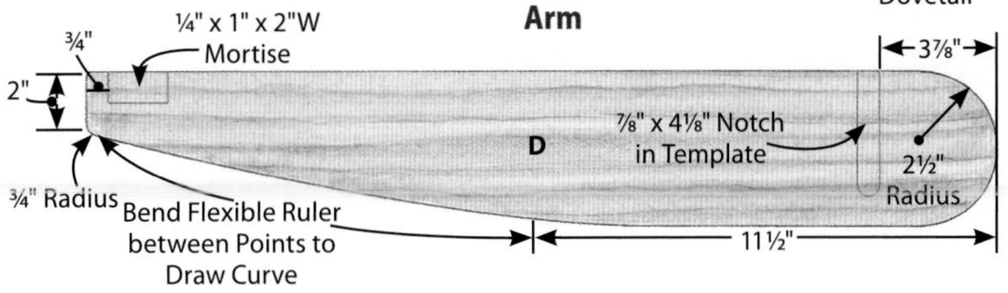
¼" x 1" x 2"W Mortise
¾"
2"
3⅞"
⅞" x 4⅛" Notch in Template
D
2½" Radius
¾" Radius
Bend Flexible Ruler between Points to Draw Curve
11½"

Back Rail

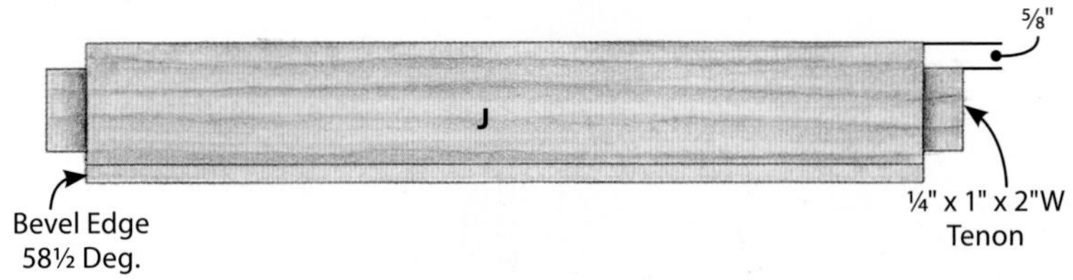
⅝"
J
Bevel Edge 58½ Deg.
¼" x 1" x 2"W Tenon

Cutting List

Part	Name	Qty.	Dimensions
5/4 Mahogany			
A	Front Leg	2	1" x 5½" x 20⅜"
B	Back Leg	2	1" x 7" x 37½"
C	Stretcher	1	1" x 4½" x 19¾"
4/4 Mahogany			
D	Arms	2	¾" x 5" x 30⅜"
E	Center Back Slat	1	¾" x 4" x 32"
F	Tall Back Slats	2	¾" x 4" x 32"
G	Short Back Slats	2	¾" x 4¼" x 26"
H	Seat Slats	8	¾" x 3" x 21"
J	Back Rail	1	¾" x 3⅜" x 23"
K	Splines	4	¼" x 3" x ⅞"

by TOM CASPAR

Adirondack Love Seat

A dirondack chairs represent all that's best about American design: they're practical, with no unnecessary parts; they're accessible, because just about anyone who can cut wood can make one; and they're perfectly suited to their setting, the great outdoors.

An Adirondack's low seat and broad arms invite you to slow down and take it easy. Most Adirondacks are single chairs, of course. A two-seater is something special. Sharing the Adirondack experience with a friend makes it all the better.

Begin building the love seat by sawing out the back legs from a western red cedar 2x6. You'll get the most accurate cuts by using a bandsaw, but you could use a jigsaw, instead.

Joinery is simple: just screws and glue. You'll cover every screw hole with a plug later on. As you build the love seat, drill holes for the plugs and screws simultaneously with a combination bit.

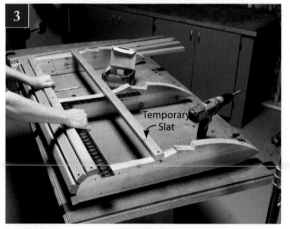

Assemble the seat. Fasten the first four seat slats, which are made from 5⁄4 cedar boards. Check for square as you go. Temporarily add a slat to space the legs the correct distance.

Screw and glue together the front legs. Use a water-resistant glue to assemble all the parts of the project.

Materials and Tools

This project is built from western red cedar construction lumber, which is commonly available at home centers and lumberyards. You'll need two 2 × 6 boards, 8 ft. long, and nine pieces of 5/4 lumber, 1 in. thick, 5½ in. wide, and 12 ft. long. Dust from cutting western red cedar can be irritating, so wear an appropriate dust mask and work in a well-ventilated shop or outdoors. Use rust-resistant deck screws to assemble the project. You'll need about 100 1½-in. screws and 50 1¼-in. screws. You'll also need two inside-corner braces and 100 screw-hole plugs.

You'll use a tablesaw, bandsaw (or jigsaw), router table, ⅜-in. roundover bit, 30-degree chamfer bit, cordless drill and a file for the project. A miter saw is also handy.

Make the Legs and Seat

1. The love seat sits on three back legs: two on the sides (A1, Fig. A, page 99) and one in the center (A2). They're virtually identical, except for one important detail: the notch for the lower back rail (A5) is positioned farther back on the center leg than on the outer legs (Fig. H). To ensure that all the legs come out the same, make one paper pattern based on the measurements given for the outer back leg (A1). Trace around the pattern on three leg blanks cut to the same length, omitting the notches. Then draw the notches directly on the legs. In addition, set your miter saw to 18 degrees and cut a miter on a scrap piece of 1 × 6. Use this piece to draw the angled lines that indicate the location of the front legs. Draw these lines on both sides of each outer leg.

Glue and screw the front legs to the seat assembly. Then add the rest of the seat slats and the lower back rail, which sits in the notches on the back legs. Assembly is much easier if you work on a large, flat surface, such as a door.

Glue the arms together from two pieces of 5/4 material. To make a tight, invisible joint, first remove the rounded edges of this construction lumber by ripping the boards on the tablesaw.

30° bevel

Rout a 30-degree bevel on the upper back rail using a router table. The love seat's back slats lean against this piece; with an accurately made bevel, you'll get tight, strong joints.

2. Saw the legs (Photo 1). Smooth the saw cuts with a file or 80-grit sandpaper wrapped around a block.

3. Make the seat slats (A3). Discard pieces with large knots—they'll weaken the slats. Drill holes for screws and plugs in the ends and middle of all the slats using a ⅜-in.-dia. combination countersink/counterbore bit (Photo 2). Make the plug holes about ¼-in. deep. Round the top edges of the slats, and all other exposed edges as you build the project, using a ⅜-in. roundover bit mounted in a router table.

4. Line up the front edges of all three legs. Temporarily fasten a slat to the middle of each leg. Glue and screw the first four slats (Photo 3).

5. Make the two pieces that comprise each front leg (B1 and B2) from one long board. Rip the board to remove its rounded edges. This makes a better-looking joint when you glue the pieces together. Cut one end of the blank at 18 degrees, then cut the inner leg to exact length (Fig. E). Cut the outer leg to length, then glue and screw together the leg pieces (Photo 4). Note that the two front legs are mirror images of each other.

6. Apply glue to the front legs and clamp them to the back legs. Use the lines you drew in Step 1 to position the front legs. Drill holes in the front legs for screws and plugs, then run in the screws (Photo 5).

7. Make the back seat slat (A4, Fig. F) and lower back rail (A5, Fig. G). Note that the inside curve on each end of the lower back rail consists of three flat sections, to receive three back slats. The straighter these sections are, the stronger your joints will be. After sawing, use a file to straighten these cuts, if necessary. Use a file to flatten the rail's center straight section, too. Drill holes for screws and plugs in the back seat slat and lower back rail, then round over the edges of both parts with a ⅜-in. router bit. Don't round over the inner edge of the lower back rail, where the back slats (D1, D2) go.

8. Remove the seat slat you temporarily screwed to the back legs. Glue and screw the lower back rail in position. Screw the back seat slat next to it, but don't glue it. Add the rest of the seat slats. Space them about ¼-in. apart. Temporarily clamping some slats in position makes it easier to space them.

9. Remove the back seat slat.

Add the Arm Assembly

10. Rip two 5/4 pieces for each arm (C1) and glue them together (Photo 6). Cut each blank to length, then saw out the curves (Fig. J). Sand the glue joint, then round over both sides of the arm with a ¼-in. roundover bit. Don't round the curved section where the arm overlays the back rail.

11. Make the upper back rail (C2). This piece has three straight sections on either side (Fig. M), like the lower back rail. Trace the curves of the arm pieces on the ends of the rail. Cut out the rail using a bandsaw, with the table set at 90 degrees, and straighten the flat sections with a file. Rout a 30-degree bevel on the inside edge of the rail (Photo 7). Leave a ⅛-in.-thick blunt edge to guide the bit's bearing.

12. Glue and screw the arms to the upper back rail. Note that the inside edge of each arm is square to the back rail (Fig. C), and that the screws go from underneath the back rail and into the arms (Fig. A).

13. Cut two temporary support pieces (C3) to hold and level the arm assembly. Prop the assembly on these pieces and the front legs (Photo 8). Once the assembly is correctly positioned front-to-back and side-to-side (Fig. D), clamp it to the front legs, so it can't shift.

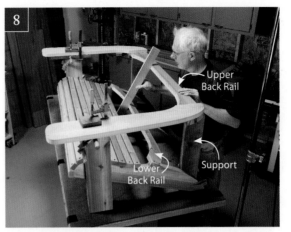

Add the arm and upper back rail assembly. Stand it on two supports and adjust its position until the bevel you routed is in line with the lower back rail. Check this with a straightedge.

Taper the back slats using a jig for your tablesaw. Mount toggle clamps on the jig to keep your fingers away from the blade.

Spacing the love seat's back slats requires careful measuring and marking. Begin by temporarily installing the four slats that define the two halves of the back.

Fasten the middle slats next. Then install two slats between the middle and outer slats. Adjust these slats up or down to make the spacing even.

Draw a curve across the back using a shop-made trammel. That's just a stick with a nail at one end and a pencil stuck in a hole on the other end. Remove the slats and cut the curve on each piece.

Fit the Back Slats

14. Make a set of back slats (D1 and D2). You can rough-cut two slats from one 5½-in.-wide 5/4 board using a bandsaw. Build a tapering jig and cut each slat using the tablesaw (Photo 9 and Fig. K). The exact angles on the slat's ends are not important.

15. Drill screw-and-plug holes in the lower ends of the outer slats (D1). Mark the positions of these slats on the lower back rail (Fig. B). Clamp the slats in position (the top ends of the centermost slats touch each other) and mark locations for the screws that will go into the upper back rail. Remove the slats, drill the screw-and-plug holes, then attach–but don't glue–the slats in place (Photo 10).

16. Install one of the inner back slats (D2) midway between the outer back slats. It should be vertical. Fit the remaining slats (Photo 11). Make the gap between them about ¼-in. After these slats are fitted, mark their screw-and-plug holes and cut off any excess length at the bottom. Then install the slats with screws, but don't use glue. Repeat this process on the other side of the back.

17. Make a trammel and find the center point of each half of the back (Fig. L). Turn the trammel around and draw each curve (Photo 12).

18. Mark the position of all slats and remove them. Bandsaw their top ends and round over all their edges. Glue and screw the slats back in place. Cut a piece of paper to fit the gap between the two back sections. Fold the paper in half and use it as a pattern to make two pieces (D3) to fill the gap. Install these pieces.

Support the Arms

19. Connect the arms and legs with inside corner braces (Fig. A). Use #10 or #12 pan head screws to install them.

20. Cut two corbel blanks (B3). Rout stopped grooves on the inside edge of each blank to accommodate the corner brace and screw heads (Photo 13). Saw the corbel's shape (Fig. N) and round over its outside edges. Make sure each corbel's top fits tight under the arm. Drill screw-and-plug holes through the front legs and screw and glue the corbels to the front legs (Photo 14).

Rout grooves on the ends and inner edges of the corbels, the wing-shaped pieces that support the love seat's broad arms. These grooves hide metal braces under the arms.

Fasten the corbels to the legs with glue and screws. The brace allows you to safely lift the love seat by its arms.

Finishing Steps

21. Install the back seat slats. Glue plugs in all the screw holes. Cut and sand them flush.

22. Apply two coats of exterior oil finish. It's best to do this outside, for good ventilation. Sit and enjoy!

Once every part is in place, glue plugs in each screw hole. Cut the excess with a flush-cutting saw.

Figure A: Exploded View

Figure B: Slat Location

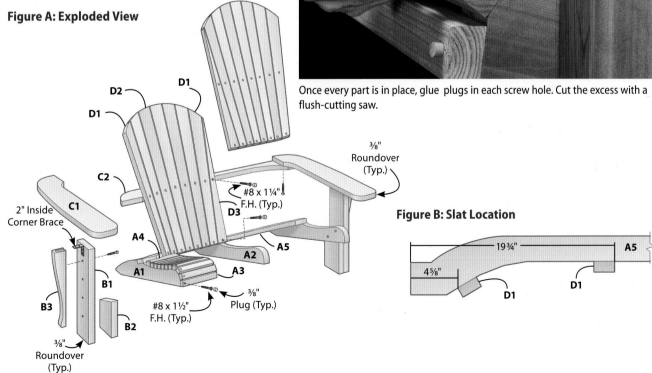

Figure C: Arm and Back Rail Assembly

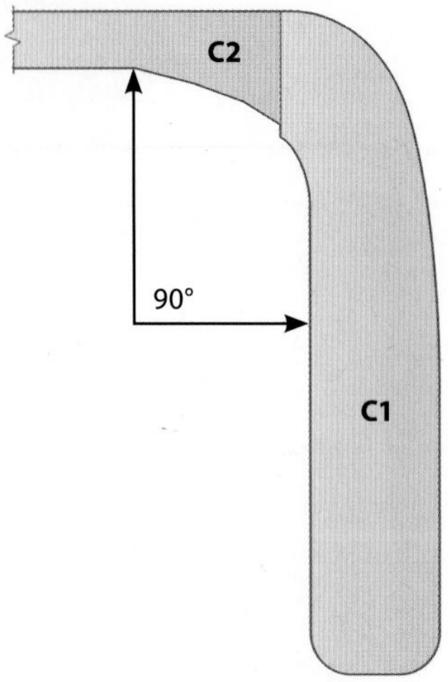
C2
90°
C1

Figure D: Cross Section

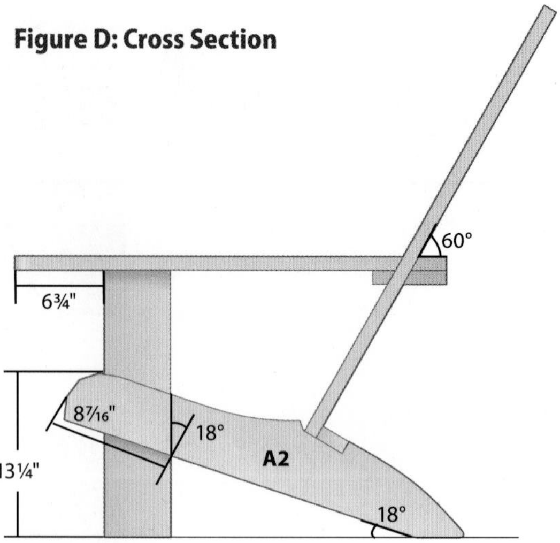
60°
6¾"
8 7/16"
18°
13¼"
A2
18°

Figure E: Front Leg

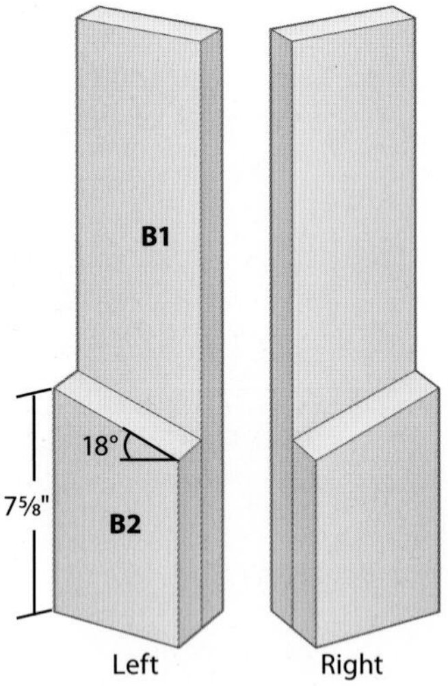
B1
18°
7⅝"
B2
Left
Right

Figure F: Back Seat Slat

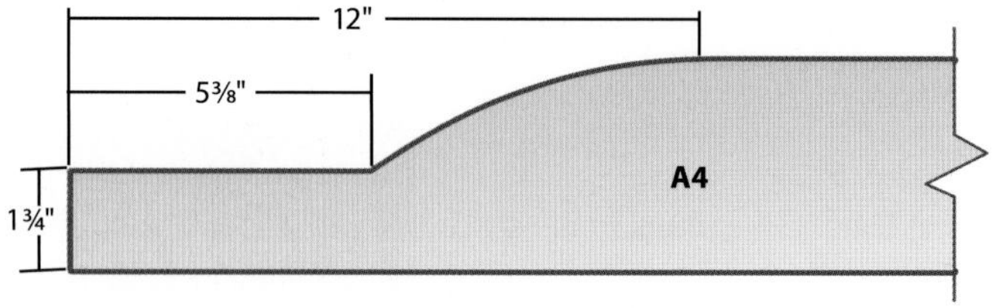
12"
5⅜"
1¾"
A4

Figure G: Lower Back Rail

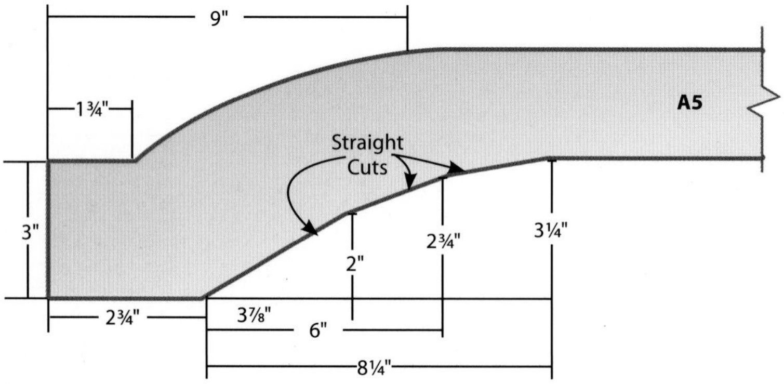
9"
1¾"
A5
Straight
Cuts
3"
2"
2¾"
3¼"
2¾"
3⅞"
6"
8¼"

Figure H: Back Legs

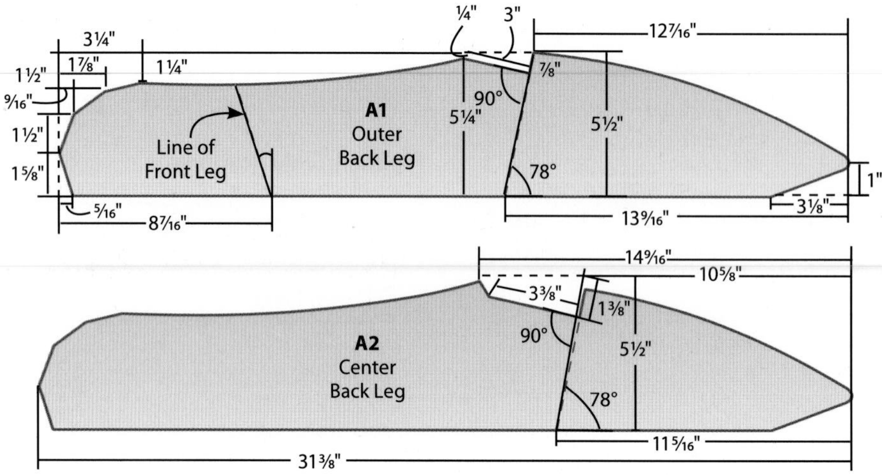
¼"
3"
12 7/16"
3¼"
1⅞"
1¼"
1½"
9/16"
1½"
1⅝"
5/16"
8 7/16"
Line of
Front Leg
A1
Outer
Back Leg
⅞"
90°
5¼"
5½"
78°
1"
3⅛"
13 9/16"
14 9/16"
10⅝"
3⅜"
1⅜"
90°
A2
Center
Back Leg
5½"
78°
11 5/16"
31⅜"

Figure J: Arm

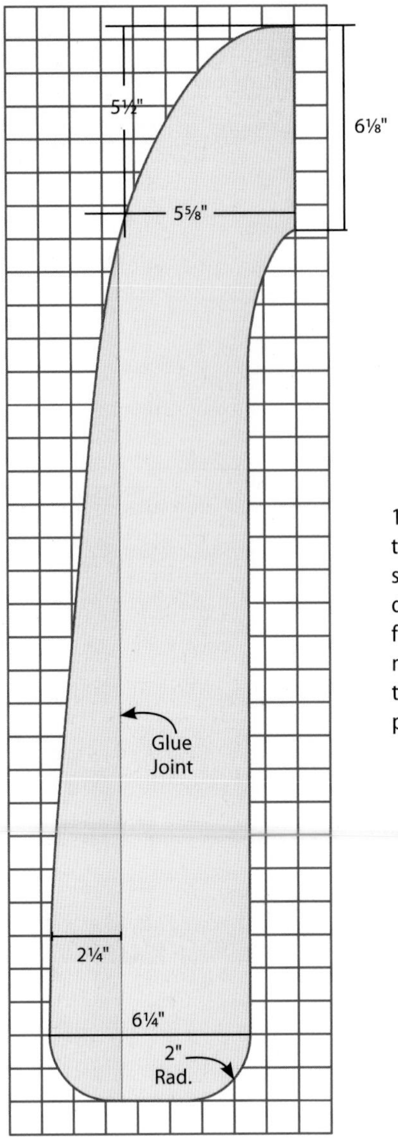
5½"
6⅛"
5⅝"
Glue Joint
2¼"
6¼"
2" Rad.

Figure K: Back Slats and Tapering Sled

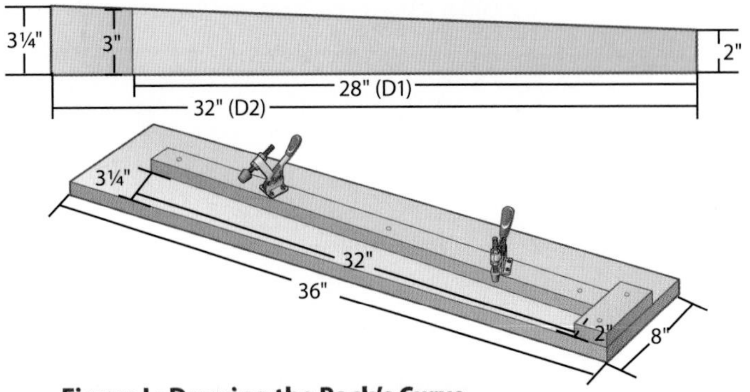
3¼"
3"
2"
28" (D1)
32" (D2)
3¼"
32"
36"
2"
8"

Figure L: Drawing the Back's Curve

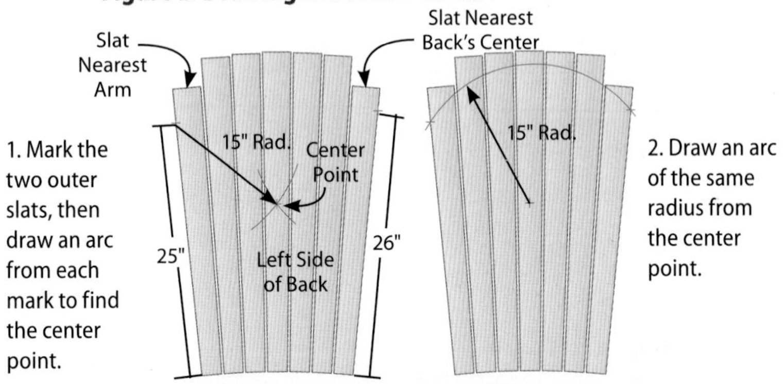
Slat Nearest Arm
Slat Nearest Back's Center
1. Mark the two outer slats, then draw an arc from each mark to find the center point.
15" Rad.
Center Point
25"
Left Side of Back
26"
15" Rad.
2. Draw an arc of the same radius from the center point.

Figure M: Upper Back Rail

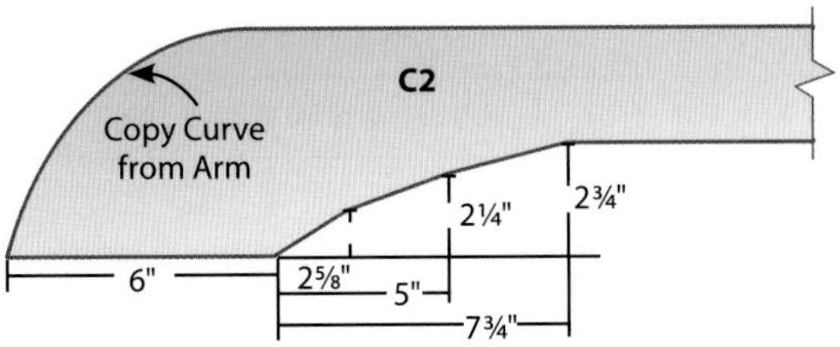
C2
Copy Curve from Arm
2¼"
2¾"
6"
2⅝"
5"
7¾"

Figure N: Corbel

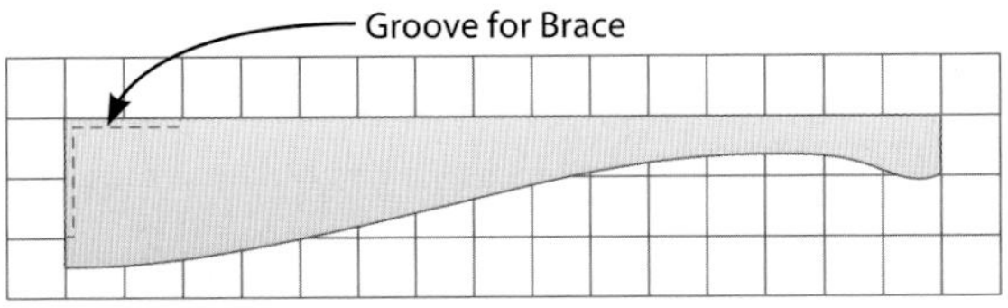
Groove for Brace

Cutting List

Overall Dimensions: 58" W x 37" D x 34½" H

Part	Name	Qty.	Dimensions	Material
Seat				
A1	Outer back leg	2	1½" x 5½" x 31⅜"	2 x 6
A2	Center back leg	1	1½" x 5½" x 31⅜"	2 x 6
A3	Seat slat	10	1" x 1½" x 47"	5⁄4
A4	Back seat slat	1	1" x 3¾" x 47"	5⁄4
A5	Lower back rail	1	1" x 5½" x 47"	5⁄4
Front legs				
B1	Outer leg	2	1½" x 5" x 19½" (a)	2 x 6
B2	Inner leg	2	1½" x 5" x 7⅝"	2 x 6
B3	Corbel	2	1" x 2½" x 15"	5⁄4
Arms				
C1	Arm	2	1" x 8" x 32⅜" (b)	5⁄4
C2	Upper back rail	1	1" x 5½" x 53"	5⁄4
C3	Assembly support	1	1½" x 5½" x 18½"	5⁄4
Back				
D1	Outer back slat	4	1" x 3" x 28" (c)	5⁄4
D2	Inner back slat	10	1" x 3¼" x 32" (d)	5⁄4
D3	Center slat	2	1" x 3½" x 25"	5⁄4

(a) Cut B1 and B2 from 30" long blank.
(b) Glue up from two pieces, 5" and 3" wide.
(c) Cut two pieces from one 5½" x 28" blank.
(d) Cut two pieces from one 5½" x 32" blank.

EDITOR: DAVE MUNKITTRICK • ART DIRECTION: EVANGELINE EKBERG • PHOTOGRAPHY: MIKE KRIVIT • ILLUSTRATION: FRANK ROHRBACH

by LUKE HARTLE

Garden Bench

GRACEFUL, COMFORTABLE, AND BUILT TO LAST

It dawned on me the other day that every single project I've made resides in my house. Since I spend a lot of time in my back yard garden, I decided it was high time I made something to enjoy in my outdoor living space as well. This backless bench is the perfect project. The bench is now the centerpiece of my yard. Stout mortise-and-tenon joinery and naturally rot-resistant mahogany ensure that it will retain its exalted position for years to come. Traditional joinery holds the framework together; the seat slats are secured with a newer joinery technique, the Miller Dowel system (see "Miller Dowel Joinery System," page 105). The bench seemed to be the perfect project on which to try these high-tech dowels. I really liked how quick and easy they were to use compared with the traditional screw-and-plug approach.

Project Requirements at a Glance

Materials:

- 18 bd. ft. of 4/4 mahogany
- 5 bd. ft. of 8/4 mahogany

Tools:

Tablesaw, jointer, cordless drill, planer, drill press

Hardware:

28 Miller Dowels, 1X size

Cost: About $165

Cutting List *Overall Dimensions: 55" L x 16¼" W x 17¼" H*			
Part	**Qty.**	**Dimensions**	**Material**
A Leg	4	1⅞" x 1⅞" x 16½"	8/4 mahogany
B Long rail	2	⅞" x 3" x 50¾"	4/4 mahogany
C Seat rail	2	⅞" x 3" x 13¾"	4/4 mahogany
D Spreader	2	⅞" x 3" x 14"	4/4 mahogany
E Lower rail	2	⅞" x 1¾" x 13¾"	4/4 mahogany
F Brace	1	⅞" x 1¾" x 51"	4/4 mahogany
G Slat	7	¾" x 2⅛" x 55"	4/4 mahogany

Figure A: Exploded View

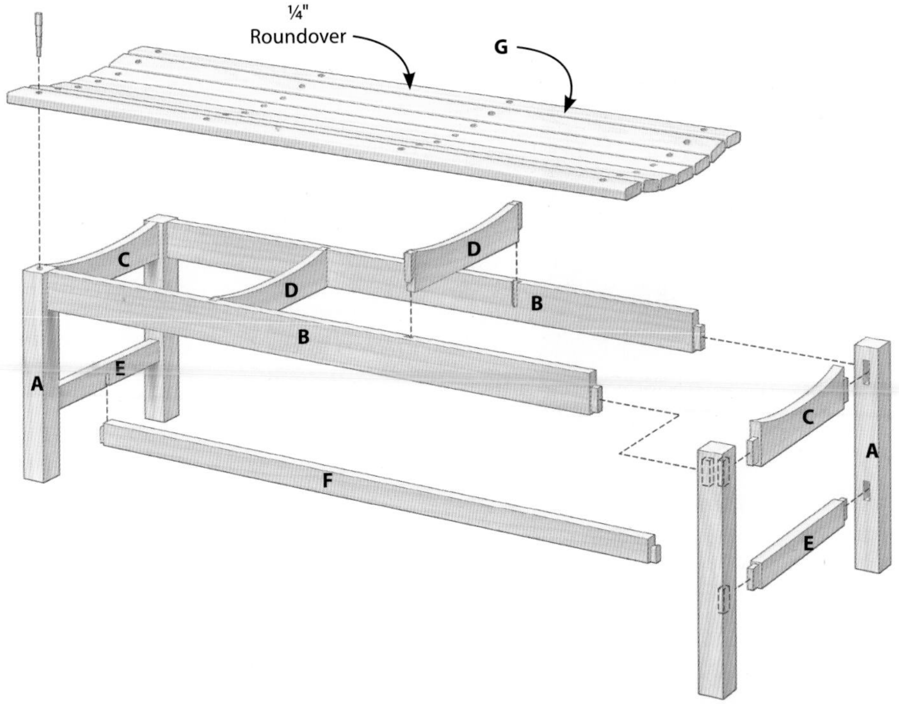

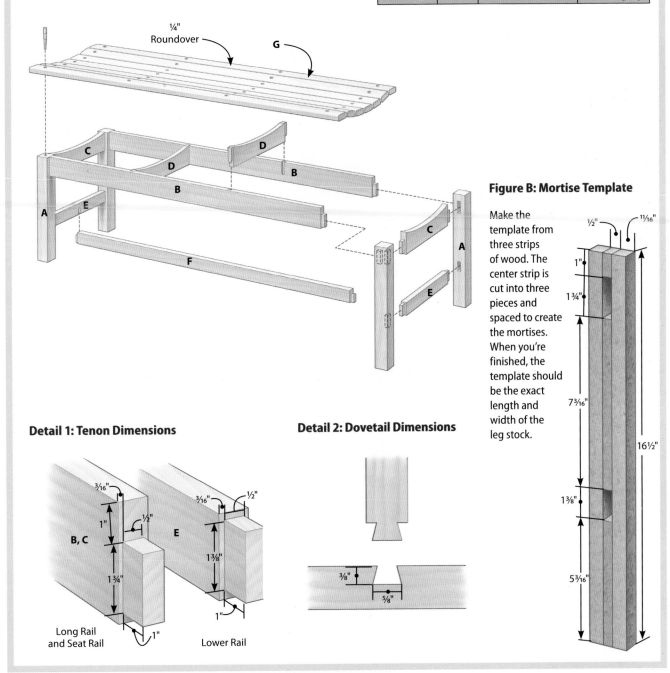

Figure B: Mortise Template

Make the template from three strips of wood. The center strip is cut into three pieces and spaced to create the mortises. When you're finished, the template should be the exact length and width of the leg stock.

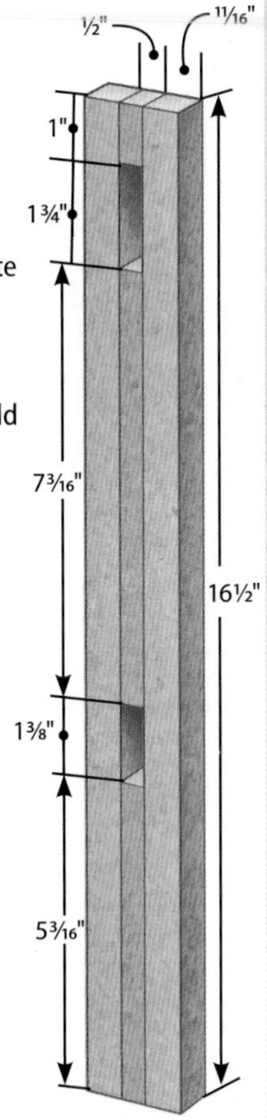

Detail 1: Tenon Dimensions

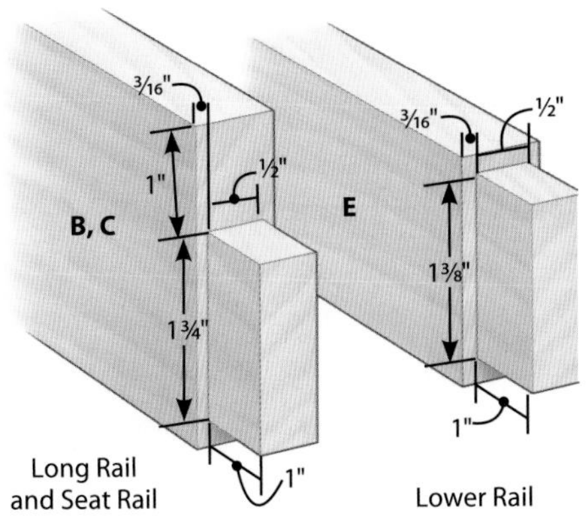

Detail 2: Dovetail Dimensions

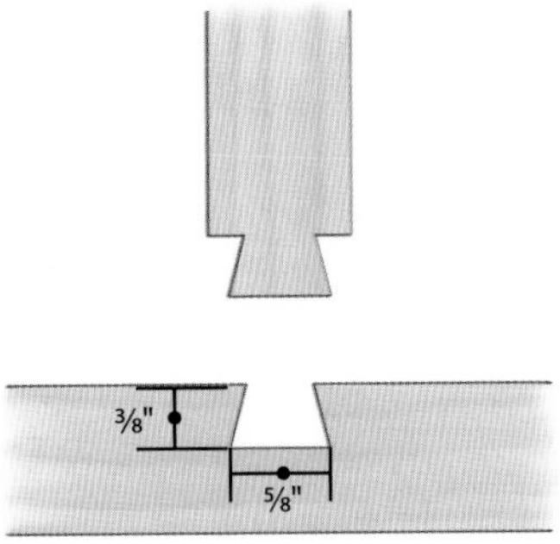

Square the corners of the mortise with a chisel before removing the template. The template serves as a guide to square the corners and ensure a perpendicular cut.

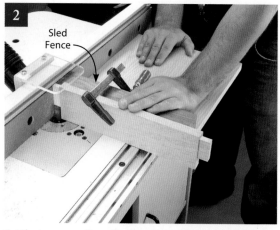

Cut the tenons on the rails with a ¾-in.-dia. straight bit. A plywood sled with an attached hardwood fence ensures the shoulders of the tenon are cut square and keeps your hands away from the spinning bit.

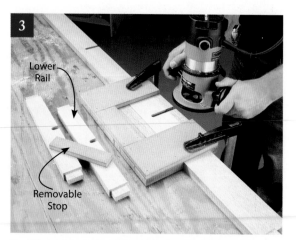

Rout the stopped-dovetail sockets for the seat supports using a simple shop-made jig. Clamp the jig to the stock and the workbench. Add a stop-block to the jig to cut the shorter sockets for the brace in the lower rails.

1. Mill all pieces to their final dimensions, except for the spreaders (D) and brace (F).

2. Make a template (Fig. B) to route the mortises.

3. To avoid mistakes, label each leg as front or back, left or right (Fig. A, page 103). Use the template to lay out the mortises.

4. Drill out the mortises on the drill press.

5. Rout the mortises in the bench legs using a template and a top-bearing pattern bit.

6. Use a chisel to square the mortise's corners.

7. Rout the tenons on the long rails (B), seat rails (C), and the lower rails (E) (Photo 2). Use a large-diameter straight-cut bit for a smooth cut.

8. Use the dovetail jig to rout the stopped-dovetail grooves in the long rails (Photo 3). Match the centerline of the socket with the centerline on the jig. Clamp everything firmly to the workbench.

9. Insert the stop block in the jig and rout the dovetail sockets in the lower rails.

10. Rough-cut the seat template pattern (Fig. C, page 105) on the bandsaw and sand smooth.

11. Rough cut the curves in the seat rails on the bandsaw. Finish the profile with the seat template and a pattern-cutting bit (Photo 4). Center the template on the rail with the back edges flush.

12. Sand all the parts to 180 grit.

13. Glue the bench frame in stages, using a waerproof glue, such as Titebond II or III. Assemble the legs, seat rails and lower rails first

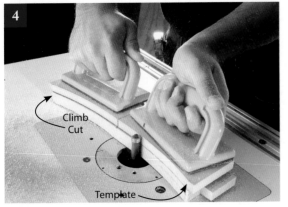

4

5 End Frame

Dovetail Groove

Rout the curve in the seat rails and spreaders using a template. Center the template on the rail and secure it with double-sided tape. Climb-cut the last portion of the curve first to prevent tearout.

Glue the long rails to the assembled end frames. Keep the dovetail groove opening faceup (that is, down on the bench) on the long rails. The grooves on the lower rails face the opposite direction to hide the dovetail joint.

to create an end assembly. Then join the end assemblies with the long rails (Photo 5).

14. Determine the exact length of the seat spreader (D) by measuring the distance between the long rails where they join the legs and adding the length of each dovetail. Cut the spreaders to length. Measuring near the legs rather than in the dovetail grooves eliminates measuring any slight bow in the long rails.

15. Measure and cut the brace (F) to length.

16. Route the tails of the dovetails on the seat spreaders and on the brace (Photo 6). Run a few test cuts on scrap lumber to get the perfect fit.

17. Use a handsaw to notch each tail so they are about ⅛ in. shorter than the sockets.

Miller Dowel Joinery System

The Miller Dowel system combines the strength of wood joinery with the ease of a screw. Drill the hole, add the glue, tap the peg and you're finished. The secret to the dowel's success lies in its stepped design. The shoulder on the head of the dowel seats before the other shoulders do, driving the parts together much like a nail does. Horizontal ribs on the dowel absorb moisture from the glue, causing the dowel to swell in the hole and lock in place. The head of the dowel serves as a plug in the hole, but unlike traditional plugs, the Miller Dowel leaves dark-looking end grain exposed for a decorative look after the plug is sanded and finished.

Miller Dowels are available in three sizes and a wide variety of species. A companion stepped drill bit is specifically designed for each size of dowel.

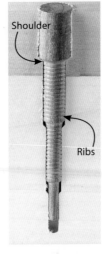

Shoulder

Ribs

Figure C: Seat Template

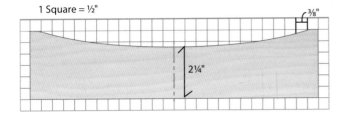

1 Square = ½"

⅜"

2¼"

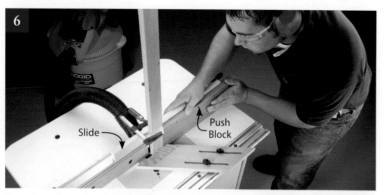

Rout the tails on the ends of the brace and the seat spreaders. Stabilize the stock using a push block with a slide attached. Fasten the slide so it runs along the top of the fence. Clamp the stock to the slide so it butts against the push block.

Glue the spreaders and the brace to the bench frame. Slide the dovetails together by hand as far as possible. Use a rubber mallet to tap the joint home. Alternate tapping each end to prevent binding.

Install the slats to the bench frame using Miller Dowels. When the first board has been doweled, use a ¼-in. spacer to set the gap between the slats. Clamp the end of each slat as you drill and dowel, working your way across the bench.

18. Rout the curves in the spreaders, as done on the seat rails in Step 11. Make sure to use the centerline for reference. Unlike the rails, the spreaders will have short flats on each end of the curve (Fig. A, page 103).

19. Sand the seat spreaders and the brace.

20. Glue in the spreaders (Photo 8). Then, flip the bench and add the brace.

21. Shape the seat slats on the router table with a ¼-in. round-over bit.

22. Lay out all dowel locations on the seat slats (Fig. A).

23. Attach the seat slats to the bench (Photo 9). First clamp an outside slat so it overhangs the leg by ⅛ in. Run the drill at the maximum rpm level with a slow feed rate to prevent tearout around the hole.

24. Use a framing square to keep the slats' ends aligned.

25. Trim the dowel heads with a flush-cut saw.

26. Sand the slats to 180 grit.

27. Finish the bench with an outdoor finish to preserve its color and appearance or skip the finish and let it age naturally to a silver-gray color.

by DAVE MUNKITTRICK

Cypress Chest

BEAUTIFUL OUTDOOR STORAGE MADE TO TAKE THE ELEMENTS. I DESIGNED THIS CHEST TO KEEP OUT BOTH THE ELEMENTS AND UNWELCOME ANIMALS

This beautiful chest is designed to store the smaller outdoor amenities we use everyday, such as cushions for deck furniture, pool toys, or even gardening supplies. The cream-colored cypress is similar in appearance to a light-colored cedar or fir. Cypress is about 50 percent harder than clear cedar but about half the cost. Cypress is a rot-resistant member of the pine family native to swampy areas in the Southern United States. It's a stable wood, meaning it won't expand and contract a lot with the seasons. Cypress also machines well and takes any finish.

ART DIRECTION: RICK DUPRE • PHOTOGRAPHY: PAGES 62–63, RAMON MORENO; OTHERS, PATRICK HUNTER • ILLUSTRATION: FRANK ROHRBACH

Built to Last in the Great Outdoors

The **top sheds rainfall** because the lid has a broad overhang and its hinge creates a gentle slope.

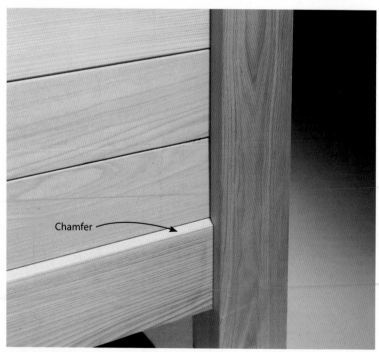

A chamfered bottom rail prevents rainwater from pooling and eventually causing decay.

Build the Legs and Rails

1. Sort your wood and select the best-looking pieces for the lid (A) and front panel (B). Rough-cut your stock according to the Cutting List (see page 113), but leave everything oversize by at least ½-in. in length. Parts made from glued-up stock (G through L) should initially be cut an extra ½ in. wide.

2. Use a waterproof glue to face-glue three pieces of ¾-in. stock for each leg (G). Glue up two pieces for the rail stock (H through L). Make an extra leg blank and an extra rail to test setups. Mark the best-looking face on each piece.

A deck-like bottom with gaps between the boards allows air to circulate to prevent mold or mildew. A galvanized metal screen called hardware cloth is mounted under the decking to keep unwanted critters out.

3. Trim the leg blanks to size after the glue has dried (Photo 1).

4. Lay out the groove location and the taper (Figs. B and C, page 111) on each leg. Position the legs on your bench just as they'll be on the chest to make sure you've got everything oriented correctly.

5. Cut the stopped grooves on each leg (Photo 2; Fig. B). It takes two fence settings to complete the two grooves. The first groove is cut with an outside face against the fence. The other groove is cut with the newly grooved edge against the fence. Be sure both grooves are equally set back on the legs.

6. Use a ½-in. chisel to square the corners where each routed groove ends.

7. Head to the drill press to cut the mortises (Photo 3; Fig. C). The mortise is really just a deeper part of the groove that accepts the tenon.

8. To finish machining the legs, cut the taper on the bandsaw. This can easily be done freehand. Use a ½-in. or wider blade and follow the line carefully. Sand the sawn surface smooth.

9. Now that the legs are finished, turn your attention to the rails. Lay out the tenons (Figs. D and E, page 111) on each end and cut them on the tablesaw. Use a test piece to check the fit of the tenons in the leg grooves. Shoot for a snug fit accomplished without a mallet.

10. Lay out and cut the tenon haunches on the bandsaw (Photo 4).

11. Dry-fit all the legs and rails to ensure all goes well at assembly. If a tenon bottoms out in the mortise before the joint is tight, trim ¹⁄₁₆-in. off the tenon length.

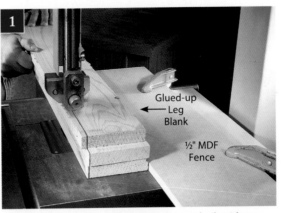

This entire project, even its stout legs, is built with rot-resistant cypress, a lightweight, weatherproof wood. To make the leg blanks, glue three pieces together and cut the stack on the bandsaw. Guide the cut with a ½-in.-tall fence that will contact only the bottom board.

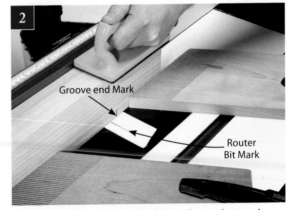

Rout stopped grooves on the legs to house the panels and the rail's tenons. The grooves are too long to use a stop block. Instead, mark where the groove ends on the edge of the leg. Make another mark on the router table across from the front of the bit. When the two marks meet, stop the router and remove the leg.

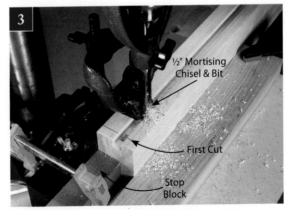

Cut the mortises on the drill press with a mortising attachment and a ½-in. chisel and bit. The groove guides the chisel so you don't get slightly staggered holes. A stop block ensures each mortise is the same distance from the end.

PROJECT REQUIREMENTS AT A GLANCE

Figure A: Exploded View

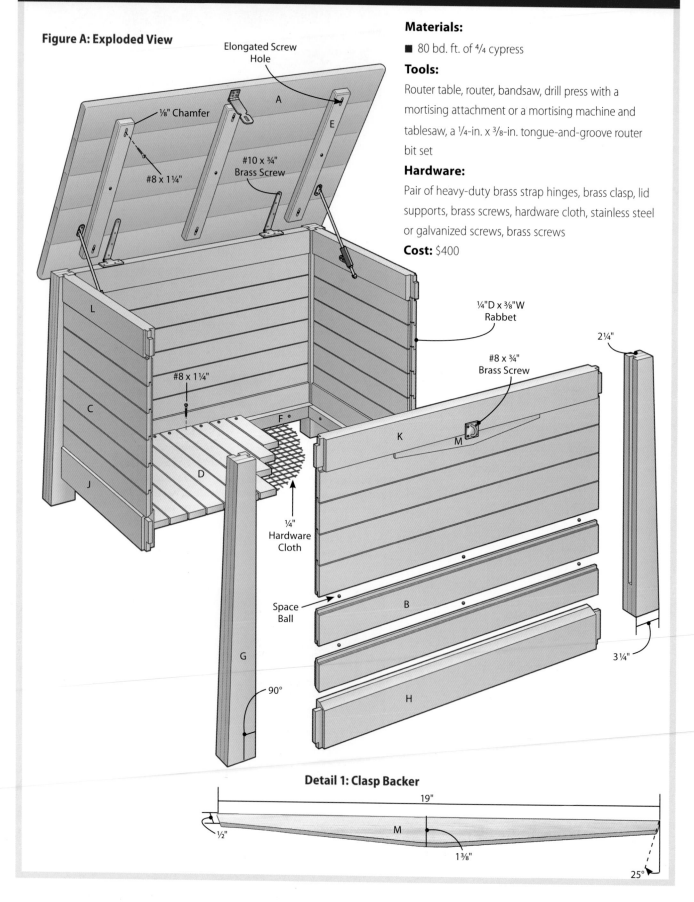

Elongated Screw Hole

⅛" Chamfer

A

E

#8 x 1¼"

#10 x ¾" Brass Screw

L

#8 x 1¼"

C

F

J

D

¼" Hardware Cloth

Space Ball

G

90°

¼"D x ⅜"W Rabbet

#8 x ¾" Brass Screw

K

M

2¼"

B

3¼"

H

Materials:

■ 80 bd. ft. of 4/4 cypress

Tools:

Router table, router, bandsaw, drill press with a mortising attachment or a mortising machine and tablesaw, a ¼-in. x ⅜-in. tongue-and-groove router bit set

Hardware:

Pair of heavy-duty brass strap hinges, brass clasp, lid supports, brass screws, hardware cloth, stainless steel or galvanized screws, brass screws

Cost: $400

Detail 1: Clasp Backer

19"

½"

M

1⅜"

25°

Machine the Panels

12. Machine the tongue-and-groove joints in all the panel pieces (Photo 5; Fig. F, page 112).

13. Don't forget to machine the groove in the bottom of the upper rail (Fig. D) and to put a 30-degree bevel on each bottom panel board where it mates with the 30-degree bevel on the bottom rail (Fig. F).

14. On the tablesaw, shave ⅛ in. off the length of each tongue. This is necessary to make room for the Space Balls that fit between each tongue-and-groove panel board. Cypress is a stable wood, but it still moves, and these panels are trapped in their frames. Space Balls are like little rubber blueberries that keep an even gap between the boards but allow for seasonal expansion and contraction of the wood.

15. Cut rabbets on the ends of each panel board so they fit snugly into the leg grooves (Fig. F).

The rails have haunched tenons. The haunch fills the groove made on the router table and strengthens the joint by increasing the glue surface. Cut the tenons on the tablesaw; then bandsaw a notch to create the haunch on each tenon.

Cut the panel boards with a tongue-and-groove router bit set. Use a chamfer bit to ease the edges where the boards meet. Featherboards keep the stock flat on the table to ensure straight tongues and grooves.

Figure B: Leg Groove

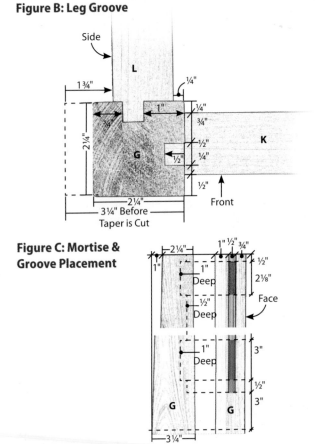

Figure C: Mortise & Groove Placement

Figure D: Top Rail Tenon

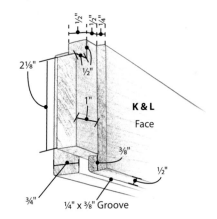

Figure E: Bottom Rail Tenon

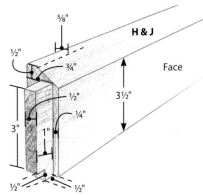

Assemble the chest upside down. Glue the top rail into one leg. Then stack the panel boards adding three or four Space Balls in each groove. Space Balls are little rubber balls that compress and expand to compensate for seasonal wood movement. Slip the bottom rail into the leg, add the second leg and clamp the assembly.

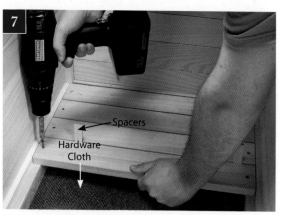

Screw down the decking using ¼-in.-thick spacers to maintain even gaps. Hardware cloth is screwed to the bottom of the deck cleats to keep critters out of your chest, yet allow air circulation.

Figure F: Panel Tongue-and-Groove Joint

¼"
¼" x ⅜" Backside
Groove
3¼"
⅜"
¼"
¼"
Space Ball
3/32" B & C
Gap ¼" ½"
1/16"
Chamfer
30°
H & J
¼" x ¼"
Tongue

Trim the tongue to ¼" to make room for space balls.

Assemble the Chest

16. Sand all the box parts through 120 grit.

17. Assemble the two end panels with waterproof glue and clamps (Photo 6).

18. After the two end panels are complete, assemble the rest of the chest in the same fashion. Set both front and back rails and panels into one end panel, add the second end panel and clamp. Be sure to check that your assembly is square.

Build the Lid

19. While the glue dries, edge-glue the boards for the lid. Take care to align each board flush. It's best to glue one board at a time for this operation.

20. Sand the top to 120 grit.

21. Cut the battens (E) and chamfer the outside edges (Fig. A, page 110).

22. Predrill countersunk holes in each batten on the drill press. **Note:** Be sure to elongate the screw holes on the ends of each batten to allow the lid to expand and contract (Fig. A).

23. Attach the battens to the lid with screws.

Install the Bottom

24. Cut the hardware cloth and screw it onto the bottom of the deck cleats.

25. Cut the deck cleats (F) and install them with screws along the bottom edge of the bottom rails (Fig. A).

26. Cut the decking (D) to fit. Predrill countersunk holes in the ends of each deck board and attach to the deck cleats (Photo 7).

Add the Hardware

27. Mount the hinges on the chest (Photo 8).

28. Glue the clasp backer (M) to the upper panel board and add the clasp (Fig. A, Detail 1).

29. Position and attach the lid closers.

30. I painted the bottom of each leg with a couple coats of two-part epoxy. This seals the leg ends and keeps them from wicking up any moisture. This is especially important if the chest sits on a concrete or brick patio.

31. You may choose to leave the wood raw. Cypress will age to a beautiful silver-gray color. If you want to preserve the color, look at some of the outdoor finishes designed for decks. Just remember, these finishes require frequent maintenance to keep their good looks. If you plan to put the chest in an enclosed porch, you're free to use your favorite finish.

Brass screw

Steel Screw

Mount the hinges with steel screws first. Then replace them with the brass screws. The steel screws pave the way, making it easier to drive the softer brass screws without breaking them.

Cutting List
Overall Dimensions: 29" H x 44½" W x 26½" D

Part	Name	Qty.	Dimensions
A	Lid	1	¾" x 26¾" x 44¾"
B	Tongue-and-groove panel	12	¾" x 3⅜" x 36¾"
C	Tongue-and-groove panel	12	¾" x 3⅜" x 19¾"
D	Decking	12	¾" x 2¾" x 19½"
E	Lid batten	3	¾" x 2" x 18"
F	Deck cleat	2	¾" x 1½" x 60"
G	Leg	4	2¼" x 3¼" x 28¼"
H	Bottom rail front and back	2	1½" x 4" x 38"
J	Bottom rail side	2	1½" x 4" x 21"
K	Top rail front and back	2	1½" x 3" x 38"
L	Top rail side	2	1½" x 3" x 21"
M	Clasp backer	1	¼" x 1⅜" x 19"

by CARROLL DAVIDSON

Patio Chair

A CURVED SEAT AND BACK MAKE THIS CHAIR EXTRA-COMFORTABLE

With a set of outdoor chairs like this on your patio or deck, you and your guests can enjoy the open air in comfort and style. This chair is comfortable (the seat contours were patterned after a Mercedes Benz seat!), and so simple to build you can put one together in a weekend. You'll need only basic tools: a tablesaw (or radial-arm saw), bandsaw, drill press, and router.

Because I live on the coast of Florida, I designed my patio chair to stand up to the ravages of salt-laden air, hot sun, and heavy rain. And I didn't want a patio full of chairs that required heavy maintenance. You can enjoy these without worrying about scraping and painting every year.

One of the tricks to building a low-maintenance chair is to select the right wood. I made these chairs from vertical-grain cypress. The grain pattern is visually appealing, and cypress holds up extremely well outdoors,

without any finish. Other suitable woods are teak, mahogany and cedar. Another secret to a long-lasting chair is to select the right hardware. I used square-drive stainless steel screws, which won't rust or stain the wood. Also, be sure to use a weather-resistant glue. I've had good luck with a yellow wood glue; it's easy to work with and holds up well in moist conditions. Alternative glues are resorcinol, epoxy and plastic resin. Finally, to protect the end grain of the legs and to keep them out of any surface water, I added plastic feet.

Cutting the Frame Parts

Begin construction by cutting the legs. They have an L-shape in cross-section, which I made by ripping the center out of 1½ by 2¼ in. stock, leaving a ¾ by 1½ in. recess. You could also glue together two pieces of 1½ by ¾ in. stock. Once you have the L-shaped stock, cut a 12-degree miter at both ends so the legs are 23 in. long. When cutting the miters, remember to make two right legs and two left legs!

Next, make the front and back rails, which have a 12-degree beveled top and bottom edge.

Starting with 1¾ in. stock, bevel-rip the first edge of both pieces at 12 degrees. Next, flip the boards over, reset the saw's fence and bevel-rip the other edge of both boards. The width of the board's face should be 1½ in. Crosscut the two rails to length and keep the offcuts to use later as spacer blocks (Photo 1).

Cut the foot rail to length, then cut the arm and side rails to the rough length shown in the Cutting List (p. 119). They will be cut to final length during assembly.

Figure A: Patio Chair

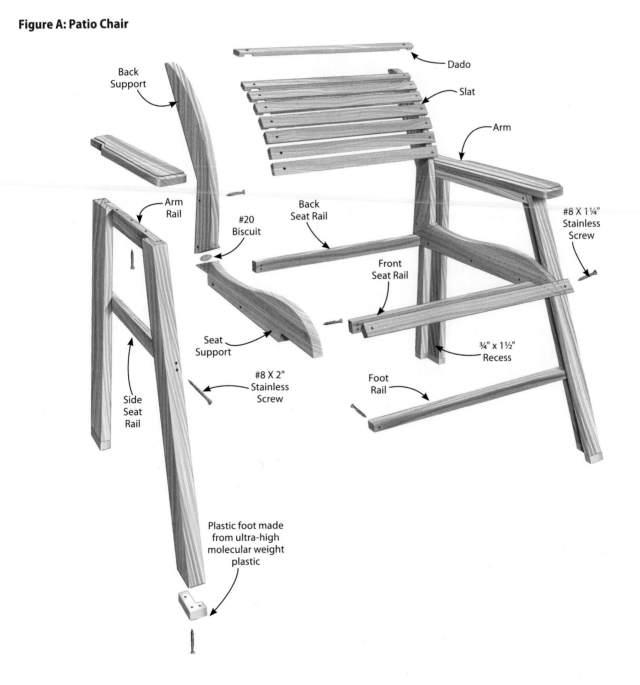

Back Support

Dado

Slat

Arm

Arm Rail

#20 Biscuit

Back Seat Rail

#8 X 1¼" Stainless Screw

Seat Support

Front Seat Rail

#8 X 2" Stainless Screw

Foot Rail

¾" x 1½" Recess

Side Seat Rail

Plastic foot made from ultra-high molecular weight plastic

Assemble the sides on a jig to keep the legs in position. The side rails are cut to fit, using spacer blocks to stand for the front and back rails.

Construct the frame by attaching the front and back rails to the two side assemblies. A couple clamps and a spacer between the back legs will help.

Frame Assembly

I made a jig (Photo 1) to help assemble the sides. The jig has blocks to position the legs so the outside corners are 27½ in. apart at the bottom, and the legs slope inward at 78 degrees. A horizontal block locates the side rail at the correct height (Photo 1).

Place two legs on the jig, and cut one end of an arm rail to 12 degrees. Put the arm rail in position, mark the opposite end, and make the opposing miter cut so the rail fits tightly. Drill and countersink the arm rail, then attach it with glue and 1¼ in. screws. To assemble the seat rail, first retrieve the two beveled pieces of scrap that you saved earlier and position them on the jig (Photo 1). These are stand-ins for the front and back rails. Cut one end of a seat rail to 12 degrees, then cut the rail to fit between the legs as you did the arm rail. Remove the spacers.

With the two sides assembled, you're ready to attach the front, back and foot rails. This can be awkward for one person, so get another set of hands, if you can. A piece of scrap cut to the same length as the rails will also help.

On a perfectly flat surface, clamp the two sides, the three rails and the spacer, without glue. If everything fits, glue and screw the rails in position, foot rail first (Photo 2). Be sure to drive the screws that go through the front and back legs and into the ends of the side rails to lock the joint together.

The Seat Supports

The shape of the seat supports is the key to the comfort of the chair. To get a comfortable curve, I traced the seat contour of my neighbor's Mercedes, a seat revered for its relaxed fit. I made a full-size template of the curve from heavy card stock.

To make the blank for the seat support, make a 75-degree cut on the end of a 1 × 4, as shown in Fig. C. There are two ways to do this: Mark out the cut, bandsaw it roughly and then plane to the line; or make a jig to clamp down the stock at a 45-degree angle, then make the cut with a tablesaw, radial-arm saw or miter saw set at 30 degrees. Save the offcut. Attach a 1 × 6 to the 75-degree cut face with a biscuit, using the offcut to help you clamp the joint tight (Photo 3).

When the glue is dry, saw out the shape of the seat support on the bandsaw and smooth it. Glue and screw the seat supports to the side rails, making sure that the bottom edge of each seat support is flush with the side rail. Clamping the seat support to the frame before driving the screws will make the joint tight.

The Armrests

First make a template for the shape of the arm out of card stock (Fig. C). Bandsaw the arms to shape and sand the edges smooth. Rout the decorative cove on the upper edges.

Secure the armrest to the arm rails with glue and screws. The arm should overhang the front leg by 1½ in. (Fig. B). Once again, clamping the joint before screwing will result in a tighter joint.

The Slats

To make the slats, first cut some wide boards to 21½ in. Allow enough material for 23 slats per chair, plus a couple extras. To strengthen the chair, each slat has a dado that fits over the seat support. I cut these dadoes in the wide boards using a radial-arm saw, with a stop block to ensure that each dado is ¾ in. from the board's end (Photo 5). Once you've cut the dadoes, rip the wide boards into 1½-in. strips and bevel-rip at 12 degrees to a final width of 1⅜ in. Trim two of the slats to 20 in.—these two fit between the legs and arms.

Drill and countersink two holes in each slat, using a simple jig to keep the holes positioned correctly (Photo 6). Drill holes in the shorter slats without the jig.

Next, install the slats. Start with the three slats in front, including the 20-in. one that goes between the legs. Use glue and screws, predrilling the seat supports for the screws. Then, install a slat at the top of the back, two slats at the "crook" of the seat support, and the short one between the armrests (Photo 7). The upper edge of this slat should line up with the top of the decorative cove cut in the arms. Install the remaining slats, spacing them by eye.

Make the rough blank for the seat support from a 1x4 with a 75-degree cut and a 1x6, joined with a biscuit. An angled wedge allows you to clamp the joint tight. When the glue is dry, bandsaw the seat support to shape.

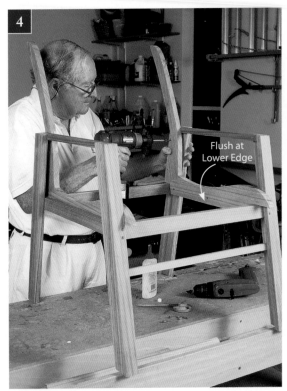

Screw the seat supports to the seat rail and the rear leg, checking to make sure they are parallel and ⅛ in. in from the back edge of the leg. Shape the armrests, then glue and screw them on.

Figure B: Chair Elevation

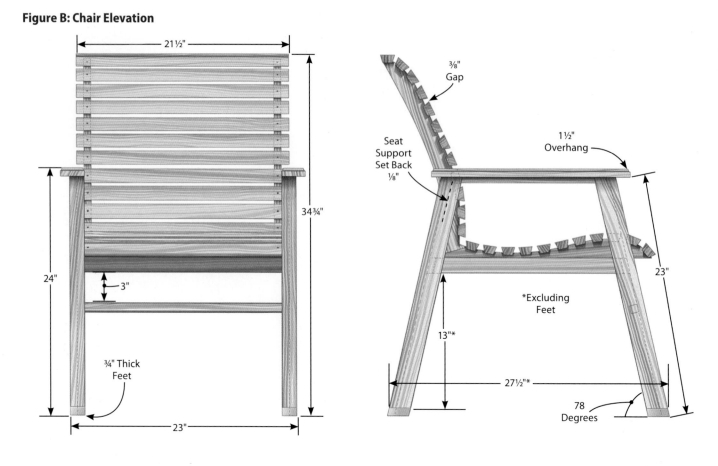

21½"

34¾"

24"

3"

¾" Thick Feet

23"

⅜" Gap

Seat Support Set Back ⅛"

1½" Overhang

23"

*Excluding Feet

13"*

27½"*

78 Degrees

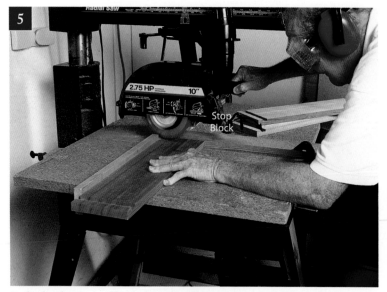

Stop Block

Dado the slats before they're ripped to width, using a stop block to ensure consistent location. Then rip the slats and bevel their edges.

Drill and countersink the slats, using a drill press and simple jig to get the holes properly located. Two slats must be cut short and drilled separately. One fits between the legs and one between the arms.

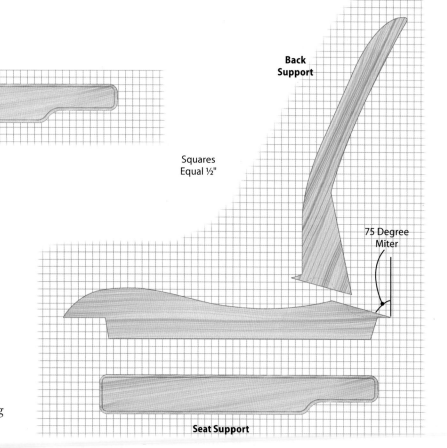

Figure C: Chair Parts

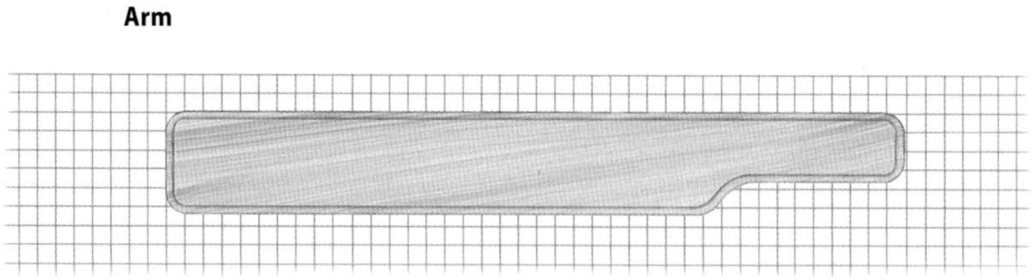

Arm

Back Support

Squares Equal ½"

75 Degree Miter

Seat Support

Finishing

Cypress naturally weathers to a beautiful silver gray. An annual coat of a water-repellent preservative with UV inhibitors and a fungicide will keep the wood looking its best.

7

Install the slats beginning with the three in front, then the top of the back, the two in the "crook" of the seat, and the short slat between the arms. Fill in the remaining slats, spacing them by eye.

Cutting List		
Parts	**Pcs.**	**Description**
Legs	4	1½ x 2¼ x 23
Arms	2	¾ x 2½ x 20
Arm rails	2	¾ x ¾ x 17*
Side seat rails	2	¾ x 1½ x 19½*
Front seat rail	1	¾ x 1½ x 21½
Back seat rail	1	¾ x 1½ x 21½
Foot rail	1	¾ x ¾ x 21½
Back supports	2	¾ x 5½ x 20
Seat supports	2	¾ x 3½ x 23
Slats	21	¾ x 1⅜ x 21½
Back slat	1	¾ x 1⅜ x 20
Seat slat	1	¾ x 1⅜ x 20
Plastic feet	4	¾ x 1½ x 2½
		(bevel to finished length of 2¼)

Hardware

2 #20 biscuits
#8 x 1¼ stainless-steel screws, as needed
#8 x 2 stainless-steel screws, as needed

*Cut to final length during assembly

CARROLL DAVIDSON IS AN ENTHUSIASTIC HOME WOOD-WORKER. HE LIVES SOUTH OF MIAMI, FLORIDA WITH HIS WIFE, HELEN.

by TOM CASPAR

Outdoor Rietveld Chair

AN ICON OF MODERN DESIGN BECOMES AN EASY-TO-BUILD OUTDOOR PROJECT

In 1918 the Dutch cabinet-maker Gerrit Rietveld reduced the idea of a chair to a 3D grid of painted sticks and boards. His revolutionary design became one of the most famous pieces of 20th-century furniture—the Red-Blue chair.

Although his chair appears easy to put together, getting all those sticks precisely located is tough, especially if you have only two hands. To make this jigsaw puzzle simpler to put together, I've figured out a building system based on two plywood boards and a few spacing blocks.

The Design

I've revised Rietveld's elegant design to make a chair that's stronger, easier to build, more comfortable to sit in and rugged enough to put outdoors. I've used screws instead of Rietveld's dowels to hold it together, increased the size of the sticks and added a stretcher. We tested our chair with both large and small people, and it gets two thumbs up for comfort.

Tools and Materials

Building this chair requires only a minimum of tools and experience. You'll need a tablesaw, planer and router to mill the wood, and a #2 square-drive bit for your drill to put it together. That's it. A drill press and a router table are helpful, but not necessary.

Honduras mahogany is a good choice for this chair. It's easy to cut, sands quickly and is weatherproof, even without a finish. Alternative woods include teak and white oak. Softwoods that are often used for outdoor furniture like cedar, redwood and cypress are probably too weak for this chair and do not hold screws well.

One chair requires about 12 board feet of $\frac{5}{4}$ wood and about 10 board feet of $\frac{4}{4}$ wood. That's about $150 per chair for mahogany, $50 for fir.

If your chair will be outdoors, use stainless steel screws and water-resistant glue. Unlike stainless steel, standard screws will leave unsightly stains on the wood. I prefer water-resistant varieties of yellow woodworking glue for kiln-dried hard-woods such as mahogany, but if you're using construction lumber, polyurethane glue would be a better choice because it works well on wood with a high moisture content.

Getting Started

Begin by cutting all the parts to size (see Cutting List). Rout a bevel or roundover on every edge, including the ends (Fig. C, Detail 1). A router table makes this repetitive job go much faster. Make some extra legs and rails, too. You'll need them to make spacers and stop blocks. The spacer you'll use over and over again, spacer #1, is simply a scrap piece of rail. I added a tab to it to make it easy to use (Photo 3). Most of this chair's dimensions are based on multiples of this block of wood.

Don't sand the sticks before you glue them together, or you might accidentally round over the flat surfaces. They must remain flat for a good glue joint.

Now build the two gluing and screwing fixtures (Fig. E) and follow the photo sequence 1 through 12.

Cutting List

Dimensions: 40" H x 30¼" W x 32" D

Part	Name	Qty.	Dimensions
A	Front Leg	2	1⅜" x 1⅜" x 14¾"
B	Arm Support	2	1⅜" x 1⅜" x 20⅛"
C	Back Leg	2	1⅜" x 1⅜" x 20⅛"
D	Rail	5	1⅜" x 1⅜" x 27⅝"
E	Arm Rail	1	1⅜" x 1⅜" x 30⅜"
F	Rail	2	1⅜" x 1⅜" x 24⅞"
G	Arms	2	1⅜" x 4⅛" x 19"
H	Cleat	1	⅝" x 2¾" x 15⅛"
J	Outer Back	2	⅝" x 5¼" x 42"
K	Inner Back	1	⅝" x 5⅜" x 42"
L	Outer Seat	2	⅝" x 6⅝" x 16⅝"
M	Inner Seat	1	⅝" x 5⅜" x 16⅝"
Fixtures			
A	Between Legs	1	¾" x 14" x 22⅛"
	Stop Stick A	1	1⅜" x 1⅜" x 24⅛"
B	Between Arms	1	¾" x 16" x 19⅜"
	Stop Stick B	1	1⅜" x 1⅜" x 21⅜"
Spacers			
#1	Basic	3	1⅜" x 1⅜" x 3"
#2	Bottom Rail	1	1⅜" x 4⅛" x 19"
#3	Top Rail	1	1⅛" x 1⅜" x 18"
#4	Rail and Leg	2	¾" x 6⅝" x 9"
#5	Seat and Back	1	⅝" x 2" x 16"
Hardware			

Hardware
2   Corner Brackets 1" x 1"
4   Corner Brackets 1½" x 1½"
38 #10 X 2½" L Stainless Steel Screws
20 #8 X ¾" L Flathead Screws
24 #8 X 1½" L Flathead Screws
6   #8 X 1¼" L Flathead Screws
Materials: Mahogany or Douglas Fir

Figure A: Guide Block for Screw Holes

The overlapping joints in this chair are screwed and glued together. This block lays out diagonal pairs of screw holes in five rails (D). Use one side to mark either end of a rail. Flip the block over to mark the other end. Then the two diagonals will run in opposite directions.

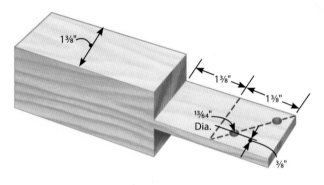

1⅜"
1⅜"
1⅜"
13/64" Dia.
3/8"

Figure B: Good Screw Joints

For this chair to last, the screwed and glued joints must be as strong as possible. That means drilling two holes of different sizes before the joint goes together. First, a large diameter "slip hole" goes all the way through the top piece. The screw must be able to slip through it without threading into the wood. A small diameter hole, or "pilot hole," goes into the bottom piece. It should be about the same size as the shaft of the screw, less the threads.

Countersink both sides of the top piece. Here's why: When the screw is driven into the pilot hole a small mound of wood is formed. You create a cavity for this mound by countersinking. Without a cavity, the mound would prevent the two pieces of wood from closely mating, thus creating a weak glue joint.

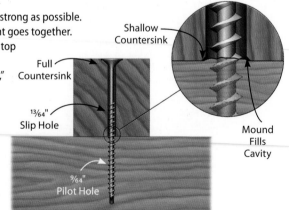

Shallow Countersink

Full Countersink

13/64" Slip Hole

9/64" Pilot Hole

Mound Fills Cavity

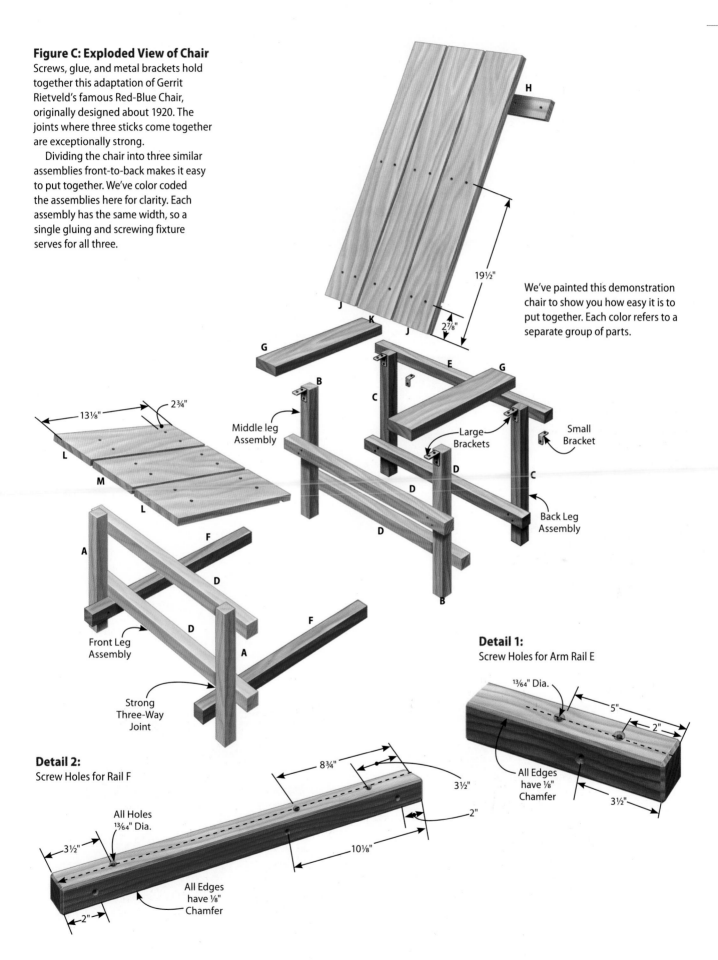

Figure C: Exploded View of Chair
Screws, glue, and metal brackets hold together this adaptation of Gerrit Rietveld's famous Red-Blue Chair, originally designed about 1920. The joints where three sticks come together are exceptionally strong.

Dividing the chair into three similar assemblies front-to-back makes it easy to put together. We've color coded the assemblies here for clarity. Each assembly has the same width, so a single gluing and screwing fixture serves for all three.

We've painted this demonstration chair to show you how easy it is to put together. Each color refers to a separate group of parts.

19½"

2⅞"

H

J

K

J

G

B

Middle leg Assembly

E

C

G

Large Brackets

Small Bracket

D

D

D

D

C

Back Leg Assembly

B

13⅛"

2¾"

L

M

L

A

F

D

F

A

D

A

F

Front Leg Assembly

B

Strong Three-Way Joint

Detail 1:
Screw Holes for Arm Rail E

¹³⁄₆₄" Dia.

5"

2"

All Edges have ⅛" Chamfer

3½"

Detail 2:
Screw Holes for Rail F

8¾"

3½"

All Holes ¹³⁄₆₄" Dia.

2"

3½"

10⅛"

All Edges have ⅛" Chamfer

2"

1

Mark the ends of all the D rails with this reversible guide block (Fig. A). Drill holes on your marks by hand or with a drill press. The screws must easily slip through these holes. Countersink both sides (Fig. B).

While you have the drill set up, put holes in rails E and F as well (Fig. C, Details 1 and 2) and countersink both sides.

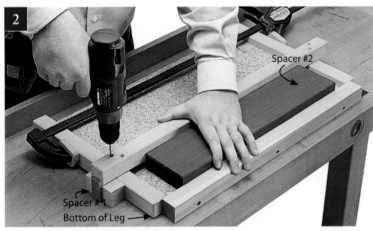

2

Assemble the front legs and bottom rail. Lock them in place on Fixture A (Fig. E). Spacer #1, at the end of the rail, sets the overhang. Spacer #2 (which is actually a chair arm) fixes the rail's distance from the bottom of the leg. Drill pilot holes into both legs, then remove the rail and blow off the wood dust. Apply water-resistant glue to the joints. Then replace the rail and drive in the screws.

Repeat this operation for the middle and back assemblies.

3

Flip the leg assembly around and re-install it in the fixture. Then insert spacer #3 to position the upper rail. (See Cutting List, p. 122, for size.)

Figure D: Side View of Chair

Steel brackets connect the arms to the legs. This joinery is far better than running screws from the top of the arm into the end of the leg. Screws do not hold well in end grain.

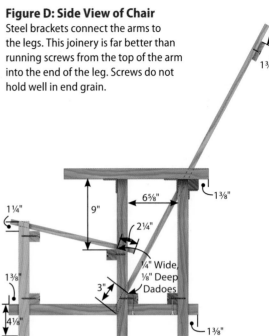

Figure E: Screwing and Gluing Fixtures

Fix the distance between each of the three pairs of legs by the width of a single piece of Medium Density Fiberboard (MDF) or plywood. Attach an extra leg or rail to the end of the fixture as a stop stick. This registers both the ends of the legs and the spacers that determine where the rails go.

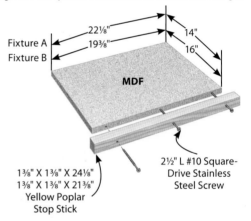

4

Install the upper rail of the middle assembly with two #4 spacers. (See Cutting List for size.)

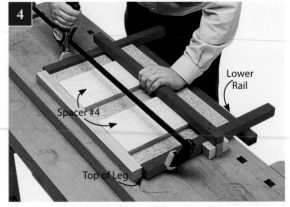

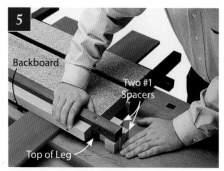

Butt rail E of the back assembly against the stop stick. Place two seat boards under the fixture to raise the stop stick to the level of the rail. Use two spacer blocks #1 to set the overhang.

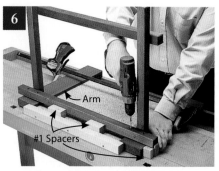

Screw the back leg assembly to the arms. Clamp the arms in place across Fixture B. Spacer blocks #1 position the arm rail from the stop stick and set the overhang.

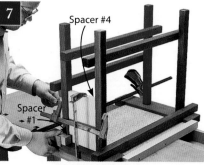

Clamp the middle leg assembly in place with spacer #4 (the same spacer you used in Photo 4, but turned the other way around). Spacer #1 sets the legs in from the arm's edge.

Drill pilot holes through rail F, then screw and glue it in place. Repeat the same process on the other side of the chair and remove Fixture B.

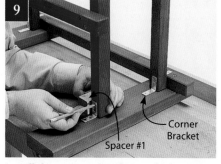

Install three corner brackets on both arms (Fig. C). Use stainless steel screws if your chair's going outside.

Clamp the front leg assembly in place. Drill pilot holes into the legs and drive in two screws to temporarily hold the assembly in place. Then remove the clamps, drill the pilot holes into the front assembly's rail and remove the temporary screws. Apply glue to the assembly and drive in all the screws.

Add the backboards. Tilt the chair back on a support block made from the spacers. Pre-drill the holes in the backboards and cut registration dadoes in them (Fig. D). Then drill pilot holes into the chair rails and drive in the screws. This is not a glued joint.

Insert a thin spacer between the seat boards to keep them parallel. The seat is not glued to the rails.

Glue and screw the cleat behind the top of the backboards.

Vine Trellis

Make any climbing plant happy with this 6-ft. tall, free-standing trellis. We used dadoes, glue and screws to fasten the slats because trellises take a beating each year when you tear off the old vines. We built our trellis from cypress, one of the longest-lasting outdoor woods. Ours was recycled from old water tanks and cost about $175. White oak, at $60, would also be a good choice.

Marking the legs for the dadoes can be confusing, but if you follow our marking procedures (Photos 1 through 4), you can't mess up. Even with our easy-to-make jigs, routing 68 dadoes is noisy, dusty, and tedious (Fig. B and Photo 5). But once they're done, the dadoes make assembly foolproof. There's only one angle to remember: Everything slopes 6 degrees.

You'll need an angled template, made with the miter gauge on your tablesaw, to make the dadoing jigs. You'll also need a router with a straight bit to cut the dadoes, and a drill with a slotted tip for all the screws. We used a jointer and planer to mill our parts to thickness, but they could also be ripped to size on a tablesaw. The slats are thin, so be sure to use a push stick.

How to Build It

1. Mill the legs (A) to thickness and cut them to length.

2. Mark the leg dadoes (Photos 1 through 4). The sides of the trellis are tapered, so the dadoes are angled.

3. Cut an 84-degree angled template, about 10-in. long and at least 4-in. wide. Use it to set the fence angle on the dadoing jigs (Fig. B).

4. Dado the legs (Photo 5). One jig will slope the right direction for the 3/16-in. deep dadoes on one side of each leg. The mirror-image jig will be correct for the other side.

1

Mark the bottoms of the legs. Bundle the legs together and mark the front and back faces as one pair and the two side faces as the other.

2

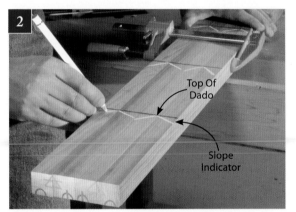

Top Of Dado

Slope Indicator

Mark the first pair of faces. The dadoes on the front and back faces match, so they can be marked at the same time. Arrange the legs with the triangles at the top. After aligning the ends, draw reference lines every 8 in. to mark the dadoes. Then go back and mark the slope, which runs outward from the center of each pair.

3

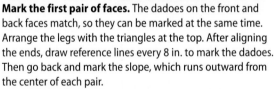

4"

Earlier Mark

Mark the second pair of faces. Rearrange the legs with the circles at the top, and align the ends. Then mark the dadoes, using the same 8-in. spacing. This time, however, start 4 in. from the bottom. As you can see from the mark on the right, these dadoes are offset from the other pair of faces.

4

Your bundle should look like this. Check to see that each leg has its two outside faces marked, that the marks are staggered, and that the slope of the dadoes is clearly indicated.

Figure A: Exploded View

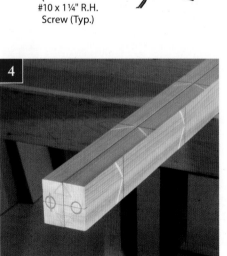

G

H

E

E

C

8" Spacing (Typ.)

F

F

A

8" Spacing (Typ.)

B

³⁄₁₆"D x 1⅛"W Dadoes (Typ.)

D

B

8"

4"

D

#10 x 1¼" R.H. Screw (Typ.)

#10 x 1" Screws

18"

1" Aluminum L-Angle

Detail 1: Optional Anchor Spikes

For windy conditions, you may want to anchor your trellis with aluminum spikes on each leg. For longer life, soak the ends of the legs in wood preservative or coat them with epoxy.

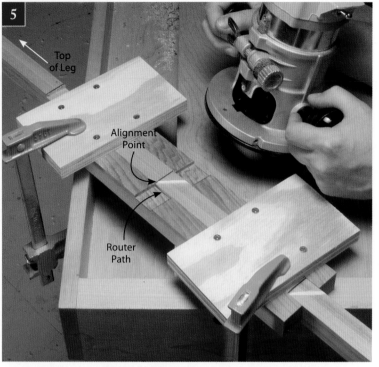

Cut angled dadoes in the legs. Slide the leg in, top end first, making sure that its slope indicators run the same direction as the jig. Align the dado reference line on the leg with the top inside shoulder of the jig's dado, clamp and rout. Remember: The reference line always marks the top of the dado and the slope indicator should always be in the router's path.

Assemble one face at a time. Frame each face by fastening the top and bottom slats to a pair of legs. Then mark, cut and install the middle slats.

Vine Trellis

5. Mill slat material to thickness and rip it into lengths, slightly oversize in width. Then plane (or rip) the slats to fit the leg dadoes.

6. Cut the bottom and top slats (B through E) for all four sides to length, with a 6-degree bevel on both ends. You can cut the slats to length in pairs because opposite sides of the trellis are the same.

7. Frame the front and back faces of the trellis (Photo 6). Align the beveled ends of the slats with the edges of the legs and drill pilot holes. Then drill out the holes in the slats so the screws slip through. Apply glue and assemble.

8. Cut the internal slats (F) to fit, and fasten them, following the procedures in Steps 6 and 7.

9. Stand the assembled front and back faces back-to-back in an "A," and assemble the sides, following Steps 7 and 8.

10. With a handsaw, square off the legs at the top of the trellis.

11. Bandsaw the spire (Part G, Fig. C). Lay out the pattern on two adjacent faces of a glued-up blank. Make the blank a foot long to keep your fingers a safe distance from the blade. After cutting the first two sides of the pyramid, tape the offcuts back onto the blank. Rotate the blank 90 degrees and cut the other two sides of the pyramid. Cut the second set of tapers the same way. After sanding, cut the spire from the blank.

12. Glue and screw retaining blocks (H) to the bottom of the spire, then soak it in preservative.

13. Screw the optional anchor spikes (Fig. A, Detail 1) onto the legs.

Figure B: Jigs for Routing Angled Dadoes

Because the sides taper, you need two mirror-image jigs, both angled 6 degrees from perpendicular. Use a template cut at 84 degrees to set the angle. Make the arms from extra leg stock. To get the proper spacing, slide another piece of extra leg stock between the arms when you mark the angles, fasten the fences and rout the dadoes. Use a spacer to keep the fences parallel so the dadoes are the same width on both jigs. The spacer's width depends on the diameter of the bit you use and the size of your router's baseplate. For example, to make the 1⅛-in.-wide dadoes, using a ½-in. straight bit in a router with a 6-in. diameter base, the spacer is 6⅝-in. wide.

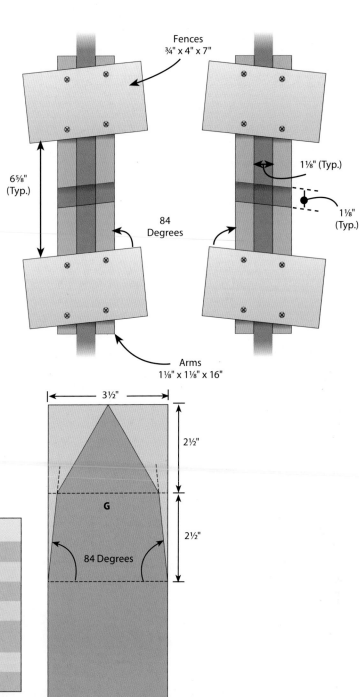

Fences
¾" x 4" x 7"

6⅝"
(Typ.)

1⅛" (Typ.)

1⅛"
(Typ.)

84
Degrees

Arms
1⅛" x 1⅛" x 16"

Figure C: Tapered Pyramidal Spire

The lower half of the spire continues the 6-degree taper of the sides. The top half accentuates the pyramidal shape. Ready-made spires, some with copper details, are also available at home centers and garden stores.

3½"

2½"

2½"

G

84 Degrees

Shopping List

35 lin. ft. (five 7-ft. lengths) of 1½ x 1½ stock
8 bd. ft. of ⁴⁄₄ stock
68 #10 x 1¼-in. R.H. brass screws (for the slats)
4 #8 x 1¾-in. F.H. stainless steel screws (for the spire)
16 #10 x 1-in. F.H. stainless steel screws (for the optional aluminum spikes)
Weatherproof glue
8 lin. ft. of 1-in. aluminum L-angle (optional)

Patio Planter

ENJOY THE GREAT OUTDOORS ON YOUR DECK OR PATIO!

If you can build a box, you can build this planter. It's much sturdier than most commercial versions, so it should last for many years. It's also the perfect opportunity for you to try your hand at shingling!

The opening accommodates a 30-in. drop-in plastic window-box planter. They're available at any garden store in several lengths. You could easily alter the design to fit a different-size box, or to accommodate individual pots. A square version of this planter would also look great.

All the materials you need lie waiting at a full-service lumberyard. You don't have to be choosy about the CDX exterior-grade plywood, but it pays to look through the cedar stock for straight, knot-free boards. If you invest in a bundle of top-grade red cedar shingles (about $45), you'll easily have enough to cover two planters. Lower grade bundles cost half as much, but have lots of knotty pieces that you

won't use. Our total cost, including the plastic planter and top-grade shingles, was about $95.

We cleaned up the 2 × 6 stock and 5/4 decking with a jointer and planer and cut all the pieces to size on a tablesaw. We used a bandsaw to cut the wide bevels on the top pieces, and a biscuit cutter and biscuits to reinforce the top's miter joints.

However, you can make a simpler version of this planter without having a shop full of tools. Except for the wide bevels, all of the cuts can be made with a circular saw and a 10-in. miter saw. Just make the top out of thinner stock and leave it flat (substitute ⅞-in.-thick cedar siding, the stuff with one rough and one smooth side, for the top and the legs). You don't have to use biscuits in the miters. Keep the pieces aligned by pin-nailing the corners and let the weatherproof glue hold the joint. A drill, hammer and clamps complete the gotta-have tool list.

Figure A: Exploded View

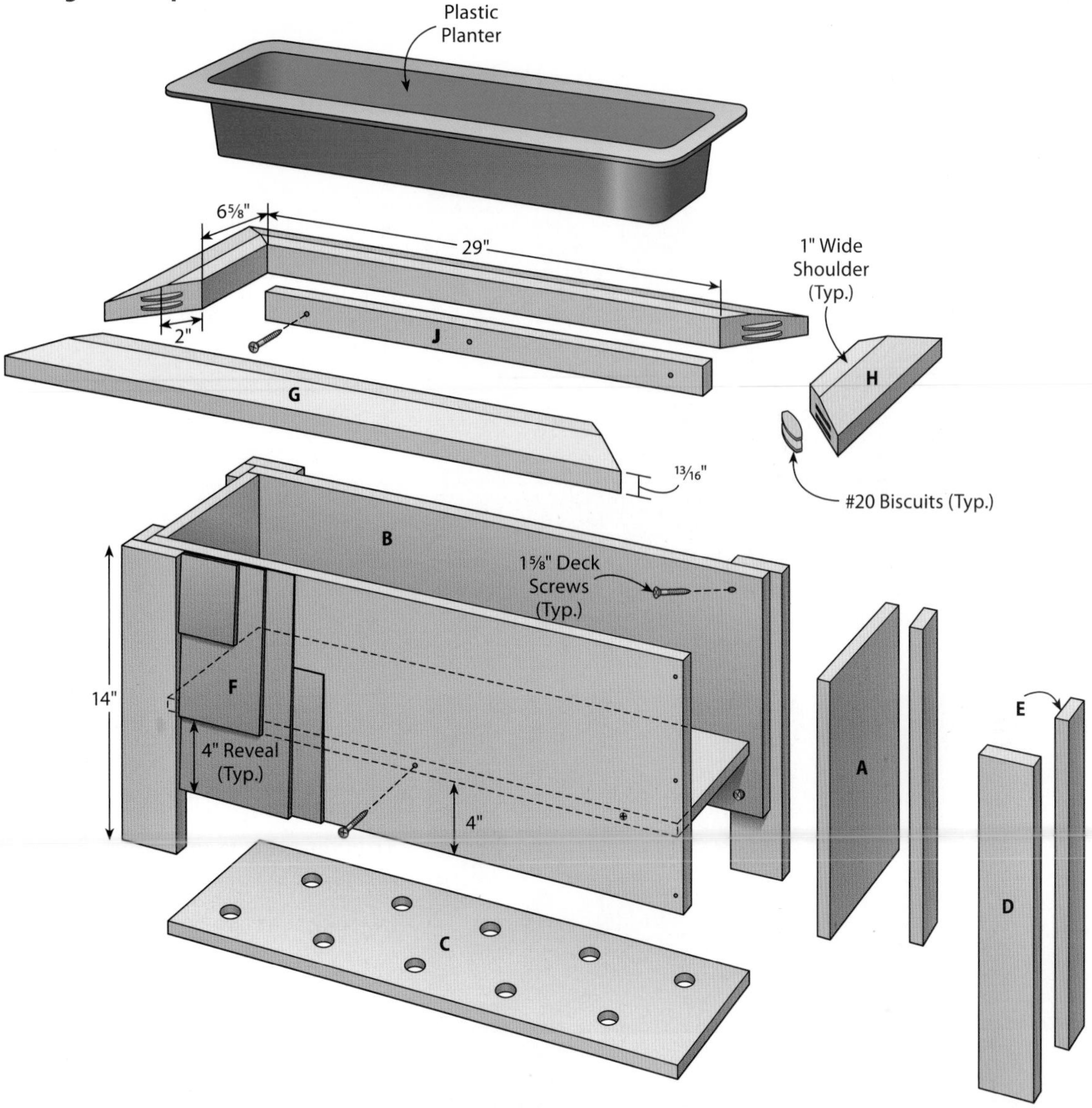

Plastic
Planter

6⅝"

29"

1" Wide
Shoulder
(Typ.)

2"

J

H

G

13/16"

#20 Biscuits (Typ.)

B

1⅝" Deck
Screws
(Typ.)

14"

F

4" Reveal
(Typ.)

A

E

4"

D

C

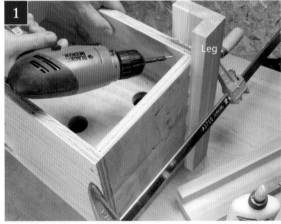

1

Leg

Fasten the legs with the box upside-down. Keep the legs flush with the top of the box, and the planter will sit square. Apply glue and hold the leg with a clamp so it doesn't slip when you drive the screw. Flip the assembly over and install another screw near the top. Remove the clamp and move on to the next leg.

Cutting List
Dimensions: 13⅛" x 35½" x 15⅜"

Part	Description	Qty.	Dimensions
A	Box ends	2	¾" x 8" x 11¾"
B	Box sides	2	¾" x 11¾" x 30½"
C	Box bottom	1	¾" x 8" x 29⅛"
D	Leg sides	4	⅞" x 3" x 15"*
E	Leg ends	4	⅞" x 1⅛" x 15"*
F	Shingles	many	Cut to fit
G	Top sides	2	1⅜" x 3¼" x 38"* #
H	Top ends	2	1⅜" x 3¼" x 15"* +
J	Top cleats	2	11/16" x 1¼" x 28"

*Oversize rough length   # Cut to 29-in. between miters
+ Cut to 6⅝-in. between miters

Patio Planter

Install the shingles in four courses. Lay the second course directly on top of the first, so there's enough pitch to make water run off. Stagger the seams from course to course, so water won't seep in behind. Locate nails or staples so they'll be covered.

Double layer

Stagger Seams

Spacer

Cut stacked slots for biscuits, to reinforce the miter joints. Use a spacer to lift the second slot above the first.

Glue the mitered top on a flat surface. Draw the joints together by alternately adjusting the pressure on the three clamps. Waxed paper keeps the top from gluing itself to your bench!

How to Build It

1. Cut plywood box pieces to size.

2. Assemble the box. Exterior-grade plywood is often twisted, so clamp the ends (A) between the sides (B) to help get all the edges flush. Fasten one corner at a time and drill pilot holes before driving the screws.

3. Square up the box by installing the bottom (C).

4. Glue the L-shaped legs (D and E) together. Square the ends and trim them to 14-in. final length.

5. Fasten the legs to the box (Photo 1).

6. To match the scale of the planter, the shingles (F) have to be made smaller. Shorten them all to 8 in., measuring from the thin edge, except for the second course, which runs full length (Photo 2). Trim the shingles to width as you go and stagger the seams. Keep the fasteners covered—those on the last course are protected by the overhanging top.

7. Mill the top pieces (G and H, Fig. A). Clean up the wide bevels by sanding or planing, after cutting them on the table- or bandsaw.

8. Measure under the rim of your plastic planter to determine the correct size for the opening in the top. Make adjustments to the dimensions given in the Cutting List and Fig. A, if necessary.

9. Cut the miters. Measure from the *inside* edges. Make sure both pairs of pieces (sides and ends) are the same length.

10. Reinforce the miter joints with #20 biscuits (Photo 3).

11. Glue up the top (Photo 4).

12. Add cleats (J) and install the top.

EDITOR: DAVE MUNKITTRICK · ART DIRECTION: EVANGELINE EKBERG · PHOTOGRAPHY: VERN JOHNSON

by BRAD HOLDEN

Outdoor Finishes

SIMPLE TO SUPER DURABLE

Outdoor finishes have one thing in common; they all require maintenance. Of course, paint is unequaled at protecting the wood from its two biggest enemies: moisture and ultraviolet (UV) light. Moisture causes the wood to rot, and sunlight bleaches out its natural color. Still, who wants to cover-up beautiful wood with paint? If you want the wood to show through on your outdoor projects, you need a clear finish.

There are three basic clear finishes for outdoor furniture: exterior oil, exterior varnish, and an epoxy sealer with an exterior varnish topcoat. Application ease and service life are the two major differences between these finishes.

Of the three clear exterior finishes, exterior oil is by far the simplest finish to apply. Just flow it on, let it soak in, and wipe off the excess. Unfortunately, oil offers the least amount of protection and it must be reapplied every season. Exterior varnish, on the other hand, is more difficult to apply: up to 8 coats have to be carefully brushed on. While exterior varnish offers excellent protection from moisture and UV light, it has to be recoated every few years to maintain that protection. An epoxy sealer with an exterior varnish topcoat is the most durable outdoor finish and can last for many, many years. However, the initial application does take longer then exterior varnish.

EXTERIOR OILS

Garden Sprayer

EXTERIOR VARNISH OR URETHANE

Natural Bristle Brush

An exterior oil finish is definitely the simplest, quickest way to treat an outdoor project. On the downside, it will only give you about a year of protection from the ravages of outdoor life. Oil finishes don't provide a protective film that sits on top of the wood like varnish does. Instead oil soaks into the wood fibers and dries. Exterior oils have added trans-oxide pigments for UV protection and mildewcides to protect against mold and mildew. You'll find colors ranging from dark brown to light amber.

Application is simple: a garden sprayer and a rag are all you need. First, flood the surface of your project with oil. I use an inexpensive hand pump garden sprayer. Its fast, easy and only costs about $8.00. Let the oil soak in according to the manufacturer's directions, then wipe it off. That's it. Done! Depending on local conditions, you'll have to reapply about once per year. The built-in UV protection should keep your wood looking natural for many years (as long as you keep up with the applications).

Exterior varnish or urethane (both finishes are technically "varnishes") builds a protective layer over the wood. It offers superior protection and durability over an oil finish. Often, the term "Spar" is found in the name, but this does not indicate any additional or special ingredient. The term "Spar" originates with its use as a coating for the spars on sailing ships. All exterior varnishes are formulated to protect against moisture and UV radiation.

Exterior varnish is applied with a natural bristle brush in multiple coats. Manufacturers recommend eight thin coats for maximum protection and a deep lustrous finish. Sand the hardened varnish lightly between each coat.

Exterior varnishes cure to a more flexible film than ordinary varnish. The flexible coat is not as likely to crack from seasonal wood movement caused by humidity extremes in an outdoor environment.

Exterior varnish will usually last 2-3 years before it starts to look chalky. As soon as you see a chalky film start to develop, it's time to freshen the finish. Simply sand the topcoat smooth, and apply a new coat of varnish. Don't put this important maintenance step off too long or cracks will develop in the finish allowing moisture to penetrate and degrade the wood. That will necessitate a complete strip and refinish to restore the furniture. You don't want to go there.

Cut up
Foam
Roller

An epoxy sealer with exterior varnish topcoats is the most durable, but also the most labor-intensive finish you can apply to outdoor furniture. This is the finish favored by boat builders so you know it's going to last a long time. Epoxy and exterior varnish enjoy a symbiotic relationship: The epoxy forms an impenetrable moisture barrier that prevents seasonal swelling and shrinking of the wood. This dimensional stability in turn gives longer life to the exterior varnish because it no longer has to stretch and shrink with the wood The exterior varnish returns the favor by providing UV protection, without which the epoxy would rapidly deteriorate.

Apply three thin coats of epoxy. The best way to get thin, even coats is to use a foam roller cut in half. It works kind of like a squeegee. Epoxy cure times vary depending on their formulation and the ambient temperature. Be sure to use an epoxy with a long enough open time (approximately 30 minutes), so it doesn't set up before you're done putting it on. For large projects, mix the epoxy in small batches so you can finish an area before the epoxy sets. Also, for optimal

flow out and penetration into the wood fibers, make sure the epoxy you use doesn't contain any thickeners. Always read and follow the instructions that come with your epoxy. If possible, apply the epoxy undercoat prior to assembling the parts. You can recoat without sanding while the previous coat is still soft but not sticky. If the epoxy seems uneven or bumpy, allow it to harden. Then, sand it smooth and apply the next coat.

Before applying the varnish topcoats, I use a card scraper or sanding block with 100–120 grit sandpaper to level the cured epoxy (see photo below left). The sanded surface also provides some tooth for the spar varnish to adhere to.

Rinse the sanded epoxy with clean water and dry with paper towels. The rinse water should not bead on the surface. Beading indicates that contaminants from the epoxy curing process are still on the surface and could interfere with the varnish bond. To remove the contaminants, wipe down with mineral spirits and dry with paper towels or a rag. Follow this with eight coats of exterior varnish, sanding lightly between coats.

Sand out any unevenness and defects in the cured epoxy before applying the exterior varnish topcoats.

Furniture Projects

If you want to build your skills or are looking to build a fine piece of furniture for your home, then this is the section for you. It includes ten great projects ranging from a natural slabwood bench to a Stickley sideboard reproduction with handmade copper hardware. If you're new to woodworking and looking for a project that covers some of the basics, check out the speaker stand. It doesn't take much wood or many tools to build, yet it incorporates several joints and techniques that you can later apply to larger projects. For something more involved, try the stowaway bench or kitchen work table. If you're really looking for a substantial project using traditional joinery and design, consider the Stickley-style chest of drawers. Made of quartersawn oak with mortise and tenon joinery, it might become a family heirloom that the kids wrestle for. If you're truly the engineering type with a penchant for math, angles, and precision, the Arts and Crafts table lamp should be enough to get you into your shop with calculator and miter gauge in hand. Designed with lines that are reminiscent of Frank Lloyd Wright, the lamp provides a more technical challenge than some larger furniture projects.

by GREG WOOD

Natural Bench

HOW TO MAKE STRONG JOINTS IN SLABWOOD

When I need wood for a project, my first stop is a small mill near my shop that specializes in local hardwoods. On one particular visit I noticed a pile of offcuts sitting out in the rain. As I pawed through the pile, a slab of white oak caught my eye. The sawn surface was wet and the grain just popped. The bark was almost completely gone on the flip side, leaving a smooth, natural surface that was miraculously free of damage from chainsaws and harvesting equipment. Turns out the slabs were free for the taking so I took several slabs back to my shop to dry.

For months I kept wondering what to make with the slabs. The undulating line where the flatsawn surface met the natural edge of the log intrigued me. From some angles, the plank's thickness was almost invisible. Eventually, I

EDITOR:DAVEMUNKITTRICK•PHOTOGRAPHY:LEADIMAGE,JASONZENTNER.ALLOTHERS,GREGWOOD•ILLUSTRATION:FRANKROHRBACH

The first step is to create a smooth, flat surface on the roughsawn face of the log. I used a hand plane and power sanders.

Saw the legs from the plank. Then fine-tune the cuts until each leg stands on its own at 90 degrees.

A flap sander quickly removes oxidation and loose debris from the slab's bark side. Don't try for a perfect surface. Just sand smooth to about 180-grit.

decided a bench would be the best way to retain the natural look of the slab and highlight its best features. The slab's 14-in. width was wide enough to provide sufficient stability, and at over 1½-in. thick, it was plenty strong. That inherent strength and a unique joint I came up with allowed me to eliminate the typical stretcher between the legs and help keep the design as clean and natural looking as possible.

I still had to figure out how to orient the legs to the slab. I turned the natural sides of the legs inward to keep all of the natural surfaces facing one another.

Leg position was another big decision. I once had a bad experience with a cantilevered bench like this. There were three of us on a bench, two got up and guess who ended up on the floor? The lesson was that there are limits to how far you can safely

Build a bridge over the seat to rout the mortises. The bridge acts as a straightedge to guide the cut and a platform to support the router.

Use a template to lay out the mortise for each leg on the seat plank. Make the template by tracing the top of the leg onto a piece of paper.

Rout the center portion of the mortise with a top- bearing flush-trim bit. The stepped ends of the mortise will be finished later. Use the edge of the bridge to guide the bit along the mortise's straightedge. Move the bridge slightly to rout the rest of the mortise.

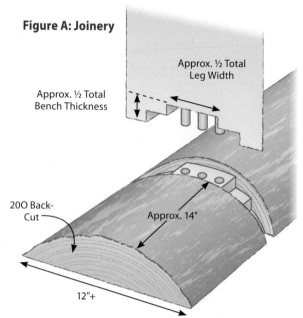

Figure A: Joinery

Approx. ½ Total Leg Width

Approx. ½ Total Bench Thickness

200 Back- Cut

Approx. 14"

12"+

cantilever a bench seat. I adjusted the legs on a prototype bench and made some test sittings until I found a point where the legs were offset enough to look visually pleasing without making the bench tippy or unstable.

Prep the Slab

The first step is to flatten and smooth the sawn face of the slab (Photo 1). You can use a hand plane to remove milling marks and any twist or warp. If there's a lot of material to remove, a handheld power plane is easier. Sand to 180-grit, using a random orbit sander. This provides a flat reference surface and establishes the plank's final thickness.

The next step is to cut the legs off the slab. I turn the plank flat side down on my radial arm saw to make the cuts. Due to the curvature of the log's edge, you'll have to approximate a square cut. This first cut doesn't need to be perfect. Once the legs are removed, fine-tune the cut until each leg stands square (Photo 2). Next, make a 20-degree angle cut on either end of the seat blank (Fig. A). If you don't own a radial arm saw, you can make all these with a circular saw or jigsaw and a straightedge.

Lightly sand the bark side of the slabs by hand with 100-grit sandpaper. Sand just enough to remove the oxidation on the surface and smooth any rough edges. Sand up to about 150-grit. Then switch to a flap sander chucked in an electric drill (Photo 3).

Cut the Joints

First, build a simple jig to bridge the width of the seat plank and provide a level platform for your router to ride on (Photo 4). Then lay out the location of the legs on the plank with a paper pattern of the leg's top (Photo 5). Set the jig to remove most of the wood in the first step of the mortise (Photo 6). Stop routing short of the natural edge of the mortise and use a chisel to pare to the pencil line.

Next, tap the leg into the mortise until it bottoms out. Then calculate how deep the notch must be to bring the outside edges of the leg flush with the top of the seat (Photo 7).

A crosscut sled on a tablesaw works well to cut the notch (Photo 8). By tapping the leg into the seat plank once again, you can see where to begin the second and third steps of the mortise. Use a chisel to chop the steps in the seat plank. Return to the tablesaw and sled to finish the notches in the leg.

Attach the Legs

Lay out and drill holes in the mortises for the ¾-in. dowels. Insert dowel centers in the holes and tap the leg in place (inset Photo 9). The centers transfer the hole locations to the top of the leg. Drill dowel holes in the legs and the joint is ready to assemble (Photo 9).

Use epoxy to glue the bench together. Epoxy is gap-filling and slow-setting, perfect for a glue-up like this. First, glue the dowels into the legs, then the legs in the seat. Tap the legs in place with a mallet until they bottom out. Carefully rotate the bench upright and use two cauls and four clamps to apply clamp pressure (Photo 10). Allow the epoxy to dry overnight.

Finish sanding the flat portions of the bench to about 220-grit. Apply your favorite finish. I used four coats of a poly/oil finish on the flat surfaces to give these surfaces a satin finish. I used one coat of paste wax on the natural surfaces to give them a flat finish.

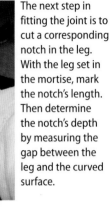

7 — The next step in fitting the joint is to cut a corresponding notch in the leg. With the leg set in the mortise, mark the notch's length. Then determine the notch's depth by measuring the gap between the leg and the curved surface.

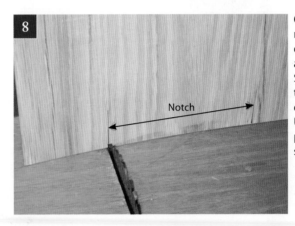

8 — Cut the stepped notch at the top of each leg using a tablesaw sled. Secure the leg to the fence with clamps and wedges. Use your marks to position the leg and set blade height.

Notch

9 — Use dowel centers to transfer the hole locations to the leg. Drill the dowel holes in the leg and glue them in. Now you're ready for the final glue-up.

10 — Glue the bench together on a flat surface, so it sits properly. Use cauls to transfer light clamping pressure.

Caul

by GARY WENTZ

Speaker Stand

WITH HIDDEN STORAGE

Don't you love hearing great sound with your movies at home? A pair of these oak stands puts today's small speakers at the ideal height—3 ft. above the floor. We've built cabinets under the speakers that hold a total of 60 DVDs behind secret doors. And we've tucked the speaker wires out of sight—they run inside the stands.

EDITOR: TOM CASPAR • ART DIRECTION: VERN JOHNSON • PHOTOGRAPHY: BILL ZUEHLKE • ILLUSTRATION: FRANK ROHRBACH

PROJECT REQUIREMENTS AT A GLANCE

Tools:

- Tablesaw
- Biscuit joiner
- Router
- Drill

Materials:

- (to make two stands) 15 bd. ft. of oak
- ½ sheet of ¼-in. oak plywood
- 10 6 x 6-in. pieces of ¾-in. plywood
- 1¼-in. and 2-in. No. 8 flat head screws

Cost: $100 for two stands

Detail 1: Grooves in Rails and Stiles

Detail 2: Side View of Top

Figure A: Exploded View
(See Cutting List, page 147)

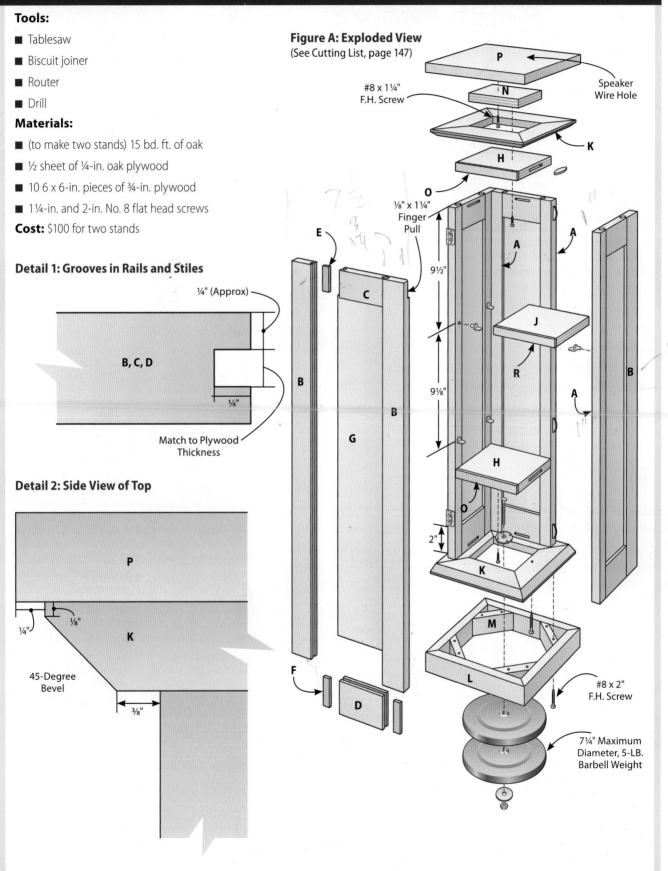

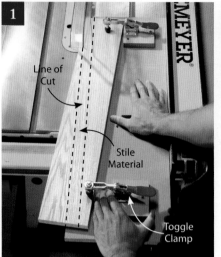

Straight-grained wood complements the simple lines of this project. This simple jig with toggle clamps lets you rip straight-grained pieces from ordinary boards.

Cut grooves in the rails and stiles to hold plywood panels and splines. The rails are very short and unsafe to hold by themselves, so push them with a shop-made jig (Fig. B).

Glue each side of the cabinet using ¼-in. plywood splines. The back and the door are built exactly the same way, although the back is narrower.

Start with Straight-Grained Wood

Wood selection makes all the difference in this project. Straight-grained pieces emphasize the stand's simple lines. Wild or angled grain is distracting, but often it's the norm in oak. No problem. If you don't mind wasting some wood, you can make your own great-looking straight-grained boards.

Begin by selecting boards for the stiles and rails. You don't need many. It doesn't matter what angle the grain runs at in these pieces, as long as some of it is straight. Save the parts of these boards with really wild grain for the frames (K) and top (P) since their faces don't show. Rip the boards at an angle that follows the grain (Photo 1). Use the new edge to cut your stiles and rails.

Rails, Stiles, and Panels

The storage cabinet is basically four frame-and-panel assemblies with similar stiles and rails. They are grooved to hold plywood panels (G) and splines (E, F). The splines join each assembly. We'll use a standard blade to cut the grooves, rather than a dado blade, because ¼-in. plywood is usually undersized.

1. Rip and crosscut the stiles (A, B) and rails (C, D). Hang on to your offcuts to use as trial pieces when making the grooves. Note that the stiles are two different widths. The back has two narrow stiles; the door has two wide ones. The sides have a narrow stile in front, a wide stile in back.

2. Cut the plywood panels (G) and use leftover scraps to make splines.

3. To make assembly easier, use sandpaper to slightly round the edges of the panels.

4. Select and mark the best-looking side of each rail and stile as its face. Place the face against the fence each time you cut a groove. That way, any slight variations in wood thickness will create uneven joints on the inside rather than the outside of the speaker stand.

5. Set your blade to ¼-in. cutting depth and set your fence ¼ in. from the blade. Cut one kerf in some trial pieces and every stile and rail (Photo 2; Fig. A, Detail 1). Move the fence and make a second pass in one of the trial pieces. Use a spline to check the fit of the groove. The spline should slip in easily, allowing room for glue. Adjust the fence if necessary and finish grooving all the pieces.

Figure B: Rail Jig

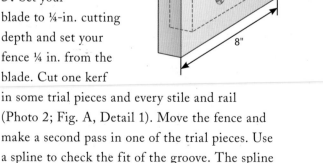

Cut biscuit slots; then drill holes in the sides for shelf supports. This jig indexes the holes and acts as a depth stop. The chuck of the drill hits the jig before the bit goes too deep.

Assemble the cabinet using the subtop and subbottom to square the sides to the back. Place spacers between the stiles so they don't flex under clamping pressure. Biscuits make aligning the parts a no-brainer for this critical step.

Assemble the Cabinet

Make a dry-run assembly to ensure everything goes together smoothly. You're assembling rails and stiles of different widths and each part has a face and a backside, so take a moment to double-check the configuration before you spread any glue. Pay special attention to the face sides when cutting biscuit slots and assembling the left and right sides of the cabinet. Otherwise, you might end up with a side that's inside out.

6. Assemble the door, sides and back of the cabinet (Photo 3).

7. Cut the subtop and subbottom (H) of the cabinet from ¾-in. plywood. We covered the front edges of these parts (and the shelves) with ¼-in.-thick strips of oak banding (Q, R).

8. Cut slots for No. 0 biscuits. Biscuits aren't vital to the strength of the cabinet, but they hold the parts in alignment and make assembly much easier.

9. Drill the holes for shelf pins before assembly (Photo 4).

Glue the mitered frames that go on the top and bottom of the cabinet. This awkward glue-up is a cinch with a band clamp.

10. Glue up the cabinet in two stages. First, glue and clamp the back to one of the sides. Immediately add the subtop and subbottom to square the assembly (Photo 5). When the glue has set, add the other side.

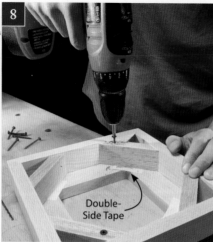

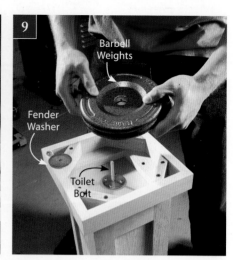

Bevel the mitered frames with the blade tilted *away* from the fence. It's safer to run your workpiece over a tilted blade rather than under the blade. Plus, this leaves a cleaner cut.

Attach the mitered frame to the base with double-sided tape. Drive a couple of screws and check the alignment. Back out the screws, remove the tape and reassemble using screws and glue.

Mount two 5-lb. barbell weights inside the base so the stand is more stable. Make a sturdy post for the weights from a toilet bolt and a fender washer with four holes drilled in it for screws.

The Top and Base

The top and base are attached to identical mitered frames that are beveled to 45 degrees.

11. Miter the frame sides (K) and cut slots for No. 0 biscuits.

12. Glue up the frames (Photo 6).

13. Bevel the frames by running them over the tilted blade (Photo 7).

14. Cut the sides (L) and corner blocks (M) for the base and glue up.

15. Attach the frame and base with double-sided carpet tape. Screw and glue together (Photo 8).

16. Use the same tape-screw-glue method to fasten the beveled frame to the cabinet.

17. Make the top (P) by gluing three boards together. A single, wide board is less likely to stay flat.

18. Attach the beveled frame to the top using screws, but no glue. Drill oversize clearance holes in the frame so the top can move freely with changes in humidity.

19. Screw a scrap of ¾-in. plywood (N) to the top, inside the frame, to attach the top to the cabinet.

20. Fasten weights to the base to stabilize the stand (Photo 9).

Hang the Door

At this point, the door is the same height as the cabinet. The top and bottom ends need to be trimmed to leave ⅛-in. gaps above and below the door.

21. Trim the door just enough so that you can set it in place and check the fit. Adjust the angle to compensate if the cabinet is slightly out of square.

22. Cut a ⅛-in.-deep, 1¼-in.-long finger pull at the top of the door using a router and chamfer bit.

23. Hang the door using no-mortise hinges (Photo 10). Install a magnetic catch (not pictured) to keep the door shut.

Finishing Touches

24. Drill holes in the top and bottom for speaker wire. Set a speaker on the stand to determine the best hole position.

25. Finish the speaker stand with golden oak stain followed by three coats of spray-on polyurethane.

26. Stick adhesive-backed felt pads to the underside of the base.

10

Support Stand

Attach the door to the cabinet. First screw the hinges to the cabinet. Stick double-sided tape to the loose side of the hinges. Set the door in place and gently swing it open. Support the door with stands as you screw the hinges to the door.

Cutting List

Overall Dimensions: 9½" x 9½" x 31¾"

All materials are ¾"-thick solid wood, unless otherwise noted. Quantities are for one stand.

Part	Name	Qty.	W	L	Notes
A	Narrow stile	4	1"	28"	Groove one side.
B	Wide stile	4	1¾"	28"	Groove one side.
C	Upper rail	4	2"	3¾"	Groove three sides.
D	Lower rail	4	2⅜"	3¾"	Groove three sides.
E	Upper spline	8	⁷⁄₁₆"	1¾"	¼" plywood
F	Lower spline	8	⁷⁄₁₆"	2"	¼" plywood
G	Panel	4	4⅛"	24"	¼" plywood
H	Subtop and subbottom	2	5½"	5¾"	¾" plywood
J	Shelf	2	5⅜"	5⅝"	¾" plywood
K	Frame side	8	2"	9"	Miter ends. Cut slots for No. 0 biscuits.
L	Base side	4	1½"	9½"	Miter ends.
M	Corner block	4	1½"	3⅞"	Miter ends.
N	Screw block	1	4⅞"	4⅞"	¾" plywood
P	Top	1	9½"	9½"	Make from edge-glued boards.
Q	Subtop and subbottom banding	2	¾"	5¾"	Make from ¼"-thick solid wood.
R	Shelf banding	2	¾"	5⅝"	Make from ¼"-thick solid wood.

by TIM JOHNSON

Walnut Coffee Table

SIMPLE JOINERY ALLOWS TIME TO ADD COOL DESIGN DETAILS

Pocket screw joinery won't win any aesthetic awards, but it does a good job with minimal fuss. If you can fit a butt joint, you can master this method. Butt joints, of course, are notoriously weak; pocket screws effectively reinforce them. To give pocket hole joinery a go, you'll need a pocket screw jig, a specialized drill bit, and pocket screws.

Playing with tradition

The table's design continues the play on tradition. The tapered legs are turned upside down and inside out from their traditional pose (Fig. A). And rather than standing at 90°, the aprons follow the slope of the legs. Thanks to pocket screw joinery, these changes present only minimal building challenges.

1. If you're working with roughsawn lumber, mill all your boards to thickness. Then decide how each board will be used.

2. Choose the best boards for the top (Part A, Fig. B). Cut them slightly oversize in length and joint the edges square. When you glue these boards together, make sure their faces are flush, to minimize sanding. Remove all squeezed-out glue before it hardens. Leave the top clamped up overnight.

3. If you're gluing up the leg stock, do it now.

4. Unclamp the top and set it aside for the time being. Stand it on end, so air can circulate freely all around, or raise it on stickers if you store it flat.

5. Make the front apron assembly (B1-B4) from a board that's oversize in both width and length (Photo 1). Start by marking a centerline across the board's width. First, rip a 1" wide length, to create the top rail (B1). Reset the fence and rip a 4" wide length, to create the piece that includes the drawer front and end spacers (B2 and B3). The offcut from this second rip, which must also be at least 1" wide, is the bottom rail (B4).

6. Crosscut the middle piece to create the drawer front. Measure from the centerline to locate both ends. Then make each cut on the

Make the drawer and its frame from a single oversize board. First, rip the board into three pieces. Next, crosscut the middle piece to create the drawer front. Locate the drawer ends by marking from a centerline.

Glue the pieces back together, using the centerline for alignment and the unglued drawer front as a spacer. Set this assembly aside—you'll rip it to width later, along with the other aprons.

Assemble the legs and aprons with pocket screw joinery. A pocket screw jig positions the workpiece and guides the drill bit, which automatically drills a counterbored shank hole.

outside edge of the line. The two offcuts become the end spacers.

7. Create the front apron frame by gluing the board back together with the unglued drawer front trapped inside (Photo 2). Use the centerline to locate the drawer front and rails, and snug the end spacers against the drawer front ends. Use waxed paper to keep the drawer front from getting stuck by squeezed-out glue. Make sure the rail and spacer faces are flush at the glue joints. Set this assembly aside until the glue dries.

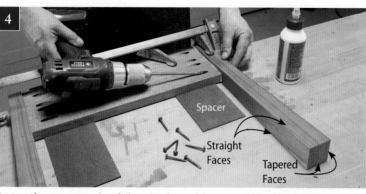

4

Spacer

Straight Faces

Tapered Faces

Fasten the aprons so they follow the slope of the tapered legs. Use spacers to create the ⅛" setback. Make sure the top edges are flush. Reinforce the joints with glue.

Figure A: Leg and Apron Details

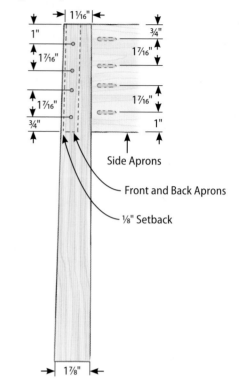

1¹⁄₁₆"

1"

1⁷⁄₁₆"

1⁷⁄₁₆"

¾"

¾"

1⁷⁄₁₆"

1⁷⁄₁₆"

1"

Side Aprons

Front and Back Aprons

⅛" Setback

1⅞"

8. Mill the leg blanks (C) square, cut them to final length, and pencil full-length tapers on two adjacent sides. Mark the inside corner on both ends of the blank—it's the only corner that will remain untouched and square after the tapers are cut.

9. Saw each taper on the waste side of the layout line. Remove the saw marks using a hand plane, a jointer, or by sanding.

10. Use one of the legs to determine the bevel angle. Note the angle (about 2½°) on your saw's bevel scale, because all of the beveled cuts used to assemble this table will be made at this angle.

11. With the saw blade tilted to the bevel angle, rip the front apron frame's top rail to final width—¾", measured on its back face. Make sure this bevel slopes toward the frame's front face. Keep the drawer front installed during the cut, to stabilize the assembly.

12. Rip the top edges of the back and side aprons (D and E) at the same angle. Again, make sure each bevel slopes toward the front face.

13. Bevel-rip the front apron frame and all three aprons to final width. On all of these pieces, the top and bottom bevels must slope in the same direction. The 5½" final width given in the Cutting List is approximate; the key is to set the fence so that the back face of the apron frame's bottom rail ends up exactly ¾" wide. (Keep the drawer front installed when you make the cut.) Once you've ripped the apron frame to final width, use the same fence setting to bevel-rip the remaining three aprons.

14. Crosscut all the aprons to final length. Measure from the centerline to locate the ends of the front apron frame and keep the drawer front installed while you make the cuts. Make sure that each pair of aprons are identical in length.

15. Drill pocket screw holes in the aprons (Photo 3). Stagger the holes so they're higher on the side aprons than on the front and back aprons (Fig. A). Then the screws won't collide when you fasten the legs.

16. Assemble the table ends (Photo 4). Clamp a side apron to your bench face-side down, with ⅛" hardboard spacers underneath. Position the legs as shown in the photo, with a square face butted against the apron and the adjacent tapered face on the bench.

17. Apply glue to both ends of the apron. Snug the legs against the apron and clamp them to the bench, making sure the top of the leg is flush with the beveled top edge of the apron. Then, gently clamp the legs to the apron. Allow the glue to tack-set (5 to 10 minutes). Then install the 1¼" fine thread, washer head pocket screws. Unclamp the assembly and remove the squeezed-out glue.

Figure B: Exploded View

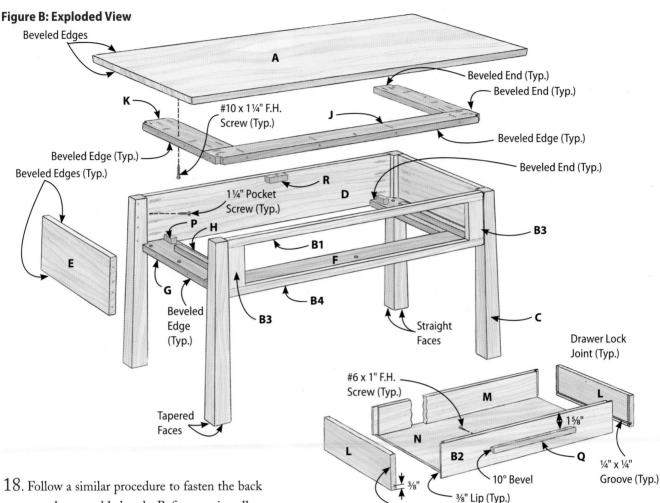

Beveled Edges

Beveled End (Typ.)

Beveled End (Typ.)

A

K

#10 x 1¼" F.H.
Screw (Typ.)

J

Beveled Edge (Typ.)

Beveled Edge (Typ.)

Beveled Edge (Typ.)

Beveled End (Typ.)

Beveled Edges (Typ.)

R

D

1¼" Pocket
Screw (Typ.)

P   H

B1

B3

E

F

G

Beveled
Edge
(Typ.)

B3

B4

C

Straight
Faces

Drawer Lock
Joint (Typ.)

Tapered
Faces

#6 x 1" F.H.
Screw (Typ.)

M

L

1⅝"

N

B2

Q

L

10° Bevel

¼" x ¼"
Groove (Typ.)

⅜"

⅜" Lip (Typ.)

Angled 2½° (Typ.)

18. Follow a similar procedure to fasten the back apron to the assembled ends. Before you install the pocket screws, make sure each assembled end is square to the back apron. Repeat the process to fasten the front apron frame.

19. Complete the table base. Cut and fit the bottom rail support (F). Bevel its front edge to match the front apron rail and both ends to match the side aprons. To determine the support's length, measure at the bottom edges of the aprons. Then cut the support to fit. Start oversize in length; then shave one end with additional cuts to achieve a perfect, snug fit. Carefully notch the front corners to fit around the legs.

20. Drill pocket holes in the bottom face of the support (Fig. C). Drill the holes for the leg screws at 45°. Don't drill these holes full-depth—leave about ½" between the end of the hole and the notch.

21. Apply glue and clamp the support to the front rail and side aprons (Photo 5). The support should be flush with both edges of the rail and with the

bottom edge of both side aprons. Let the glue tack; then install the pocket screws.

22. Cut the drawer supports (G) to fit. Bevel the outside edge and the back end of these mirror-image parts, and cut the notches.

23. Drill pocket holes in the bottom faces of both drawer supports (Fig. C) and install them with glue and screws (Photo 6).

24. Install the drawer guides, (H) using a carpenter's square.

25. Cut and fit the top rail support (J). Use the same procedure as for the bottom support, but this time, measure between the top apron edges to determine the length, and drill the pocket holes in the top face (Fig. C). Note that you don't have to drill any holes at 45°. Fasten the top rail support with glue and screws.

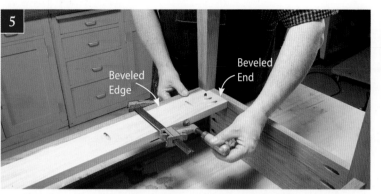

Install the bottom rail support with glue and pocket screws. To fit the sloping rails, this piece is beveled on the front edge and both ends. Allow the glue to tack-set before driving the screws.

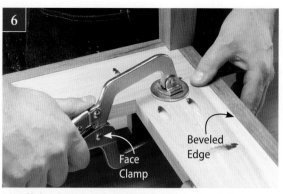

Install the drawer supports with glue and pocket screws. A special clamp holds the joint flush while you install the screws. Follow the same procedures to install the top rail support and the drawer kickers.

Cut the front end of the drawer sides at an angle, so the drawer front will slope to match the apron, which slopes to match the tapered leg.

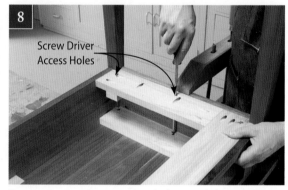

Fasten the top after centering the base and clamping it in position.

26. Cut, fit, and install the drawer kickers (K and Fig. C).

27. Cut the drawer front (B2) and drawer sides (L) to final width.

28. Cut the front ends of the drawer sides at the bevel angle (Photo 7).

29. Saw or rout grooves to house the bottom in all three pieces.

30. Cut the drawer back (M) to final width. Then cut the drawer front and back to final length, 1/16" shorter than the opening in the frame.

31. Create the drawer joints. I used a drawer lock bit (see Sources). Used in a router table with a fence, this bit allows routing all the parts from the same basic setup.

32. Cut the drawer bottom (N) to final size and finish sand the inside faces of all the drawer parts.

33. Assemble the drawer with glue and brads. Make sure the inside bottom edge of the drawer front is flush with the bottom edges of the sides. Lay a thin bead of glue in the grooves and slide in the bottom. Make sure the drawer is square. Then fasten the bottom to the drawer back with screws.

34. Test fit the drawer and make any necessary adjustments. Position the drawer so it's front is flush with the frame. Then glue on the drawer stops (P). Apply glue and butt one stop to the back end of each drawer side.

35. Make the drawer pull (Q). Bevel one edge of a wide 3/4" thick board at 10°. Return the blade to 90° and rip the pull from the board as an offcut. Cut the pull to length. Sand the pull and the drawer front.

Then glue on the pull with its beveled edge down as a finger grip.

36. Glue the screw block (R) to the back rail. Drill holes in the drawer kickers, the screw block and the top support rail for the top-mounting screws (Fig. C). Elongate all the holes but the two at the center, to allow for the top's seasonal movement.

37. Drill access holes for your screwdriver through the bottom rail and supports (Fig. C). Coincidentally (not intentionally), the outside access holes align with the diagonal screw pockets.

38. Rough sand both sides of the top, to level both surfaces.

39. Cut the top to final dimensions. I beveled both the edges and ends at 2½°, but this time, the bevels slope in at the bottom.

40. Fasten the top to the base (Photo 8). Mark centerlines on the bottom of the top and inside the base. Then use the lines to automatically center the base on the top.

41. Clamp the base to the top. Then install screws.

42. Remove the top. Then finish-sand the top and the base.

43. Apply your favorite finish. I started with a coat of SealCoat (dewaxed shellac) to bring out the rich color of the walnut. Then I brushed on two coats of polyurethane.

Cutting List
Overall Dimensions: 18" H x 21" W x 42" L

Part	Name	Qty.	Dimensions	Material	Blank Size
A	Top	1	¾" x 21" x 42"	Walnut	
B1-B4	Front apron assembly	1	¾" x 5½" x 33" (a)	Walnut	¾" x 6¼" x 35"
B1	Top rail	1	¾" x ¾" x 33" (b)	Walnut	¾" x 1" x 35"
B2	Drawer front	1	¾" x 3⅞" x 28¹⁵⁄₁₆"	Walnut	¾" x 4" x 29"
B3	End spacer	2	¾" x 4" x 2"	Walnut	¾" x 4" x 3"
B4	Bottom Rail	1	¾" x ¾" x 33" (b)	Walnut	¾" x 1" x 35"
C	Leg	4	1⅞" x 1⅞" x 17¼" (c)	Walnut	1⅞" x 1⅞" x 17¼"
D	Back apron	1	¾" x 5½" x 33" (a)	Walnut	
E	Side apron	2	¾" x 5½" x 16⅜" (a)	Walnut	
F	Bottom rail support	1		Poplar	¾" x 3½" x 35" (d)
G	Drawer support	2		Poplar	¾" x 3½" x 15" (e)
H	Drawer guide	2	½" x ¾" x 14"	Poplar	
J	Top rail support	1		Poplar	¾" x 3½" x 35" (d)
K	Drawer kicker	2		Poplar	¾" x 3¼" x 15" (e)
L	Drawer side	2	¾" x 3⅞" x 15¼" (f)	Poplar	
M	Drawer back	1	¾" x 3¼" x 28¹⁵⁄₁₆"	Poplar	
N	Drawer bottom	1	¼" x 15½" x 28"	Hardboard	
P	Drawer stops	2	¾" x ¾" x 1"	Poplar	
Q	Drawer pull	1	¾" x ⅝" x 18" (g)	Walnut	
R	Screw block	1	¾" x 1¼" x 3"	Poplar	

(a) Both edges are beveled.
(b) The width is as measured on the back face (the blade is tilted for this cut).
(c) The two outside faces taper to 1¹⁄₁₆" at top.
(d) The front edge slopes to match the front apron rail and both ends slope to match the side aprons. Cut the length to fit.
(e) The outside edge slopes to match the side apron and the back end slopes to match the back apron. Cut the length to fit.
(f) The length is measured at the bottom; the front end slopes to match the front apron.
(g) The front edge is ⅝" wide; bevel the bottom face at 10°.

Figure C: Drilling Guide

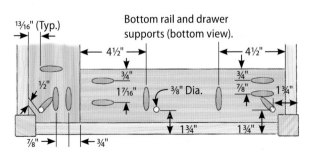

Bottom rail and drawer supports (bottom view).

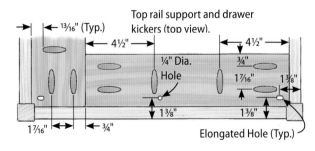

Top rail support and drawer kickers (top view).

by RANDY JOHNSON

Stickley-Style Chest of Drawers

BUILD A MASTERPIECE WITH HANDSOME QUARTERSAWN OAK

This striking chest of drawers is closely modeled after one of Gustav Stickley's most famous designs. Both bold and graceful, the wide overhanging top, slightly bowed legs and arched apron of Stickley's chest show the strong influence of his brilliant associate Harvey Ellis. My version is nearly identical in appearance, but I've modified its joinery to strengthen the case and improve the drawers' operation.

Building nine drawers is a big part of making this chest. I've used a sliding dovetail joint popular in Stickley's time. The drawers run on center-mounted wooden guides, a recent innovation 100 years ago when the original chest was built. Center guides help wide drawers track well, even when they're pushed or pulled with only one hand. I've added web frames to strengthen the chest. They also make the guides easier to install.

Stickley built most of his Mission-style furniture from quartersawn white oak. I used quartersawn red oak. It generally has less pronounced figure, but I was able to find some beautiful boards. I used quartersawn oak for everything except a couple of leg parts. I used the best-looking boards for the outside of the chest and the plainer-looking boards, which were more rift-sawn in appearance, for interior parts. Lumber that is quartersawn or rift-sawn is very stable and is a good choice for drawers and related parts.

I used heavy solid copper hardware with a hammered texture and antique finish. It cost an eye-popping $350. Less-expensive Mission-style hardware is widely available, but I love the heavy feel and authentic appearance this hardware adds to my chest. If you're up to a real challenge, you can make your own hardware.

Gustav Stickley considered his life's mission to promote the values of fine workmanship. He named his magazine and his line of furniture *The Craftsman*. When you build this chest and hammer out the hardware, you'll certainly be a craftsman, too!

PROJECT REQUIREMENTS AT A GLANCE

Materials:
- 150 board feet of ⁴⁄₄ quartersawn oak
- 20 board feet of ⁸⁄₄ plainsawn oak
- 2 sheets of ¹⁄₄-in. oak plywood

Tools:
- Tablesaw
- Jointer
- Planer
- Drill press
- Bandsaw
- Biscuit plate joiner

Hardware:
- 12 drawer pulls
- 6 tabletop fasteners
- Miscellaneous wood screws

Cost:
- About $1,250 ($900 for the wood and $350 for hardware)

Figure A: Exploded View

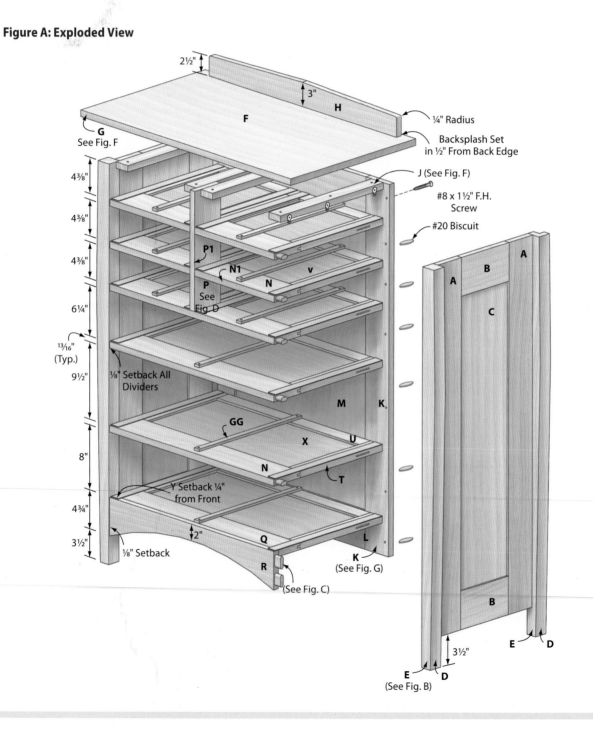

2½"
3"
F
H
G
See Fig. F
¼" Radius
Backsplash Set in ½" From Back Edge
J (See Fig. F)
#8 x 1½" F.H. Screw
#20 Biscuit
4³⁄₈"
4³⁄₈"
4³⁄₈"
6¼"
9½"
8"
4¾"
3½"
¹³⁄₁₆" (Typ.)
P1
N1
P See Fig. D
N
v
A
B
A
A
C
M
K
U
X
GG
N
T
¹⁄₈" Setback All Dividers
Y Setback ¼" from Front
2"
Q
¹⁄₈" Setback
R
(See Fig. C)
L
K (See Fig. G)
B
E
D
E
D
3½"
E
D
(See Fig. B)

ART DIRECTION: VERN JOHNSON • PHOTOGRAPHY: MIKE KRIVIT • ILLUSTRATION: FRANK RHORBACH

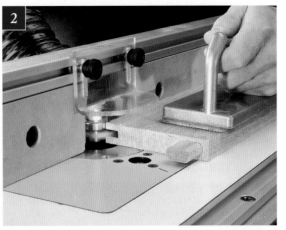

Stout mortise-and-tenon joinery make this chest strong enough to withstand many years of heavy use. I used the router-based Leigh frame-and-mortise jig to cut all the joints because it's quick and super-accurate, but many other joint-making methods will work as well.

Start with the sides. After cutting the joints, rout grooves in the rails and stiles using a slot cutter. The grooves hold the side's quartersawn oak panels. The panels are solid wood, so the grooves must be deep enough to allow them to expand and contract.

Build the Sides

1. Machine the stiles (A, K) rails (B, L), and drawer dividers (N, P, Q, and R) to final size. Cut the mortise-and-tenon joints in these parts (Photo 1; Fig. A). I used the Leigh frame-and-mortise jig and a Bosch 3¼-hp plunge router, but you can cut the same joints many other ways as well.

2. Rout grooves in the rails and stiles for the side panels (C), (Photo 2; Figs. B and C). Note that the grooves in the stiles do not extend to the end of the boards but stop at the mortises. Rout similar grooves for the back (M, Fig. G) and dust panels (V, X, Fig. A).

3. Resaw boards for the side panels and glue them together. Plane them to final thickness.

4. Sand and stain the panels (Photo 3). Sand and stain the rails' and stiles' inner edges. A one-step oil finish works well.

5. Assemble the sides and back (Photo 4).

Make the Legs

6. Saw ¼-in.-thick quartersawn veneer for the leg faces (E). Glue these strips to the leg centers (D, Photo 5). Make the faces and centers ½ in. overlong. Plane the legs to final thickness, which

Stain the panels before you assemble each side. Prestaining the entire width of a panel guarantees that no unfinished wood will show when the panel contracts in dry weather.
Tip: Stain the edges of the stiles and rails, too. This removes the risk of getting stain lap marks on the center panel later when you stain the rest of the case.

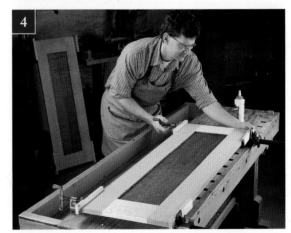

Glue and clamp the sides. The panel isn't glued in the grooves, of course. It must be free to move. Be careful in applying glue to the joints. You don't want any glue squeeze-out to make its way into the grooves and adhere to the panel.

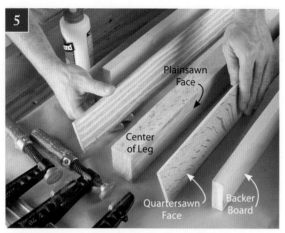

5

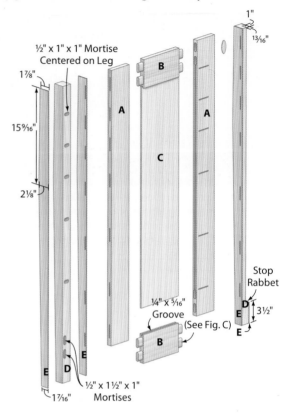

Figure B: Left Side and Leg Assembly

Make each leg from three pieces. Glue a plainsawn board between two thick strips of shop-made veneer. This classic trick makes a leg with four quartersawn faces.

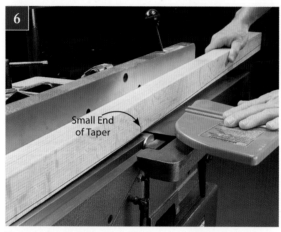

6

Taper the legs on your jointer. The legs are bow-shaped, wide in the middle and narrower at the top and bottom. With the jointer running, carefully lower the leg on the cutterhead and push the leg through. Repeat this cut until you reach the taper's layout line.

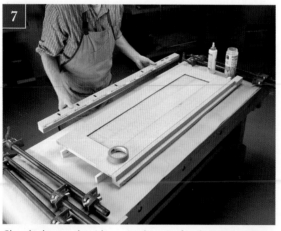

7

Glue the legs to the sides, using biscuits for alignment. Put tape next to the joints on the legs and on the sides, to catch glue squeeze-out. After clamping, pull off the tape to remove the excess glue.

Figure C: Rail Tenons

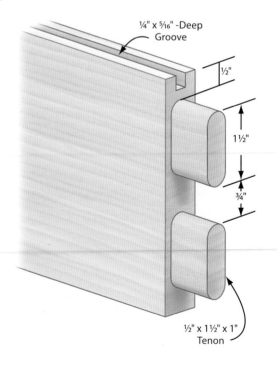

Cut notches on the vertical drawer divider. These notches interlock with complementary notches in the two top horizontal drawer dividers. You can freehand these cuts if you've got a steady hand, or use a miter gauge.

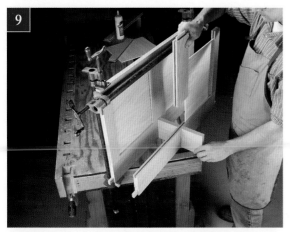

Assemble the top three web frames as a unit. The top two web frames interlock with the vertical drawer divider. The third web frame is screwed to the bottom end of the vertical divider.

Check the fit of the web frames. All must be glued at the same time, so you don't want any surprises. For the actual glue-up, it's a good idea to enlist a helper.

will reduce the veneers to ¹⁄₁₆ in. thick. (This is far easier than making ¹⁄₁₆-in.-thick veneer.) Joint and plane the legs to 2³⁄₁₆ in. wide, which is ¹⁄₁₆ in. oversize. This extra ¹⁄₁₆ in. will be removed after you taper the legs. Cut the legs to final length.

7. Mark tapers on the legs' faces (Fig. B). You can bandsaw and joint the tapers or do all the cutting on the jointer (Photo 6). With your jointer set for a ¹⁄₁₆-in. cut, the top taper should take four passes and the bottom taper 11 passes. The jointer will cut a small, sniped depression at the small end of the tapers. Sand off the sniped area that you kept on the leg in Step 6 after jointing. After sanding, the leg should be very close to a final width of 2⅛ in. at its widest spot.

8. Mark each leg to indicate in which corner it goes on the chest. Select the legs with the best faces for the front. Put the less attractive sides of the other two legs facing the chest's back.

9. Cut stopped rabbets in the rear legs using a dado set or router. Use a chisel to square the stopped ends of the rabbets (Fig. B). Lay out and machine the mortises in the front legs. Cut biscuit slots in the legs and the side panels.

10. Sand the stiles on the sides and the inside faces of the legs. These parts form inside corners, which are hard to sand after assembly. Glue and clamp the legs to the sides (Photo 7).

Assemble the Case

11. Make the horizontal drawer dividers (N) and vertical drawer dividers (P). Glue quartersawn edging (N1, P1) to their fronts (Figs. D and E). Lay out and cut bridle joints on the vertical drawer dividers and two of the horizontal drawer dividers (Photo 8, Fig. D).

12. Machine all the web frames' parts (S, T, U, V, X). Assemble the vertical and horizontal drawer dividers and web frames as a unit (Photo 9). Bandsaw the curve in the arched rail (R) and glue it to the bottom web frame.

13. Cut biscuits slots in the sides of the web frames and the leg and panel assemblies (Figs. A and B).

14. Dry-fit the web frames into the sides (Photo 10). Then clamp and glue.

Assemble and Install the Drawers

15. Build the drawers using sliding dovetails. All the part dimensions are given in the Cutting List, and in Fig. H. Note that the sides and back of the top two drawers are narrower than their fronts, unlike the other drawers. These narrow parts are necessary for the drawer to slide under the screw cleats (J) attached to the top (F). Add bottom guides (HH) to the bottoms of the drawers (Photo 11).

16. Glue wear strips (Y) to the web frames (Photo 12; Fig. A). The strips are made from plastic laminate, so you must use contact cement or epoxy.

17. Add center guides (GG) to the web frames (Photo 12). The guides are set back from the front rail by $13/16$ in., the thickness of a drawer front. The front of the guide stops each drawer so the drawer is flush with the front rail.

18. Drill the drawer fronts for the pulls (Photo 13).

Add the Top and Back

19. Glue a piece of quartersawn edging (G) to the front edge of the top (F, Fig. F). Because the top is made from quartersawn wood, its front edge will have ordinary-looking plainsawn figure. Quartersawn edging here and on the drawer dividers makes the whole case's look harmonious.

20. Make the backsplash (H). It has a tapered top edge you can make on the jointer, like the legs. Attach the backsplash ½ in. in from the back edge of the top.

21. Make the screw cleats (J) that go under the top. Drill shallow holes in two cleats for figure-eight tabletop fasteners (Fig. F). Drill oversize screw holes in all the cleats for fastening them to

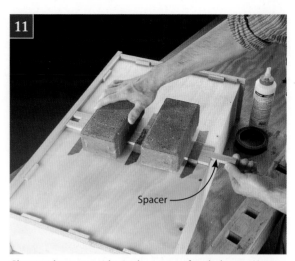

Glue two bottom guides in the center of each drawer. Use an extra strip as a spacer, but remove it before the glue sets. Bricks supply sufficient pressure and are simple to use.

Install drawer center guides from the back of the chest. To position each guide, fasten the front end first. Slide in the drawer and align the drawer front with the case. Finally, fasten the guide on the back rail.

Drill holes for the drawer hardware. Apply masking tape on which you draw clearly visible layout lines. Marking on bare wood often requires a lot of erasing later on. Here, you simply peel off the tape.

Figure D: Upper Web-Frame Assembly

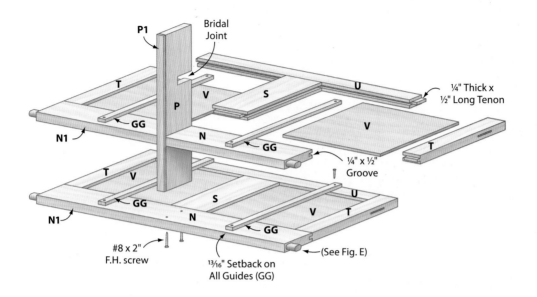

P1

Bridal Joint

T

P

V

S

U

¼" Thick x ½" Long Tenon

GG

N1

N

GG

V

¼" x ½" Groove

T

V

S

U

N

GG

GG

V

T

N1

(See Fig. E)

#8 x 2" F.H. screw

¹³⁄₁₆" Setback on All Guides (GG)

Figure E: Drawer Divider

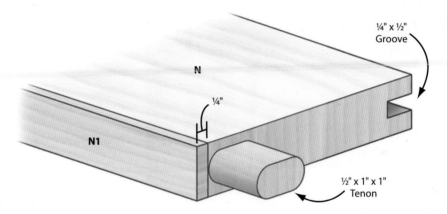

N

¼" x ½" Groove

¼"

N1

½" x 1" x 1" Tenon

Figure F: Bottom View of Top Assembly

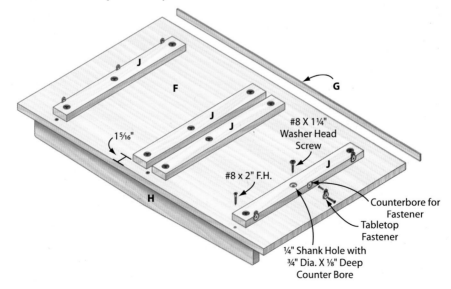

J

F

G

J

J

#8 X 1¼" Washer Head Screw

1⁵⁄₁₆"

#8 x 2" F.H.

J

H

Counterbore for Fastener

Tabletop Fastener

¼" Shank Hole with ¾" Dia. X ⅛" Deep Counter Bore

Fasten the top to the chest's sides. There are four cleats under the top. The outer two serve as braces for screwing the top assembly to the sides with low-profile figure-eight fasteners. The drawer sides are inset, so they won't hit the fasteners.

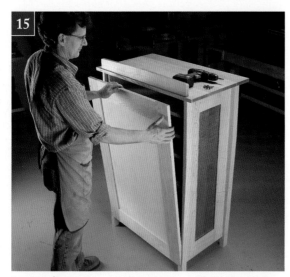

Screw on the back to complete the chest. The back adds the final rigidity to the case. Push it, lift it, slam the drawers—this beautiful chest is strong enough to last for generations.

the top. Attach the cleats to the top with washer-head screws, which allow the top to freely expand and contract. Attach the cleats and top to the sides (Photo 14).

22. Install the back (Photo 15).

Finish

23. Stain the rest of the chest, but leave the drawer boxes natural. Light-colored drawer boxes contrast nicely with the dark case.

Figure G: Back Frame and Panel

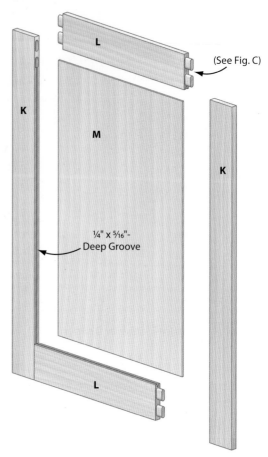

Figure H: Drawers

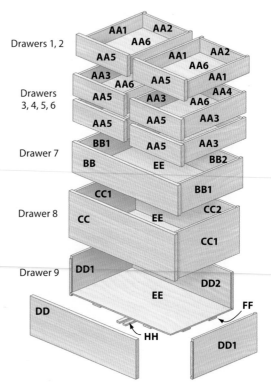

Cutting List

Overall Dimensions: 53" H x 36" W x 21¼" D

Part	Name	Qty.	Dimensions	Material	Comments
Sides, legs, top and back					
A	Side stile	4	¹³⁄₁₆" x 4" x 45¹¹⁄₁₆"	Quartersawn oak	
B	Side rail	4	¹³⁄₁₆" x 4¾" x 10"	Quartersawn oak	Includes 1-in. tenon at each end
C	Side panel	2	¼" x 8½" x 36¹¹⁄₁₆"	Quartersawn oak	
D	Leg center	4	1⅝" x 2⅛" x 49³⁄₁₆"	Plainsawn oak	
E	Leg face	8	¹⁄₁₆" x 2⅛" x 49³⁄₁₆"	Quartersawn oak	Make ¼ in. thick, then plane to ¹⁄₁₆ in. thick after gluing to leg
F	Top	1	¹³⁄₁₆" x 21⁷⁄₁₆" x 36"	Quartersawn oak	
G	Top front edge	1	¹⁄₁₆" x ¹³⁄₁₆" x 36"	Quartersawn oak	Make ¼ in. thick, then joint to ¹⁄₁₆ in. thick after gluing to top
H	Backsplash	1	¹³⁄₁₆" x 3" x 32"	Quartersawn oak	
J	Screw cleat	4	¹³⁄₁₆" x 2" x 17½"	Quartersawn oak	
K	Back stile	2	¹³⁄₁₆" x 4" x 45¹¹⁄₁₆"	Quartersawn oak	
L	Back rail	2	¹³⁄₁₆" x 4¾" x 24¼"	Quartersawn oak	Includes 1-in. tenon at each end
M	Back panel	1	¼" x 22¾" x 36¾"	Oak plywood	
Drawer dividers and web frames					
N	Horizontal drawer divider	5	¹³⁄₁₆" x 4¼" x 30¼"	Quartersawn oak	Includes 1-in. tenon at each end
N1	Edge banding	5	¼" x ¹³⁄₁₆" x 30¼"	Quartersawn oak	
P	Vertical drawer divider	1	¹³⁄₁₆" x 4¼" x 14¾"	Quartersawn oak	
P1	Edge banding	1	¼" x ¹³⁄₁₆" x 14¾"	Quartersawn oak	
Q	Bottom rail	1	¹³⁄₁₆" x 3¹¹⁄₁₆" x 28¼"	Quartersawn oak	
R	Arched front rail	1	¹³⁄₁₆" x 4¾" x 30¼"	Quartersawn oak	Includes 1-in. tenon at each end
S	Web-frame center divider	3	¹³⁄₁₆" x 4" x 13"	Quartersawn oak	Includes ½-in. tongue at both ends
T	Web-frame side rail	12	¹³⁄₁₆" x 2" x 14½"	Quartersawn oak	Includes ½-in. tongue at front end
U	Web-frame back rail	6	¹³⁄₁₆" x 2" x 25¼"	Quartersawn oak	
V	Web-frame dust panel	6	¼" x 13" x 11⅛"	Plywood	
X	Web-frame dust panel	3	¼" x 13" x 25¼"	Plywood	
Y	Wear strip	18	¹⁄₁₆" x 1¼" x 18¼"	Plastic laminate	
Drawers 1 and 2					
AA1	Side	4	½" x 3½" x 17¼"	Quartersawn oak	Includes ¼-in.-long dovetail at front end
AA2	Back	2	½" x 3½" x 12³⁄₃₂"	Quartersawn oak	Includes ¼-in.-long dovetail at each end
Drawers 3, 4, 5, 6					
AA3	Side	8	½" x 4¼" x 17¼"	Quartersawn oak	Includes ¼-in.-long dovetail at front end
AA4	Back	4	½" x 4¼" x 12³⁄₃₂"	Quartersawn oak	Includes ¼-in.-long dovetail at each end
Drawers 1–6 common parts					
AA5	Front	6	¹³⁄₁₆" x 4¼" x 13⅝"	Quartersawn oak	Allows ¹⁄₁₆-in. gap all around drawer front
AA6	Bottom	6	¼" x 16¾" x 12¹⁄₁₆"	Oak plywood	
Drawer 7					
BB	Front	1	½" x 6⅛" x 28⅛"	Quartersawn oak	Allows ¹⁄₁₆-in. gap all around drawer front
BB1	Side	2	½" x 6⅛" x 17¼"	Quartersawn oak	Includes ¼-in.-long dovetail at front end
BB2	Back	1	½" x 6⅛" x 26⅝"	Quartersawn oak	Includes ¼-in.-long dovetail at each end
Drawer 8					
CC	Front	1	½" x 9⅜" x 28⅛"	Quartersawn oak	Allows ¹⁄₁₆-in. gap all around drawer front
CC1	Side	2	½" x 9⅜" x 17¼"	Quartersawn oak	Includes ¼-in.-long dovetail at front end
CC2	Back	1	½" x 9⅜" x 26⅝"	Quartersawn oak	Includes ¼-in.-long dovetail at each end
Drawer 9					
DD	Front	1	½" x 7⅞" x 28⅛"	Quartersawn oak	Allows ¹⁄₁₆-in. gap all around drawer front
DD1	Side	2	½" x 7⅞" x 17¼"	Quartersawn oak	Includes ¼-in.-long dovetail at front end
DD2	Back	1	½" x 7⅞" x 26⅝"	Quartersawn oak	Includes ¼-in.-long dovetail at each end
Drawer 7, 8, 9 common parts					
EE	Bottom	3	¼" x 16¾" x 26⁹⁄₁₆"	Oak plywood	
All drawers, common parts					
FF	Glue block	72	⁵⁄₁₆" x ⁵⁄₁₆" x 1½"	Hardwood	Eight per drawer
GG	Center guide	9	⅜" x ¹³⁄₁₆" x 17¹¹⁄₁₆"	Quartersawn oak	
HH	Bottom guide	18	⅜" x ¹³⁄₁₆" x 16½"	Quartersawn oak	Two per drawer

by JON STUMBRAS

Stowaway Bench

This country-style bench will cut the clutter by the door and serve as a resting spot to put on your shoes. The lid opens up to reveal a handy storage area. At only 11-in. wide by 44-in. long, it neatly fits in an entryway or mudroom. And it's a good weekend project.

Tools and Materials

You'll need a tablesaw, dado blade, jigsaw, router, and beading bit. We used 15 lineal ft. of 1 × 12 Douglas fir dimensional lumber. Dimensional lumber comes planed on all four surfaces and measures ¾-in. thick by 11¼-in. wide. This is wide enough for the widest parts, so there is no edge gluing of boards required.

Cut the Parts

It's important that the lid (A) be as flat as possible. Since it's common for wide boards to be slightly warped, pick the flattest one for the lid before cutting out any other parts. Then rip and crosscut the lid, legs (B) and rails (C) to final dimensions (see Cutting List). The legs and lid are too wide to crosscut with a standard tablesaw miter gauge. A simple shop-made crosscut sled solves this problem (Photo 1). Cut the bottom (D) to final length, but leave it 1-in. oversize in width. It will be custom fit later.

Shape the Legs and Rails

Start by cutting the dadoes in the two legs (Photo 2 and Figs. A and B). Then cut the notches in the upper corners of the legs. This is a three-step process. First, make two vertical cuts in each leg (Photo 3). Second, set the miter gauge 95 degrees to the left of the blade and crosscut the left-hand notches (when facing the dado) on each leg (Photo 4).

Third, set the miter gauge 95 degrees to the right and crosscut the right-hand notches (Photo 5). Break off the waste with your hand, and clean up the remaining wood with a chisel (Photo 6). Now test fit the rails into the notches. The tops of the rails and the tops of the legs should be flush. If either is proud, trim it flush. Next, cut the angle on the sides of the legs (Fig. B) with a jigsaw and smooth the cut with a hand plane or sanding block.

The arcs at the bottom of the legs come next. Start by drawing a 4-in.- radius circle on a piece of cardboard. Cut it out and use it as a template. Position it according to the dimensions in Fig. B and draw the arc. Then cut the arc out of the leg with a jigsaw. Sand the rough edges.

Next, rout the bead on the bottom edge of the rails (Photo 7).

Then draw the arc at the ends of the rails using a cardboard circle template and saw out each arc (Photo 8). Sand the rough edges as you did before.

Next, cut mortises for the hinges in the back rail. The depth of the mortise should equal the thickness of the hinge (Fig. D). Mark the locations of the hinges (Fig. A) and use the tablesaw and a dado blade to remove the waste (Photo 9). Test fit the hinges in the mortises and drill pilot holes for the screws.

Custom Fit the Bottom

The bottom needs to be exactly the same width as the length of the dado in the legs (Fig. A). Place the oversized bottom in the dado, flush-up the edge of the bottom with the dado on one side and mark the exact width on the other side (Photo 10). Now cut the bottom to final width.

EDITOR: RANDY JOHNSON • ART DIRECTION: EVANGELINE EKBERG AND PATRICK HUNTER • PHOTOGRAPHY: RAMON MORENO • ILLUSTRATION: FRANK ROHRBACH

Figure A: Exploded View

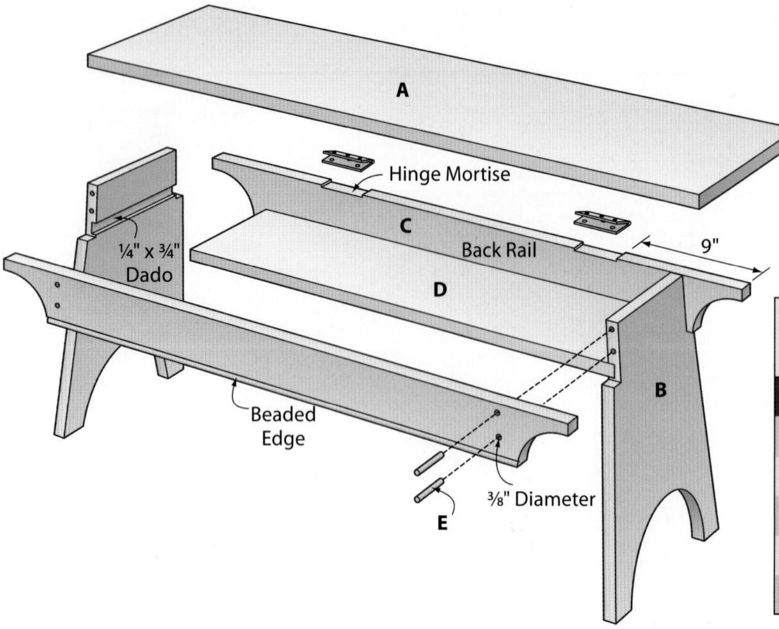
A
Hinge Mortise
C
Back Rail
9"
D
¼" x ¾" Dado
Beaded Edge
B
⅜" Diameter
E

Cutting List

Overall Dimensions: 17" H x 44" W x 11" D

Part	Name	Qty.	Dimensions
A	Lid	1	¾" x 11" x 44"
B	Legs	2	¾" x 11" x 16¼"
C	Rails	2	¾" x 3½" x 39¾"
D	Bottom	1	¾" x 7" x 30¾"
E	Pegs	8	⅜" x 1¾"

Figure B: Cutting Sequence for Legs

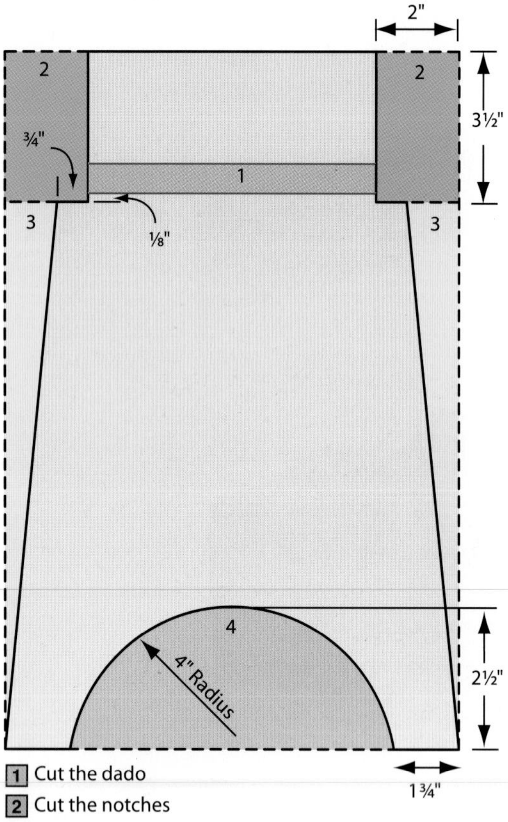
2"
2
2
¾"
1
3½"
3
3
⅛"
4
4" Radius
2½"
1¾"

1 Cut the dado
2 Cut the notches
3 Cut the angled sides
4 Cut the arc

Figure C: Rail Detail

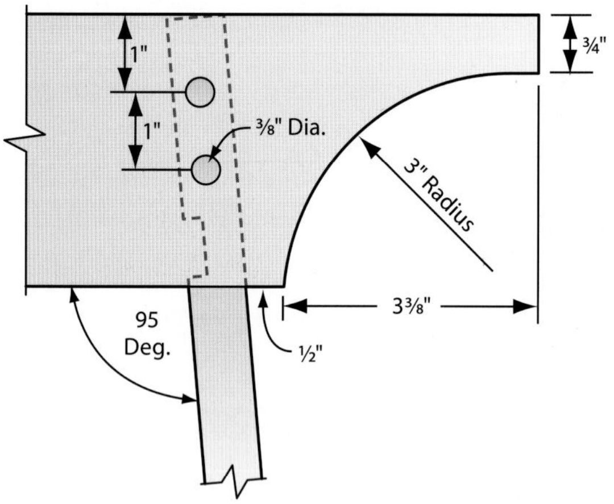
1"
1"
⅜" Dia.
¾"
3" Radius
95 Deg.
½"
3⅜"

Figure D: Hinge Detail

Measure hinge thickness with hinge closed. Cut the hinge mortises in the back rail to this depth.

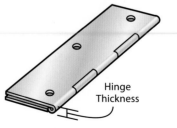

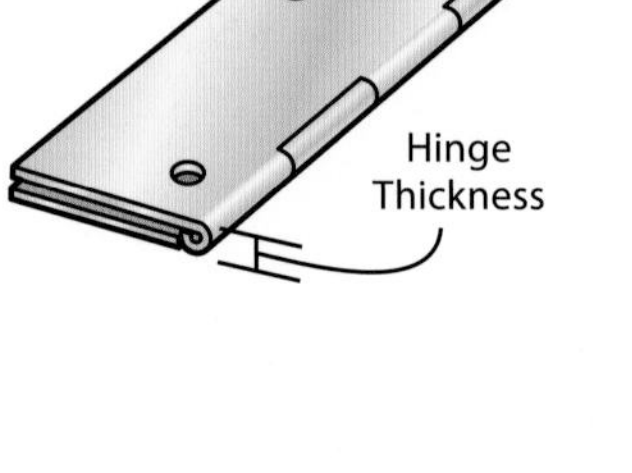
Hinge Thickness

Cut the lid and legs using a crosscut sled because it's difficult to safely and accurately cut such wide boards with a standard miter gauge.

Cut the dadoes in the legs for the bottom of the storage compartment.

Caution: Guard must be removed for this step. Use caution.

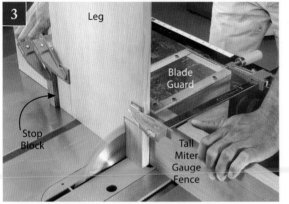

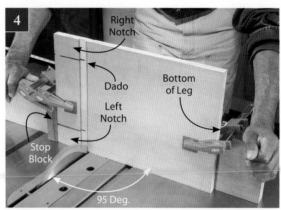

A vertical cut is the first step in cutting the notches in the legs. Set the miter gauge at 90 degrees and the blade to its maximum height. Your saw may not be able to cut the full 3½ in. that's required for this cut, but that's a good thing because the uncut part will keep the scrap from falling out in the next step. Use a tall fence on the miter gauge to support the leg and a stop block on one end to ensure identical cuts on both legs.

Crosscut the side of the left notch with the miter gauge set at 95 degrees away from the left side of the blade. Clamp the leg to the tall fence with the dado facing toward the blade and with the bottom end of the leg positioned as shown. Make this cut for the left-side notch on both legs. ***Do not cut the right-side notch with this setup!***

Assemble the Parts

Begin by building an assembly jig to hold the legs upright during the glue-up (Photo 11). A 2 × 4 sheet of plywood works fine for the base and some scrap 2 × 2 material is all that's needed for the supports. Rip the edge of the 2 × 2 lumber on the tablesaw with the blade set at a 5-degree angle. Then crosscut it so you get four 12-in.-long pieces. Orient the supports so they hold the legs angled toward each other. Double-faced tape works well to fasten the four angled scraps to the plywood. Position the supports so the bottom inside edges of the legs are 32½ in. apart. The sides are now held at the right distance from each other, angled at 5 degrees. Dry-fit the rails in the leg notches to make sure they extend by ½-in. at the ends (Fig C).

Sand all the parts before gluing. Start with 150 grit and work your way up to 320 grit if you plan to use an oil finish. You can stop at 180 grit if you plan to use varnish. Also round over any sharp edges.

To assemble, start by gluing the bottom into the leg dadoes. You'll notice that the dadoes are at a slight angle because the legs are angled in (Fig. C). It's nothing to be concerned about and the bottom will still fit fine. Clamp across the top of the legs to pull the bottom securely into the dadoes. Apply glue to the rails and set them in place. Clamp along the bottom of the rails and at the ends (Photo 12). Clean up glue squeeze-out with a putty knife after the glue becomes semi-dry. Then let the bench sit until the glue has completely dried.

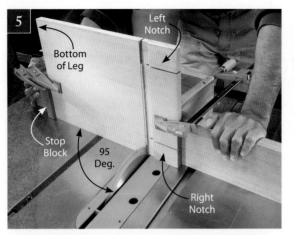

Crosscut the right notch with the miter gauge set at 95 degrees away from the right side of the blade. Again, clamp the leg to the tall fence with the dado facing toward the blade and with the bottom end of the leg pointing as shown.

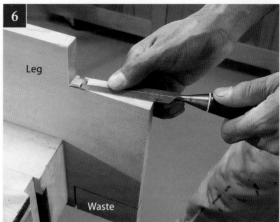

Clean up the remaining wood inside the corner of the notch that is left after you break off the waste piece by hand. A sharp chisel makes quick work of this task.

Rout a bead along the bottom of the rails. Clamp the rail to a thick board. This provides a wide surface on which to balance the router.

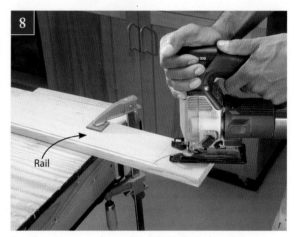

Cut the curves on the ends of the rails and sand them smooth.

Peg the Rails to the Legs

When the glue is dry, remove the clamps and drill the holes for the pegs (E) that help hold the rails to the legs (Figs. A and C). Drill the holes 1¾-in. deep. Store-bought ⅜-in. dowel rod will work fine for the pegs but making your own from the same wood as the bench adds a nice touch.

To make your own pegs, rip some scraps into ⅜-in. × ⅜-in. square strips and round them with a rasp or chisel. Next, cut the strips into 2-in. lengths. Slightly taper one end of the pegs to make them easier to drive in. Then use a small dowel or stick to smear glue inside the peg hole. Insert the peg and tap it in with a hammer (Photo 13). Trim off the remaining dowel with a handsaw and sand it flush.

Hinge the Lid

Screw the hinges into mortises in the back rail. Then mark lines on the underside of the lid for the hinges. Position these lines so when the lid is attached to the bench it is centered from side to side and front to back. Drill holes for the hinges screws. Be careful not to drill through the lid. Now snip the tips off the screws to make them ⅝-in. long. This keeps them from poking through the top of the lid. Then screw the hinges to the lid (Photo 14). Now give the bench parts a final sanding and apply a finish. We used an oil finish, which gives Douglas fir a warm amber glow.

Cut mortises in the back rail for the hinges. Use a dado blade and make multiple passes. Clamping the rail to the fence ensures accuracy and prevents the rail from slipping.

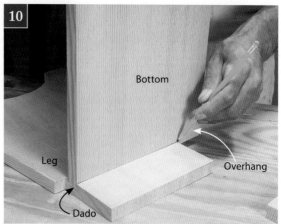

Custom fit the bottom. Insert the bottom in the leg dado so it's flush on one side and overhangs on the other. Mark the overhang and saw it off. The bottom needs to be exactly as wide as the dado is long.

Glue the bottom and rails to the legs. A shop-made jig simplifies the glue-up process. Wood scraps cut at a 5-degree angle support the legs. It's like having two shop assistants to help you.

Add clamps to hold the parts together. One clamp across the top will hold the bottom in the leg dadoes. Clamps along the lower edge of the rails and at the ends will hold the rails in place. Use little blocks of wood as clamping pads to prevent the clamps from marring the bench.

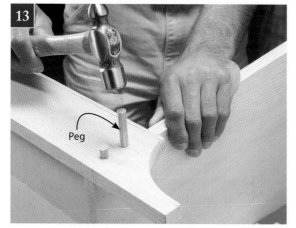

Glue and tap the pegs into predrilled holes in the rails and legs. Taper the ends of the peg with a chisel or rasp to make driving the pegs in easier. Cut off the waste with a handsaw and sand the pegs flush with the rail.

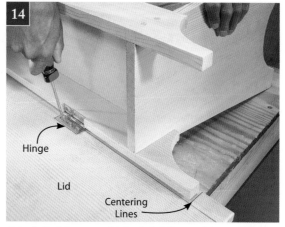

Attach the hinges to the back rail first and then to the underside of the lid. The hinges should be located so the lid sits centered on top of the bench.

EDITOR: TIM JOHNSON • ART DIRECTION: VERN JOHNSON • PHOTOGRAPHY: ANDY RAE, RAMON MORENO AND JOHN HAMEL • ILLUSTRATION: FRANK ROHRBACH, DON RAYMOND AND HEATHER BRINE LAMBERT

Kitchen Work Table

A PERFECT FIT FOR THAT SMALL SPACE IN YOUR KITCHEN

Here's a compact work table that you could tuck away in a corner or use daily as a central island. It's the same height as standard kitchen countertops, so it's perfect for food preparation and other chores.

The Cutting List on page 173 has two sets of dimensions; one for the 18-in. by 30-in. table shown here and another for a larger 24-in. by 36-in. version. You'll need a tablesaw, a stacked dado set, a bandsaw, a drill press, and a chop saw.

You'll also need a plunge router to cut the mortises and curves on the rails.

Use your favorite hardwood, but substitute hard maple for the top if you plan to use it as a cutting surface. To make the smaller version, you'll need about 12 bd. ft. of 5/4 stock for the top and slats, four 3½ ft. lengths of 2-in. square stock for the legs and 5 bd. ft. of 4/4 stock for the aprons, rails and stretcher. For the larger version, you'll need 20 bd. ft. of 5/4 and 7 bd. ft. of 4/4 stock.

Keep your router stable while plunging the mortises by ganging two legs together. Make several shallow passes until you reach full depth. To maximize the gluing surfaces, the mortises meet inside the leg and the tenons are mitered to fit (Fig. A).

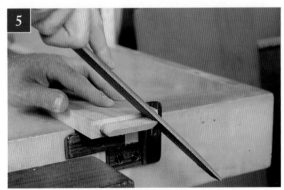

Cut tenons on the aprons and rails with a dado set and the miter gauge. Make a first pass on both sides as shown, then make the final pass using the rip fence to establish the tenon length. Hold the apron tight against the miter gauge and flat on the table. Fine-tune the tenon thickness by adjusting the blade height.

Mortise the Legs

When laying out the legs, orient the end grain in a pleasing pattern because it will be visible at the corners of the finished top. Plunge-rout the mortises, using an edge guide for your router and a ⅜-in.-dia. up-cutting spiral bit (Photo 1).

Once you've cut the mortises, switch to a ¼-in.-dia. straight bit and plunge-rout the slots in the aprons for the top fasteners, using the same gang-cutting method (Fig. A, Detail 2).

Tenon the Aprons and Rails

Cut tenons on the tablesaw using a carbide-tipped, stacked dado set (Photos 2 through 4). Any roughness on the tenon cheeks left by the cutters can be removed

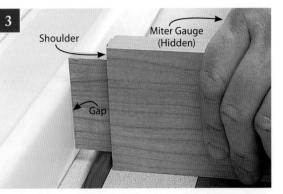

Cut shoulders on the ends of the tenon after adjusting the height of the blade. Hold the apron on its edge, tight against the miter gauge and make two passes, as in Photo 2. Keep the tenon slightly away from the fence on the final pass and pare away the remaining waste with a chisel.

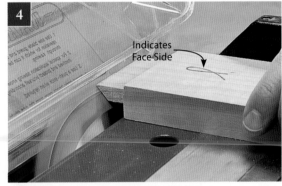

Miter the tenons, making sure the angled edges are oriented properly with the face side of the apron.

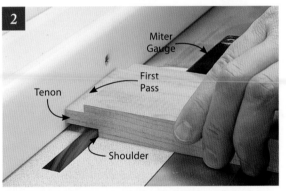

Round the shoulders of the tenons with a rasp, making firm forward strokes, so they'll fit the mortises.

Safety Warning : Using the rip fence and miter gauge simultaneously is safe only when there will be no off-cut piece. The blade guard must be removed for this cut. *Be careful.*

with a chisel or rabbet plane. After the tenons are cut and mitered, round their shoulders (Photo 5).

Rout Curves

The shallow curves on the lower rails keep the table from looking bottom-heavy. Rout them with the help of a double-sided, shop-made jig (Fig. B). First, use the jig to transfer the curves onto the rails.

Figure A: Exploded View

Detail 1: Apron and Rail Joints

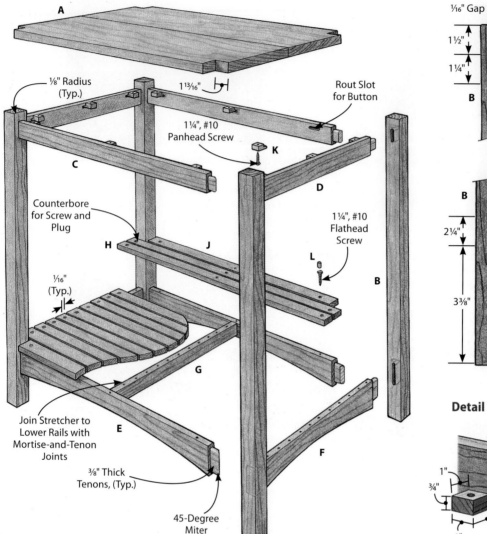

A

¹⁄₈" Radius (Typ.)

1 ¹³⁄₁₆"

Rout Slot for Button

1¼", #10 Panhead Screw

K

C

D

Counterbore for Screw and Plug

H   J

1¼", #10 Flathead Screw

L

B

¹⁄₁₆" (Typ.)

G

Join Stretcher to Lower Rails with Mortise-and-Tenon Joints

E

F

³⁄₈" Thick Tenons, (Typ.)

45-Degree Miter

¹⁄₁₆" Gap

1½"

1¼"

1"

2"

B

³⁄₈" Wide Mortise

C And D

B

1"

2¼"

3"

3³⁄₈"

E And F

Detail 2: Slots and Top Fasteners

½"

¼"

1"

¾"

¼"

1½"

1"

1"   1½"

Saw the profiles, slightly oversize, on a bandsaw or with a saber saw. Then attach the rails to the jig and rout the curves (Photo 6).

Notch the Top

The top is notched to fit inside the legs. Leave a suitable gap (min. ¹⁄₁₆ in.) around each leg so the top has room to expand during humid conditions (Fig. A, Detail 1). With the proper setup, these notches can be cut safely and precisely on the tablesaw (Photos 7 and 8).

Attach the Slats

Mill all of the slats and drill counterbored access holes for screws. To space the slats evenly, lay them in place on the lower rails with ¹⁄₁₆-in.-thick shims in between (Photo 9). You may have to joint a couple of slats or add pieces of masking tape to some of the shims to make everything fit.

With the shims in place, align the ends of the slats and clamp them all together. Drill pilot holes into the rails and fasten the slats with screws. Fill the screw holes by gluing in side-grain wooden plugs. When the glue is dry, pare and scrape the plugs flush with the slats.

Tip

Before you fasten the slats to the frame, finish their edges and bottoms.

Once installed, these surfaces are difficult, if not impossible, to reach.

Figure B: Jig for Routing the Arched Rails

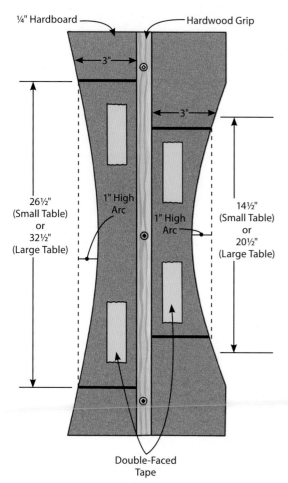

¼" Hardboard

Hardwood Grip

3"

3"

26½"
(Small Table)
or
32½"
(Large Table)

1" High
Arc

1" High
Arc

14½"
(Small Table)
or
20½"
(Large Table)

Double-Faced
Tape

Feed
Direction

Bearing

Rout the curved rails with a jig (Fig. B) and a flush-trim bit with a top-mounted bearing. First rough-saw the curve on the rail, leaving it about ⅛-in. oversize. Then mount the rail on the jig, using double-faced tape. As you rout, the bit's bearing rides on the jig's curved edge. Do half the curve, flip the rail over, and do the other half (see "Oops!," below).

Cutting List

Part	Name	Quantity	Small Table 18 x 30 x 36⅛	Large Table 24 x 36 x 36⅛
A	Top	1	1 x 18 x 30	1 x 24 x 36
B	Legs	4	1¾ x 1¾ x 36⅛	1¾ x 1¾ x 36⅛
C	Long Aprons	2	¾ x 2 x 28½*	¾ x 2 x 34½*
D	Short Aprons	2	¾ x 2 x 16½*	¾ x 2 x 22½*
E	Long Rails	2	¾ x 3 x 28½*	¾ x 3 x 34½*
F	Short Rails	2	¾ x 3 x 16½*	¾ x 3 x 22½*
G	Stretcher	1	¾ x 1¾ x 16†	¾ x 1¾ x 22†
H	Inner Slats	8	1 x 1¾ x 30 △	
	Inner Slats	11		1 x 1¹³⁄₁₆ x 36 □
J	Outer Slats	2	1 x 1¾ x 26⅜	1 x 1¾ x 32⅜
K	Top Fasteners	12	¾ x 1 x 1½	¾ x 1 x 1½
L	Side-Grain	30	⅜ diameter	
	Plugs	39		⅜ diameter

* Includes 1-in.-long tenons on both ends.
† Includes ¼-in.-long tenons on both ends.
△ Requires nine ¹⁄₁₆-in.-wide shims.
□ Requires twelve ¹⁄₁₆-in.-wide shims.

Oops!

Short
Grain

Bit
Rotation

The curve was shaping up beautifully when all of a sudden, *WHAM!*

I forgot that when you rout an arch, the short grain at the back end is likely to get blown out because of the bit's rotation. The best approach is to rout the front half of the curve, stop, and flip the rail end-for-end. Then you'll be routing *with* the grain as you finish the curve.

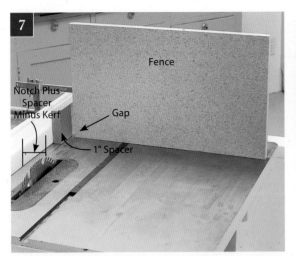

Before sawing the notches, clamp a spacer block to the rip fence, well in front of the blade. Screw a tall fence to the miter gauge, leaving a gap so it won't bind against the spacer. Set the fence to the combined widths of the notch and spacer, minus the saw kerf. Raise the blade to the height of the notch.

Attach the slats, using shims to keep them evenly spaced. Be sure to put one shim between each leg and the adjacent slat. Use a clamp to keep the slats aligned while the pilot holes are drilled and the screws are set. Wooden plugs, glued in the screw holes and sanded smooth, create a finished look.

Safety Warning: The blade guard must be removed for this cut. *Be careful.*

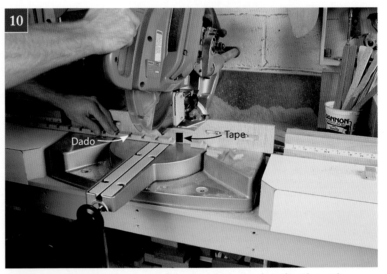

Cut notches after sliding the top against the spacer block and clamping it firmly to the tall fence. The spacer ensures an adequate gap between the top and the rip fence to keep the off-cut waste pieces from binding.

Cut wooden fasteners for the top from straight-grained stock with evenly spaced dadoes sawn across its length. Black tape on the fence indicates the correct length.

Fasten the Top

To center the top between the legs, use shims of equal thickness all around. Secure the top to the frame with wooden fasteners (Photo 10 and Fig. A, Detail 2). These fasteners allow the top to expand and contract by sliding inside the slots in the aprons.

Apply the Finish

Finish the top and frame separately so you can seal every surface. A wipe-on varnish is a good choice. Follow the instructions on the can, and put on three or four coats. After the first coat, it's a good idea to sand the surface with 220-grit sandpaper.

If you prefer a food-safe finish on the top, use Behlen's Salad Bowl Finish or Preserve Woodworker's Cream. Do not use vegetable oil, because it will turn rancid.

by JON STUMBRAS

Arts & Crafts
Table Lamp

SURE-FIRE STEPS SIMPLIFY THE INTRICATE SHADE JOINERY

PROJECT REQUIREMENTS AT A GLANCE

Materials:
- 3 bd. ft. of 8/4 mahogany
- 3 bd. ft. of 4/4 mahogany
- Electrical parts
- Stained glass

Tools:
Tablesaw, dado blade, router, 1/4 in. router guide bushing, 1/4 in. straight cutting bit and jigsaw.

Cost: $120

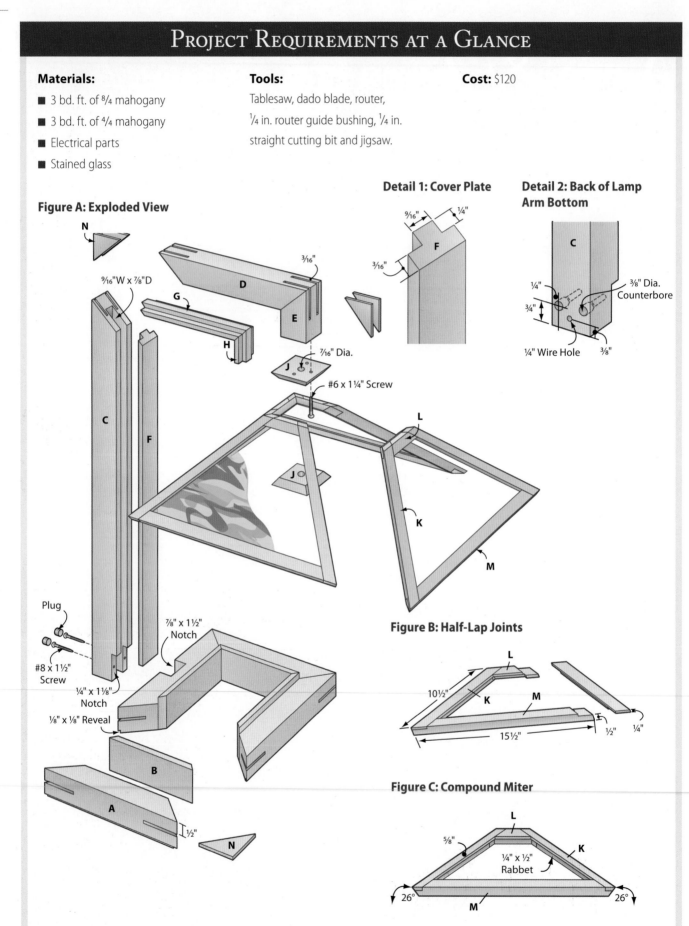

Figure A: Exploded View

Detail 1: Cover Plate

Detail 2: Back of Lamp Arm Bottom

Figure B: Half-Lap Joints

Figure C: Compound Miter

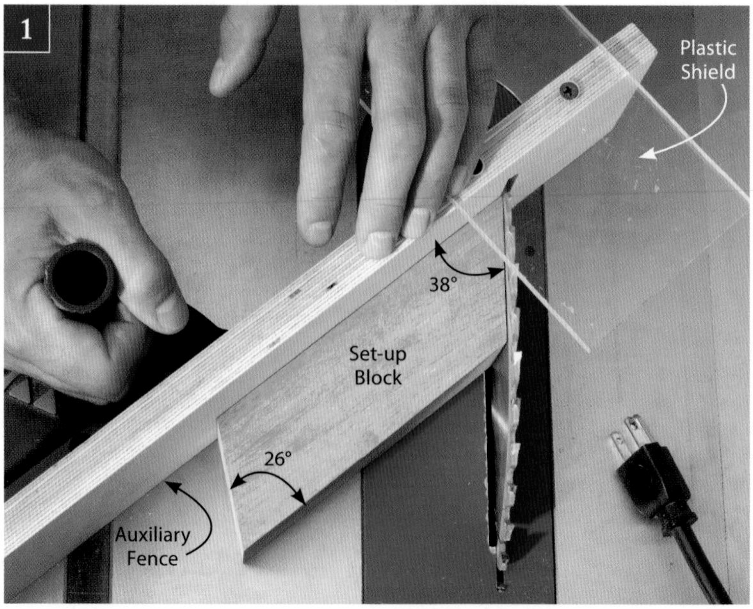

Two precisely angled cuts are key to building the lamp shade. You'll go back and forth between these cuts a number of times. To ensure accuracy, make a setup block with both angles to use every time you reset the miter gauge or the tilt of the blade.

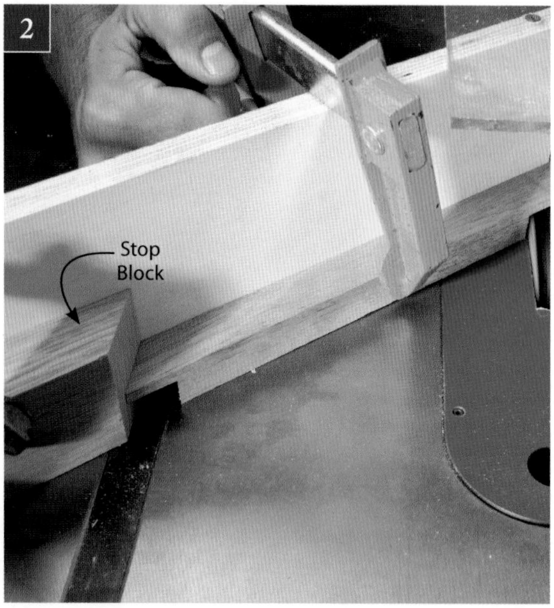

Cut the angled half-lap joints for the lampshade frame with a dado blade. Clamp a stop block to the fence so every joint comes out exactly the same size. Test the fit of scrap parts before cutting the real thing.

Caution: Fasten a piece of plastic to the top of the auxiliary fence to keep your fingers away from the blade.

Our table lamp is reminiscent of the Prairie style of design, with lines that Frank Lloyd Wright might favor. In spite of its complex-looking shade, this elegant lamp is within reach of any intermediate woodworker. We've figured out a straightforward system that tames all those nasty angles and guarantees good results. The wiring is also simple, even if you haven't done

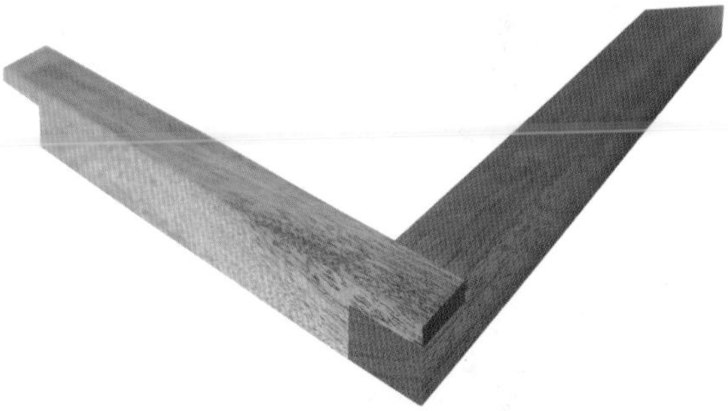

Cutting List

Overall Dimensions: 14½" W x 22½" H x 17" D

Material	Part	Name	Qty.	Dimensions	Material	Part	Name	Qty.	Dimensions
Mahogany					Electrical				
	A	Base sides	4	1⅛" x 1½" x 9¼"		Q	Lamp cord and plug	1	18 g. 8 ft. long
	B	Base lip	4	5/16" x 1⅜" x 6 5/16"		R	Rotary line switch	1	
	C	Arm (vertical)	1	1½" x 1½" x 22½"		S	Bushing	1	⅛" ips, female bushing
	D	Arm (horizontal)	1	1½" x 1½" x 10¾"		T	Steel pipes	2	⅛" ips, 10" long
	E	Arm (end)	1	1½" x 1½" x 3"		U	Couplings	3	⅛" ips, female
	F	Vertical cover plate	1	7/16" x 1⅛" x 21"		V	Steel pipe	1	⅛" ips, 9" long
	G	Upper cover plate	1	7/16" x 1⅛" x 9"		W	Armbacks (elbows)	2	90 degree, ½" ball, ⅛ ips
	H	End cover plate	1	7/16" x 1⅛" x 2"		X	Nipple	1	⅛" ips, 5" long
	J	Shade hangers	2	⅜" x 2½" x 2½"		Y	Star lock washers	2	⅛" ips
	K	Shade sides	8	¾" x 1" x 10½"		Z	Nuts	3	⅛" hex nut
	L	Shade tops	4	¾" x 1" x 12"		AA	Keyless sockets	2	
	M	Shade bottoms	4	¾" x 1" x 15½"		BB	Cluster body	1	1 1/16" x 1 1/16"
	N	Splines	8	⅛" x 2" x 3½"		CC	Brass arms	2	3½", ⅛" ips
Glass						DD	Wire nuts	2	9/16" x 5/16"
	P	Stained glass	4	⅛" x 12¼" x 6⅛"					

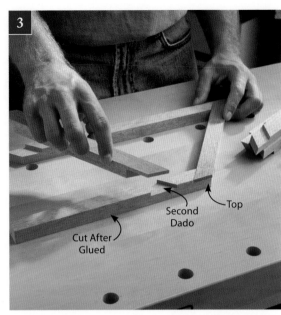

Assemble the frame without glue to determine the exact position of the top's second dado. This piece is actually quite short in the finished shade, but it's much easier to make and hold on the saw if you start with a long piece of wood. Trim the excess length after the frame has been glued up.

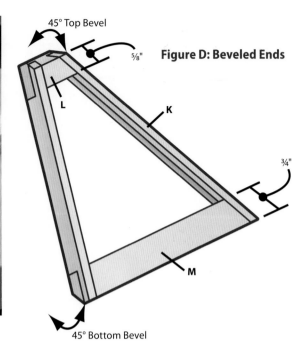

Figure D: Beveled Ends

45° Top Bevel
⅝"
L
K
¾"
M
45° Bottom Bevel

much electrical work. All the parts are readily available through the mail or at a lighting store. You may find that the hardest part is selecting the stained glass. There is a bewildering array of colors and textures to choose from, but that's part of the fun.

Build the Shade Frame

The shade is made of four identical frames. Use a stop block for all the cuts.

1. Mill the 4/4 mahogany to thickness and rip the boards into 1-in. widths. Rough-cut three 12-in. pieces and one 18-in. piece for each of the four frames (K, L, M). Cut enough parts to build an extra frame as a precaution and for setup purposes.

2. Attach a long auxiliary fence to your tablesaw's miter gauge. We added an acrylic guard just as a reminder of where not to put one's fingers.

3. Make a setup block for setting your miter gauge angles by cutting a 38-degree angle on one end and a 26-degree angle on the other one. Use an accurate miter saw to cut the block.

4. Set the miter gauge to cut at 38 degrees (Photo 1). Miter both ends of the frame sides (K) and frame bottoms (M) to final dimensions. Miter just the left edge of the frame top (L). All these cuts can be made using one miter fence setting.

5. Cut the half-lap joint on the mitered end of each piece (Photo 2; Fig. B). Use scrap wood to set the blade height and a stop block for each cut. You will need to rotate the miter gauge 38 degrees right and left of center to accomplish all the angles.

6. Dry-fit all the pieces together and mark the position of the half-lap on the right side of the frame top (Photo 3). Then cut the rest of the top half-laps.

7. Glue each frame assembly together with small C-clamps. When the glue has set, cut off the waste on the top.

Rabbet for the Glass

8. Make a template out of ¼-in. plywood to cut rabbets in each frame. Simply place a shade frame on the plywood, trace the interior and mark lines ¼ in. to the outside of the tracing lines. Cut to this line with a jigsaw. Keep the template 3 in. wide to support the router.

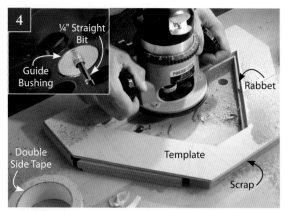

Rabbet each frame to accept the stained glass. Make a plywood template with wide edges to guide and support the router. Use double-stick tape to secure the frame to the bench and template. Tuck frame scraps under the template for support. Rout the rabbet with the template guide.

Rip compound angles on both sides of all four frames. Be sure to cut one side first on each frame before resetting the miter gauge to cut the other sides.

9. Rout the rabbet with a ¼-in. straight bit and guide bushing (Photo 4; Fig. C). Take several passes of to get the rabbet to full depth. Clean up the corners of the rabbet using a chisel.

Cut the Compound Miters

10. Use the setup block to set the tablesaw miter fence to cut at 38 degrees and angle the blade to 26 degrees.

11. Place a frame, face side up, with the bottom against the fence. Cut the compound miter (Photo 5), leaving a ⅝-in.-wide side (Fig. C). To ensure a clean joint, make two passes. The first cut is just shy of the line. For the second cut, add a shim, such as a playing card, to the stop block. This will take just a whisker off for a super-clean edge.

12. Next, place the freshly cut side against the miter fence and adjust the angle so the uncut side is parallel to the blade. This should be approximately 76 degrees on the miter gauge. Then miter the second side.

13. With a beveled side against the fence, adjust the miter fence so the frame bottom is parallel to the blade. Reset the blade to 90 degrees; rip each bottom to ¾ in. wide (Fig. C). Reset the blade to 45 degrees and bevel the underside of the frame's bottom just up to the routed rabbets (Fig. E).

Compound Miter

Figure E: Glass Stop

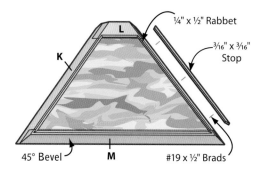

¼" x ½" Rabbet

L

³⁄₁₆" x ³⁄₁₆" Stop

K

45° Bevel

M

#19 x ½" Brads

14. Remove the miter fence, flip the frame over onto its face and use the tablesaw fence to bevel the top.

15. Glue the four frames together using spring clamps (Photo 6). When dry, clean up the glue and sand.

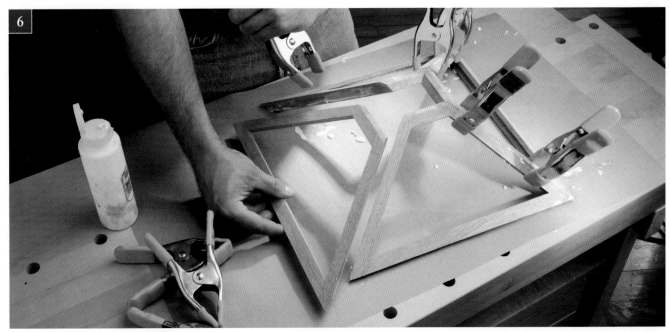

6

Glue the four sides together. You need eight spring clamps to hold them tight.

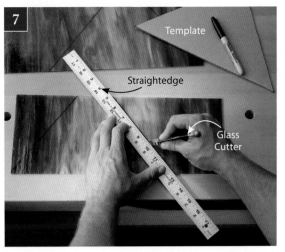

7

Template

Straightedge

Glass
Cutter

It's easy to cut your own glass for the shade. Lay out the parts with a cardboard template, then score inside the lines with a glass cutter and snap off the waste sections.

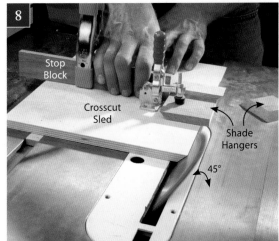

8

Stop
Block

Crosscut
Sled

Shade
Hangers

45°

Two small beveled blocks are needed to hold the shade to the arm. For safety, cut the blocks with a simple sled made out of plywood and a toggle clamp. Adjust the sled's stop block until the blocks fit perfectly.

Cut the Glass and Shade Hangers

16. Make a cardboard template $\frac{1}{32}$ in. smaller than the frame opening. Mark this pattern on the glass using a felt-tipped marker.

17. Make a single scoring cut just inside one of the lines (Photo 7). Place the scored edge over the end of the bench and, with a gentle downward motion, snap the glass at the scored mark. Repeat until all the glass is cut. Be sure to wear gloves for this step. The freshly cut glass can be razor sharp.

Tip

Minor adjustments to the glass shape can be made using an 800-grit waterstone. Do not use a grinder or power sander.

18. Cut the two shade hangers (J, Photo 8). Make a simple crosscut jig (Fig. F) to safely cut the 45-degree chamfers on the tablesaw. Cut the top hanger until it just fits inside the mitered top of the shade. Drill a hole in the center of each hanger for the nipple (X).

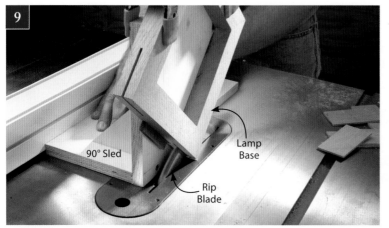

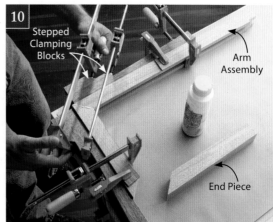

The lamp base is simply a mitered frame, reinforced with splines. Cut slots for the splines with a rip blade and a 90-degree sled. A rip blade is best because it cuts a flat bottom. That's essential for a clean-looking joint.

Glue the arm assembly one joint at a time with a pair of stepped clamping blocks. Leave the end piece extra-long for now, so there's room to attach the stepped block. Cut this piece to length after it's glued.

Figure F: Sled Jigs

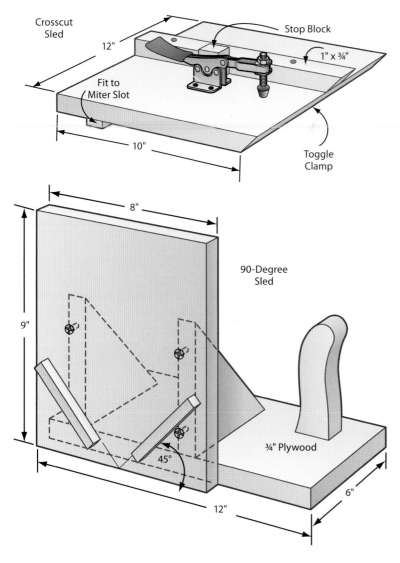

Make the Base and Arm

19. Mill 8/4 mahogany to 1½ in. Rip stock for the four base sides (A) to 1⅛ in. Miter to the final dimension.

20. Glue up the base with a band clamp. After the glue dries, cut slots for the splines (N) on the tablesaw (Photo 9) using a shop-made sled (Fig. F). Glue in the splines and trim them flush when dry. Cut the reveal around the bottom of the base (Fig. A).

21. Cut a notch in the base (Fig. A) with a dado blade.

22. Mill 4/4 mahogany to ⁵⁄₁₆-in.-thick stock and rip to 1⅜ in. for base lip (B). Miter to fit inside the base, and glue.

23. Cut a 45-in. length of 1½-in. × 1½-in. mahogany for arm assembly parts (C, D, and E).

24. Cut a deep groove for the conduit in the center of one side (Fig. A).

25. Miter the arm assembly parts. To make clamping the miter easier, leave part E long until after the glue-up.

26. Cut the notch in the bottom of Part C (Fig. A). Dry-fit the base and the vertical arm.

27. Drill two holes (Fig. A, Det. 2) for the screws that attach the base and arm. Drill a third hole for the lamp wire.

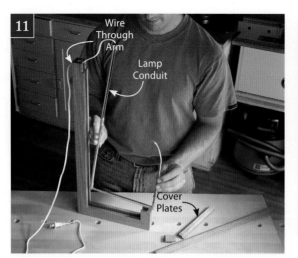

Install the lamp conduit into the arm assembly. Run lamp cord through the hole in the base of the arm first, then through each of the loose sections of conduit. Assemble the entire conduit. Cover plates conceal the conduit. They are friction-fit to allow access to the wires, should you ever have to take apart the lamp.

28. Glue the arm assembly one joint at a time (Photo 10).

29. Cut the splines' slot in the assembled upright, as in Step 19, and glue in the splines. Cut the splines and sand them flush.

30. Cut arm end (E) to final length.

31. Make cover plate F, G, and H (Fig. A, Det. 1) from a 40-in.-long strip of wood. Cut the rabbets so the cover plates fit snugly into the groove with hand pressure.

32. Miter the completed cover plates to fit the upright.

33. Sand the shade, base, upright and hangers to 220 grit and apply the finish.

34. Install the stained glass in the shade. Rip stops on the tablesaw (Fig. E). Miter the stops to fit behind the glass and attach them with No. 19 × ½-in. brads.

Screw the base onto the upright to complete the lamp. Install mahogany plugs into the screw holes for a finished look.

Figure G: Conduit Assembly

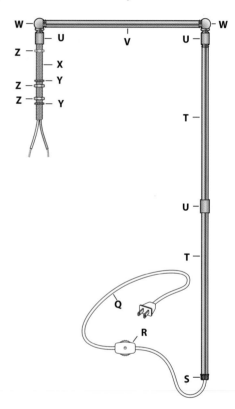

Assemble the Wiring Conduit

We've wired this lamp the safest way possible using metal conduit to protect the wires. The lamp cord has a polarized plug for safety and a add-on power switch for simplicity.

35. Cut two 10 in. pieces from the end of the lamp cord (Q) and set aside for wiring the sockets later.

36. Feed the lamp cord through the hole in the upright (Photo 11). Assembling the conduit is just a matter of screwing Parts S through X together and feeding the wire as you go (Fig. G). Don't overly tighten the two armbacks (W) as they can cut through the cord insulation. Make sure several inches of cord feed past the end of the nipple (X).

37. Lay the conduit in the upright assembly (Photo 11).

> ## Tip
> Reverse twist the cord before screwing on the last armback so the wire is not wound in the conduit.

Wire the Bulb Sockets

38. Screw the two arms (CC, Fig. H) into the cluster (BB).

39. Feed 10 in. of lamp cord from the cluster through each arm.

40. Wire the sockets (AA, Fig. I). Strip ⅝ in. of insulation from each wire end and wrap the bare wire three-quarters of the way around the screw.

41. It's standard practice in lamp wiring that the neutral wire is marked. Our wire was marked with ribbing on the insulation. Other manufacturers may use different colored insulation or a colored strand in the wire itself. No matter how it's marked, you can always tell the neutral wire; it's the one that comes off the wide blade on the plug.

42. Attach the shade to the upright (Fig. K,).

43. Twist wire nuts on the three neutral wires and the three hot wires (DD, Fig. H). Take care that all the copper wire strands are in the wire nuts. Push the wires into the cluster and screw the cap on.

44. Attach the rotary switch (R) to the cord (Fig. J).

Figure H: Cluster Wiring

Combine the three ribbed wires and the three hot wires with small wire nuts. Important: Make sure the wire nuts are rated to join three 18-gauge wires.

BB

CC

CC

Hot Wires

Neutral Wires (Ribbed)

DD

ARTS & CRAFTS TABLE LAMP

Caution: Only remove ⅜-in. of insulation from each wire end. Be sure to attach the neutral (ribbed) wire that runs from the wide blade on the plug to the silver screw and the hot wire to the brass-colored screw.

Figure I: Socket Assembly

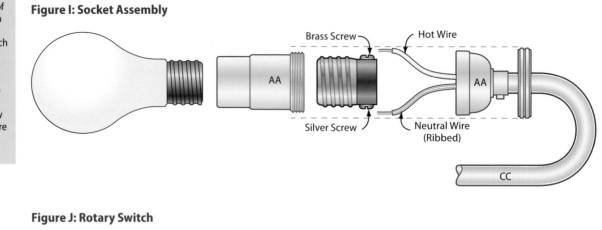

Brass Screw
Hot Wire
Silver Screw
Neutral Wire (Ribbed)

Figure J: Rotary Switch

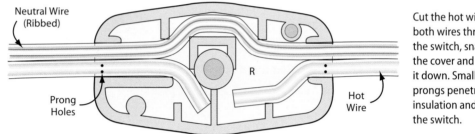

Neutral Wire (Ribbed)

Prong Holes

Hot Wire

Cut the hot wire, lay both wires through the switch, snap on the cover and screw it down. Small metal prongs penetrate the insulation and complete the switch.

Attach the Base

45. Screw the base onto the uprights (Photo 12). Check with a square to make sure the arm seats 90 degrees to the tabletop. If needed, pare the base slot with a chisel to adjust the fit. Plug the screw holes with ⅜-in. mahogany plugs. Add self-adhesive felt pads to the bottom and you're done!

Figure K: Attach the Shade

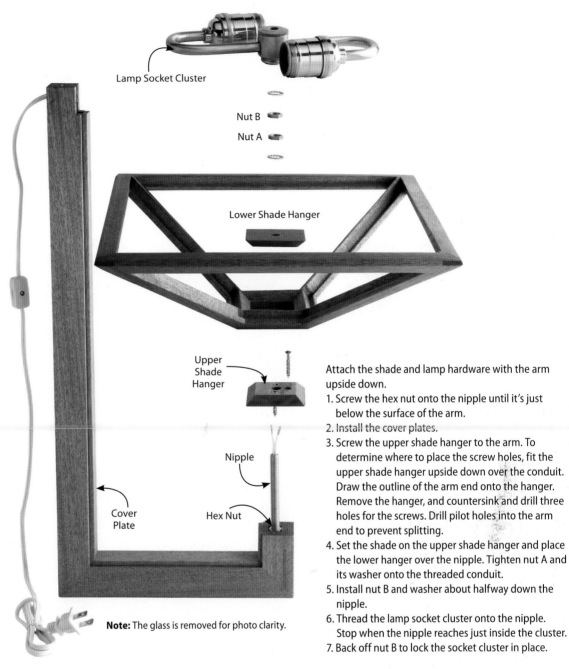

Lamp Socket Cluster

Nut B

Nut A

Lower Shade Hanger

Upper Shade Hanger

Nipple

Cover Plate

Hex Nut

Note: The glass is removed for photo clarity.

Attach the shade and lamp hardware with the arm upside down.

1. Screw the hex nut onto the nipple until it's just below the surface of the arm.
2. Install the cover plates.
3. Screw the upper shade hanger to the arm. To determine where to place the screw holes, fit the upper shade hanger upside down over the conduit. Draw the outline of the arm end onto the hanger. Remove the hanger, and countersink and drill three holes for the screws. Drill pilot holes into the arm end to prevent splitting.
4. Set the shade on the upper shade hanger and place the lower hanger over the nipple. Tighten nut A and its washer onto the threaded conduit.
5. Install nut B and washer about halfway down the nipple.
6. Thread the lamp socket cluster onto the nipple. Stop when the nipple reaches just inside the cluster.
7. Back off nut B to lock the socket cluster in place.

by TIM JOHNSON AND BRUCE KIEFFER

Stickley-Style Sideboard

A MASTERPIECE IN ARTS AND CRAFTS STYLE

This sideboard is a reproduction of one that originally appeared in Gustav Stickley's 1912 Craftsman Furniture Catalog as piece No. 814½. The cost was $50. It was factory produced, at a time when woodworking as a hobby was virtually unknown. Today, though it will cost a lot more than $50, this piece is perfect for our power tool-driven workshops.

This project is a major undertaking, but by dividing it into three stages, you'll find it easier to manage. You need to know how to make rabbets, dadoes, mortises and tenons, and machine-dovetailed drawers. The wood for this sideboard cost us $700, and the hardware, which is unique to this piece, cost $1000. However, it's possible to make your own hardware for about $100.

Quartersawn white oak, with its striking ray flake figure, is the wood of choice for this piece. The drawer fronts are solid, the doors and side panels are book-matched veneers. If veneering is new to you, our step-by-step photos will take you through the process.

Lay Out the Parts

Lay out the rough lumber so you can see it all and decide how to use each piece. On the completed sideboard, the drawer fronts (EE, FF, GG, JJ), plate rails (T and MM), back stile (U), and lower front rail (S) will be most visible, so use the boards with the best quartersawn figure. Make the drawer fronts from single boards.

Boards for the top should be matched for color first, then figure. Width isn't an issue. Choose pieces for the side rails (P and Q) last. After you've chosen the wood for these important pieces, rough cut them (including the lower back rail), about 1-in. oversized in both dimensions, and set them aside until you're ready for them.

The legs (M and N) are made from 8/4 rough quartersawn lumber, with the best-figured side as the front of each leg. It's a good idea to make an extra leg for testing tear out and milling to dimension, because you'll need to cut 1⅞-in. square legs from 2-in. rough stock. It helps to cut the legs to rough dimensions on the bandsaw, before planing, to minimize the amount of bow or cup in each leg. On a wide plank, use a cardboard pattern to help you lay out the legs.

Cut all plywood parts and web frame pieces to exact dimensions. The only web frame pieces that show are the front edges of the drawer divider webs (C). Be sure these show quartersawn grain. The same is true for the divider and shelf faces (L and AA).

Find quartersawn veneer with suitable width and figure. Faces for the 12½-in.-wide doors are made of two pieces book-matched so the flake pattern resembles a mountain peak. Each piece must be 16-in. long and at least 6½-in. wide, with ray flake extending diagonally all the way across. The side panels are bigger, 23-in. L by 18-in. W, so use four book-matched pieces for each face.

Build Web Frames

Your first constructions are four web frames. Two of them (C and D) serve as drawer dividers. Tongue-and-groove joinery is easy and allows plywood dust panels (E) to be included in the design. The lower frame (F, G, and H) is made the same way, with an added center rail. This frame will be glued between the lower front and back rails. The upper frame, (A and B), employs mortise-and-tenon joinery for extra rigidity. Position its inside rails 16⅞-in. apart, spaced 9⅜-in. from the outer rails.

The top and bottom web frames and the horizontal shelf (J) must be made square and to the same width, 47⅝-in., though they have different depths. Notch the corners of each piece to fit around the legs.

Figure A: Interior Assembly

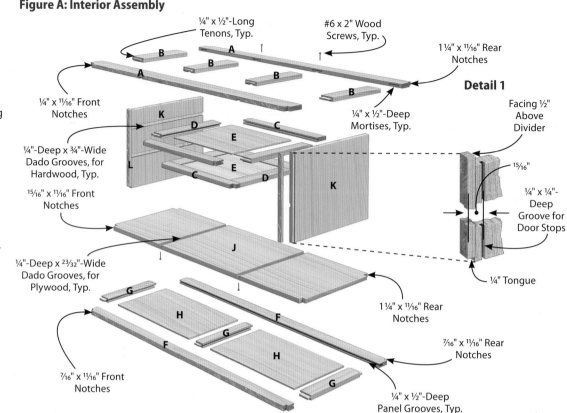

¼" x ½"-Long Tenons, Typ.

#6 x 2" Wood Screws, Typ.

1¼" x ¹¹⁄₁₆" Rear Notches

Detail 1

¼" x ¹¹⁄₁₆" Front Notches

¼" x ½"-Deep Mortises, Typ.

Facing ½" Above Divider

¹⁵⁄₁₆"

¼" x ¼"-Deep Groove for Door Stops

¼"-Deep x ¾"-Wide Dado Grooves, for Hardwood, Typ.

¹⁵⁄₁₆" x ¹¹⁄₁₆" Front Notches

¼" Tongue

¼"-Deep x ²³⁄₃₂"-Wide Dado Grooves, for Plywood, Typ.

1¼" x ¹¹⁄₁₆" Rear Notches

⁷⁄₁₆" x ¹¹⁄₁₆" Rear Notches

⁷⁄₁₆" x ¹¹⁄₁₆" Front Notches

¼" x ½"-Deep Panel Grooves, Typ.

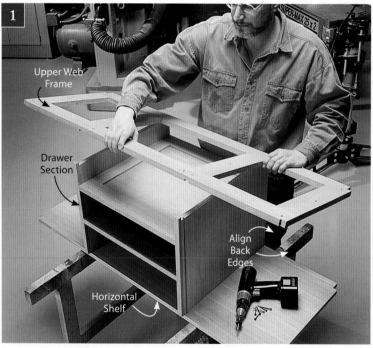

Assemble the Interior by fitting the drawer section into the dadoes in the horizontal shelf and upper web frame. Dadoes are great for easy, accurate assembly. Carefully position the three pieces so their back edges align. Secure the joints with glue and screws.

Make the Dividers

Cut dadoes in the vertical dividers (K). When you measure for these dadoes, allow for the ¼-in. tongue at the bottom of each divider. Glue facing strips (L) on the vertical dividers. At ¾ in., they'll be slightly wider than the plywood. Position them so the overhang is on the drawer (dadoed) side, and allow for the ¼-in. tongue at the bottom edge. After gluing, cut a dado on the outside of each vertical divider for door stops, (Fig. A, Detail 1).

Assemble the Interior

Notch the front corners of the drawer web frames so they fit between the facing strips on the vertical dividers. Assemble these frames and dividers to form the drawer section. Glue this assembly, taking care to make it square.

Cut dadoes in the top web frame and horizontal shelf to house the drawer section. Dadoes for plywood parts are only ²³⁄₃₂-in. wide. Fit the drawer section between the top web frame and the plywood shelf and glue and screw them together.

Veneering the doors and panels takes time, but it's not hard and the end result is worth it. Choose the two best pairs of book-matched veneer for the door fronts.

Cut the Book-Matched Pieces of veneer with a veneer saw. With its flat bottom and offset handle, the veneer saw is designed to be used while held against a fence. Here the fence is a board clamped across the pieces of veneer. It holds them in place and guides the saw. The saw's curved blade keeps a minimum of teeth engaged and allows starting the cut anywhere on the piece. Choose pieces of veneer with ray flake running diagonally across their entire widths, and cut them at least 1-in. oversize.

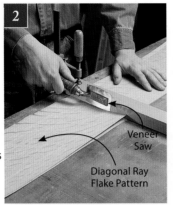

Veneer Saw

Diagonal Ray Flake Pattern

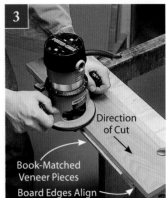

Direction of Cut

Book-Matched Veneer Pieces

Board Edges Align

Joint the Edges of the veneer. Fold the two book-matched pieces together and clamp them between two straight-edged boards so the veneer protrudes. Make sure the edges of the boards are aligned. Trim the edges of the veneer with a router and a flush-cutting bit, making a climb cut. (Advance the router from right to left. This will reduce the chance of tear out.)

Hold the Book-Matched Pieces together with a piece of veneer tape. Run this tape the length of the joint on the front surface after pieces of masking tape have been stretched across it on the back side. After the veneer tape dries, remove the masking tape. The doors require two pieces of veneer per side, the side panels need four.

Moistened Veneer Tape

Tinted Adhesive

Apply Glue to the edged door substrate. Unibond 800 is a modified urea formaldehyde adhesive designed for cold press veneering. It has a slow set, gives a good bond, won't creep, sands well, and is easy to apply. Use a foam roller to spread the glue uniformly. To hide any bleed through, tint the glue with dye powder—the same color you'll be using to dye the sideboard.

Glue the Book-Matched Joint from the back side. Bend the taped pieces to open the joint and apply a thin bead of glue. Close the joint and immediately lay it, with the veneer-taped side up, onto the glued surface of the substrate. Position it squarely, and press it flat.

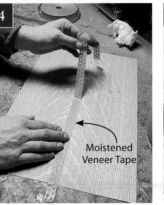

Backside of Taped Veneer Pieces

Clamp the Center First

Clamp the Veneered Panel between sheets of MDF, separated by newspaper. Even clamping pressure, working from the center to the edges, is the key to a successful glue-up. To apply pressure to the center of the panel, place boards over blocks taped to the centers of both pieces of MDF and clamp the ends of these boards together. Move the pressure out by using deep-throated clamps first and then smaller ones around the perimeter. Glue should squeeze out around all edges. By setting the assembly on saw horses, you can get clamps all around it.

Trim the Edges of the veneer with a router and flush-trim bit, using a climb cut. The oak edging gives the appearance of a solid wood door and provides solid mounting for the hinge screws. The side panels need neither edging nor trimming. Make them slightly oversized so they can be cut to final size on the tablesaw.

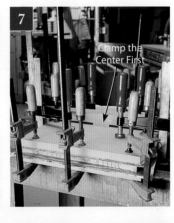

Oak Edging

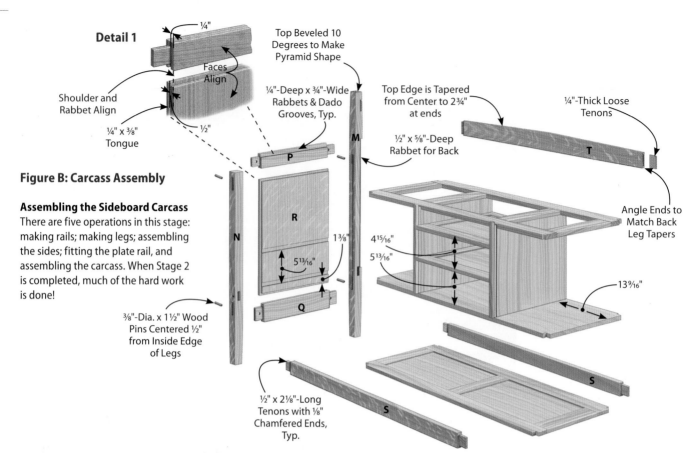

Detail 1

¼"

Faces Align

Shoulder and Rabbet Align

¼" x ⅜" Tongue

½"

Top Beveled 10 Degrees to Make Pyramid Shape

¼"-Deep x ¾"-Wide Rabbets & Dado Grooves, Typ.

Top Edge is Tapered from Center to 2¾" at ends

½" x ⅝"-Deep Rabbet for Back

¼"-Thick Loose Tenons

M

P

T

Angle Ends to Match Back Leg Tapers

Figure B: Carcass Assembly

Assembling the Sideboard Carcass
There are five operations in this stage: making rails; making legs; assembling the sides; fitting the plate rail, and assembling the carcass. When Stage 2 is completed, much of the hard work is done!

N

R

1⅜"

5¹³⁄₁₆"

4¹⁵⁄₁₆"

5¹³⁄₁₆"

13⁹⁄₁₆"

⅜"-Dia. x 1½" Wood Pins Centered ½" from Inside Edge of Legs

Q

S

S

½" x 2⅛"-Long Tenons with ⅛" Chamfered Ends, Typ.

9

Chop Through Mortises by cutting to half-depth, turning the piece over (keeping the same face registered against the fence), and finishing the cut from the other side. A mortising machine is great for this, but a mortising attachment on a drill press will get the job done too. The mortise being cut here is for a front rail. The location of both the rail and mortise are marked on the leg. After mortising, locate and drill ⅜-in. dia. by ⅜-in.-deep tenon pin starter holes in the legs.

Cutting Rails and Legs

Cut all the through tenon rails (P, Q, and S) to size, and make some scrap pieces for testing the tenon cuts. Cut the legs (M and N) to size, mark them for position (right front; left rear), and mark each side (front, back, inside, outside).

Assemble Side Rails and Panels

On a piece of leg scrap, lay out and chop one mortise 2½-in. long and another 1¾-in. long. Use scrap rail pieces to adjust the fit of the tenons to the mortises (a sliding fit without side-to-side play), then cut the through tenons on the rails. Chamfer the ends.

Cut rabbets in the upper side rails for the top web frame (Fig. B). Cut dadoes in the edges of the side rails and tongues on the panels (R) so the insides of the rails and panel are flush. Cut dadoes across the inside of the panels for the tongues on the plywood shelf and the lower web frame. Glue the rails and panels together. Align the inside rabbet on the panel with, or slightly inside of, the tenon shoulders (Fig. B, Detail 1).

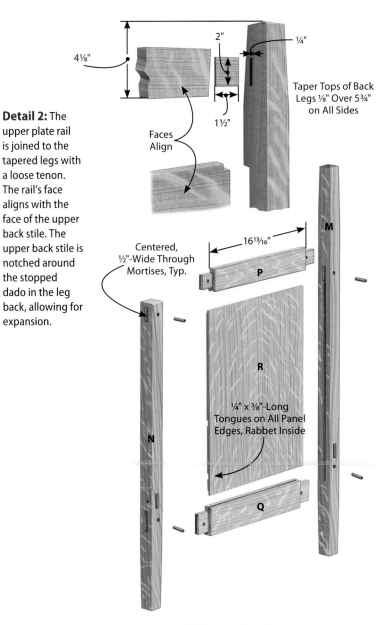

Detail 2: The upper plate rail is joined to the tapered legs with a loose tenon. The rail's face aligns with the face of the upper back stile. The upper back stile is notched around the stopped dado in the leg back, allowing for expansion.

4⅛"

2"

¼"

Faces Align

1½"

Taper Tops of Back Legs ⅛" Over 5¾" on All Sides

M

P

16¹³⁄₁₆"

Centered, ½"-Wide Through Mortises, Typ.

R

¼" x ⅜"-Long Tongues on All Panel Edges, Rabbet Inside

N

Q

10

Fence

Dado

Rout the Dadoes for the side panel tongues on the insides of the legs, between the mortises. A fence clamped to the router positions the bit accurately. Locate the dadoes by dry-fitting the legs on the rail and panel assembly and marking their positions.

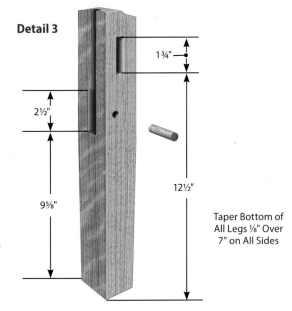

11

Lay a Bead of Glue in the leg dadoes, in the mortises and on the tenons and glue the legs to the rail and panel assembly. You can't take this step until all of the leg mortises, dadoes, rabbets, pyramids, and tapers have been completed, as well as finish sanded, so check twice to make sure you're ready.

Mortise and Dado the Legs

Use the assembled sides to locate the positions of the mortises and mark them on the sides of the legs. Mark the mortises for the front and back rails by measuring from the bottom of the legs (Fig. B, Detail 3). Chop the mortises (Photo 9) and rout dadoes for the side panels in the legs (Photo 10).

Dry-assemble the sides and legs, then add the front and back rails. Check the fit of the lower web frame between these rails and make any necessary adjustments. Remove the rails and legs. Glue the web frame between the lower rails. Rout stopped rabbets in the inside back legs for the back assembly. After all the mortises are cut, lay out and cut the tapers on the bottoms of the legs (Fig. B, Detail 3).

Detail 3

1¾"

2½"

12½"

9⅝"

Taper Bottom of All Legs ⅛" Over 7" on All Sides

Figure C: Final Assembly

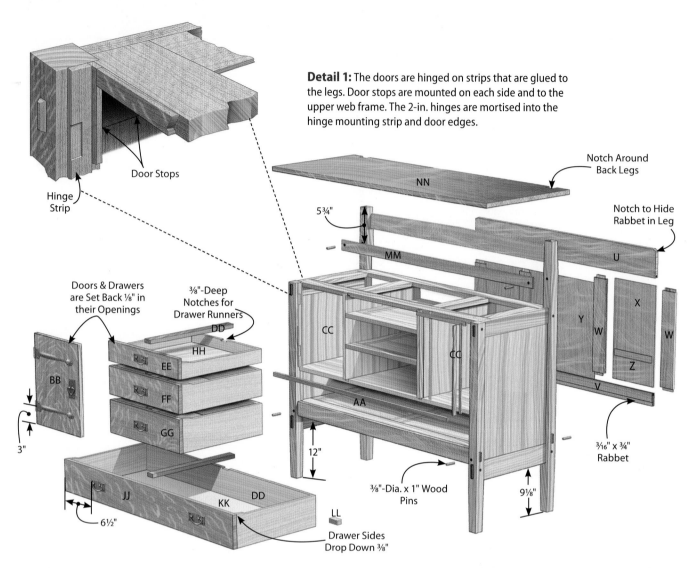

Detail 1: The doors are hinged on strips that are glued to the legs. Door stops are mounted on each side and to the upper web frame. The 2-in. hinges are mortised into the hinge mounting strip and door edges.

Door Stops

Hinge Strip

Notch Around Back Legs

Notch to Hide Rabbet in Leg

5¾"

NN

MM

U

Doors & Drawers are Set Back ⅛" in their Openings

⅜"-Deep Notches for Drawer Runners

DD

HH

CC

Y

X

W

BB

EE

CC

W

FF

Z

GG

V

3"

AA

⅜"-Dia. x 1" Wood Pins

12"

9⅛"

³⁄₁₆" x ¾" Rabbet

JJ

KK

DD

6½"

LL

Drawer Sides Drop Down ⅜"

Completing the Sideboard
Put together a beautiful piece of furniture by adding doors and drawers, the back, the top, applying the finish and mounting the hardware.

Fitting the Plate Rail and Top

This is the most difficult joint of the project (Fig. B, Detail 2). Lay out the tapers on the legs and make sure the rail stock is long enough to fit between them after they've been tapered. Cut the ¾-in. deep mortises in the legs and rail, enough to house the loose tenons after tapering. Cut the pyramid tops on the legs with a tablesaw, miter gauge, and a stop. Leave a flat spot on the top to bear on the stop. Now taper the legs.

Reassemble the carcass (without the lower rail assembly) and transfer the taper of the leg tops to the plate rail. Use a sliding bevel to transfer this angle to the miter gauge and cut the ends of the plate rail. After a good fit between rail and legs is made, cut the peak on the upper rail's top edge and glue the loose tenons into the rail.

Assemble the Carcass

Setting up the two interior assemblies and having a second pair of hands makes a difficult glue-up easier (Photo 12). After the clamps are removed, drill holes for the pins and install them.

Assemble the Carcass with glue, clamps, and a little help from some friends—a helper is one, the saw horses are another, and the box, exactly sized to the opening between the lower rail assembly and the drawer and shelf assembly, is the third. Glue and clamp one assembled side at a time, as shown, adding bar clamps at the bottom rails and upper plate rail after both sides are in place.

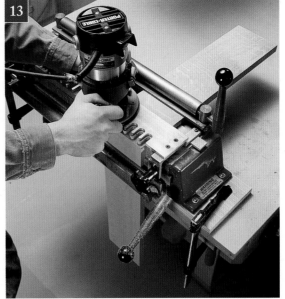

Cut Dovetails with a router and template jig and you'll have drawers that look just like the originals, especially if you make half-blind fronts and backs. After dovetailing, and evening-up the bottom edges, cut ¼-in.-deep dadoes on all four pieces for the bottom. If you locate the dadoes behind the lowest tail, it won't show from the side. Glue the drawer parts together with the bottom inside.

Doors and Drawers

The doors and drawers on this cabinet are set back, both for aesthetic and practical reasons. The set-back adds visual interest and camouflages a less-than-perfect fit.

Work from the open back when positioning the drawer stop blocks (LL), then mount the drawer runners (DD). The drawers' stepped sides and center-mounted guides are production techniques that allow extra margins of error when fitting, but do little to make the drawers work better.

Install the Back Assembly

The back (V-Z) is assembled the same way as the drawer web frames—tongue-and-groove, with panels between. You've already chosen a piece with nice figure for the top stile—it's the only piece that shows. Cut a rabbet in the bottom stile to fit over the lower back rail and fit the back into the leg rabbets. Drill counterset mounting holes and screw the back in place.

Materials
Lumber & Plywood
25 board feet of ⁴/₄ quartersawn white oak
25 board feet of ⁵/₄ quartersawn white oak
15 board feet of ⁸/₄ quartersawn white oak
20 board feet of ⁴/₄ plainsawn white oak
25 board feet of ⁴/₄ birch
1 sheet ¾" x 4' x 8' white oak veneered plywood
1 sheet ¼" x 4' x 8' white oak veneered plywood
1 sheet ¾" x 4' x 8' MDF
Quartersawn White Oak Veneer
8 book-matched pieces 7" wide x 17" long for doors
16 book-matched pieces 5" W x 24" L for panels.

Attach the Top

Notch the back edge of the top to fit the legs and screw it down through holes in the top web frame that are large enough to allow for seasonal movement.

A Beautiful Finish

We chose a finish that is easy to apply, adds rich color, brings out the figure, and has a soft luster.

Mix two shades of Transfast Wood Dye water-based dye: 5 parts Dark Chocolate Brown to 1 part Medium Red Brown, both mixed at 1 tsp. to 4 oz. water ratio. Before you use a water-based dye it is imperative that you wet all surfaces with a sponge. Let the surfaces dry and sand the raised grain smooth. Wet the surfaces again, especially end grain, before you apply the dye. You can spritz the dye on with a plastic spray bottle and wipe with a cotton cloth. After the dye has dried, seal it with a coat of 1-lb. cut dewaxed dark shellac followed by a coat of 2-lb. cut dewaxed pale shellac. This enhances the color and builds enough of a finish so you can sand it lightly before applying the top coats, Master-Gel finish.

The Hardware

The crowning touch on this sideboard is the authentic hand-hammered copper pulls and strap hinges, made by Tony Smith. This hardware is well worth the several months' wait and the $1000 cost, but you can also make your own hardware or buy similar mass-produced hardware.

After the hardware is installed, stand back, and enjoy your masterpiece!

Figure A

Ref.	Qty.	Dimensions	Parts
A	2	¾" x 3" x 47⅝" oak	top web stiles
B	4	¾" x 3" x 13⁵⁄₁₆" oak	top web rails
C	4	¾" x 2½" x 19½" oak	drawer web stiles
D	4	¾" x 2½" x 15½" oak	drawer web rails
E	2	¼" x 15½" x 15½" oak ply	drawer dust panels
F	2	¾" x 2½" x 47⅝" oak	bottom web stiles
G	3	¾" x 2½" x 13¹¹⁄₁₆" oak	bottom web rails
H	2	¼" x 13¹¹⁄₁₆" x 21¹⁄₁₆" oak ply	bottom web dust panels
J	1	¾" x 19" x 47⅝" oak ply	horizontal shelf
K	2	¾" x 19" x 15⁹⁄₁₆" oak ply	vertical dividers
L	2	½" x ¾" x 15¹³⁄₁₆" oak	facings for vertical dividers

Figure B

Ref.	Qty.	Dimensions	Parts
M	2	1⅞" x 1⅞" x 49" q.s. oak	back legs
N	2	1⅞" x 1⅞" x 37⅛" q.s oak	front legs
P	2	1" x 2¾" x 21¹⁄₁₆" q.s. oak	upper side rails
Q	2	1" x 3½" x 21¹⁄₁₆" q.s. oak	lower side rails
R	2	¾" x 17⁹⁄₁₆" x 22½" oak ply	side panels*
	4	18⁹⁄₁₆" x 23½" q.s. veneer sheets	side panel faces
S	2	1" x 2¾" x 50½" q.s. oak	front & back rails
T	1	½" x 3¼" x 46½" q.s. oak	upper plate rail

		Figure C	
Ref.	Qty.	Dimensions	Parts
U	1	5/8" x 5 3/8" x 47 1/4" q.s. oak	back top stile
V	1	5/8" x 2 1/2" x 47 1/4" oak	(back bottom stile)
W	4	5/8" x 3" x 19 1/8" oak	back rails
X	2	1/4" x 19 1/8" x 10 1/4" oak ply	outside back panels
Y	1	1/4" x 19 1/8" x 17 3/4" oak ply	center back panel
Z	2	3/16" x 1 1/4" x 9 1/4" oak	filler strips behind shelf
AA	1	1/2" x 3/4" x 46 1/4" oak	horizontal shelf facing
BB	2	3/4" x 12" x 15 3/16" particleboard	door cores
	8	5/16" x 13/16" x 16" oak	door edging**
	4	13 1/2" x 16 3/4" q. s. veneer sheets	door faces
CC	2	1/4" x 3/4" x 15 13/16" oak	hinge mounting strips
	4	1/4" x 1/2" x 15 13/16" oak	door stops
	2	1/4" x 1/2" x 12 1/8" oak	upper door stop fill strips
DD	4	11/16" x 1 1/2" x 18 5/16" oak	drawer runners
EE	1	3/4" x 3 9/16" x 19" q.s. oak	top drawer front***
	2	5/8" x 2 3/4" x 18" birch	top drawer side
	1	5/8" x 2 3/4" x 19" birch	top drawer back
FF	1	3/4" x 4 15/16" x 19" q.s. oak	center drawer front***
	2	5/8" x 4 15/16" x 18" birch	center drawer sides
	1	5/8" x 4 15/16" x 19" birch	center drawer back
GG	1	3/4" x 5 13/16" x 19" q.s. oak	lower drawer front***
	2	5/8" x 5 13/16" x 18" birch	lower drawer sides
	1	5/8" x 5 13/16" x 19" birch	lower drawer back
HH	3	1/4" x 17 3/4" x 18 1/4" birch ply	drawer bottoms
JJ	1	3/4" x 5 13/16" x 46 1/4" q.s. oak	bottom drawer front***
	2	5/8" x 5 13/16" x 18" birch	bottom drawer sides
	1	5/8" x 5 13/16" x 46 1/4" birch	bottom drawer back
KK	1	1/4" x 17 3/4" x 45 1/2" birch ply	bottom drawer bottom
LL	10	3/4" x 1" x 2" oak	drawer stops
MM	1	3/8" x 1 15/16" x 50" q.s. oak	lower plate rail
NN	1	7/8" x 21" x 56" q.s. oak	top

*Finished size—make oversize and trim after veneering.
**Extra thickness allows trimming of doors to fit.
***Drawer opening size.

by TOM CASPAR

Shaker Table

A PERFECT BLEND OF CLASSIC LINES AND MODERN JOINERY

When I first saw a drawing of this table 20 years ago in a book by Thomas Moser, I knew I had to make it. It perfectly captures the essence of classic Shaker design. Moser's reproduction has become an American icon.

Here's an up-to-date version that retains the Shaker spirit. They used mortise-and-tenon joinery, but I've substituted biscuits. For this table, the biscuits are just as strong and can be made much faster. The Shakers planed their wood by hand. For my version, you can machine all the parts and then give them a few licks with a hand plane. The Shakers also hand-dovetailed their drawers. You can make machine-cut dovetails if you wish, but I prefer the look of handmade joints.

If you've never planed wood or cut dovetails by hand before, this project is a great way to get started. I built this table in walnut, a wood that is easy to work with hand tools. Cherry, mahogany, red oak, or other woods of equal density would also be good choices. The pieces are small and easy to handle. I used a No. 4 smooth plane, a No. 5 jack plane and a No. 6 fore plane, but all three aren't necessary. A single No. 4 or No. 5 is OK.

PROJECT REQUIREMENTS AT A GLANCE

Materials:

- 2 bd. ft. of ⁵⁄₄ walnut
- 10 bd. ft. of ⁴⁄₄ walnut
- 2 bd. ft. of ⁴⁄₄ basswood

Tools:

- Jointer
- Planer
- Tablesaw
- Bandsaw
- Plate joiner

Hardware:

- Walnut knob
- Six tabletop fasteners

Cost: $100

Figure A: Exploded View

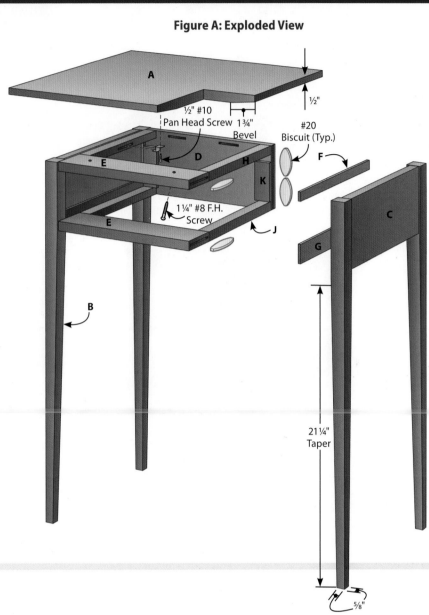

Make the Legs and Rails

1. Select straight-grained wood for the legs (B). Mill the wood into square blanks (see Cutting List). Lay out the tapers and cut them on the bandsaw (Fig. A). Note that the legs only taper on the two inside faces. Joint or hand-plane the sawn surfaces.

2. Mill the side rails (C), back rail (D) and front rails (E). Cut all these pieces the same length. Mark reference lines for biscuit slots in the legs and rails (Fig. B). Note that the front legs only have one set of slots.

3. Cut No. 20 biscuit slots in the legs and rails with their face sides down. Use the bottom of the plate joiner, not the fence, as a reference surface. Place a ⅛-in. piece of hardboard under the plate joiner when you cut leg slots (Photo 1). This automatically creates an ⅛-in. offset between the legs and rails.

4. Plane or sand the outside faces of all the rails (Photo 2). Sand with 180- or 220-grit paper to remove any small ridges left by the plane iron. Plane the outside faces of the legs.

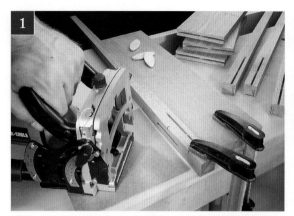

All the joints in this table are made with biscuits. They're plenty strong for this job and can be made very fast. Cut the joints while each piece is still perfectly flat and square.

Plane or sand the side rails to remove machining marks. Planing is quicker, quieter and a lot more fun than sanding. This small project, though primarily built with power tools, is a good opportunity to put your planes to work.

Plane two strips flush with the legs. They're glued to the completed side assembly. These strips provide level surfaces for the front rails' biscuit joints. Planing these pieces by hand is more precise than milling them with a planer.

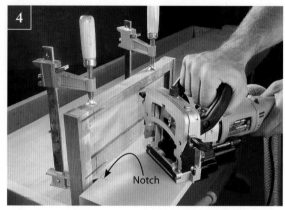

Notch

Cut a biscuit slot to receive the lower front rail. Clamp a notched board under the side rail for support. This rig guarantees that the slot is square to the leg and the same height as the corresponding slot in the lower front rail.

Build the Case

5. Glue the side legs and rails together. Be careful to align the top of the legs with the top of the rails. Make sure the legs are square to the rails. Check this is with a straightedge placed across both legs. The leg's faces must be in the same plane.

6. Make the top and bottom spacers (F, G). Glue them to the sides. Plane them exactly even with the legs (Photo 3).

7. Mark biscuit centerlines on the front rails (Fig. C). Mark corresponding centerlines on the sides. Note that the front rails are set back ⅛ in., like the side rails. Mark the top face of the upper front rail and the bottom face of the lower front rail. Cut biscuit slots in the rails, referencing from

the bottom of the plate joiner, with the marked faces down.

8. Stand each side assembly upside down and cut biscuit slots for the top front rail. Cut slots for the bottom front rail (Photo 4).

9. Plane and sand the front edges of the front rails.

10. Glue the case together. Check the ⅛-in. setback of the front rails with a combination square, or temporarily tape a piece of ⅛-in. hardboard to the front of each rail. The setback is correct when the hardboard is flush to the legs.

11. Mill the kickers (H) and drawer supports (J). The kickers prevent the drawer from tipping when opened. Glue these parts to the case (Photo 5).

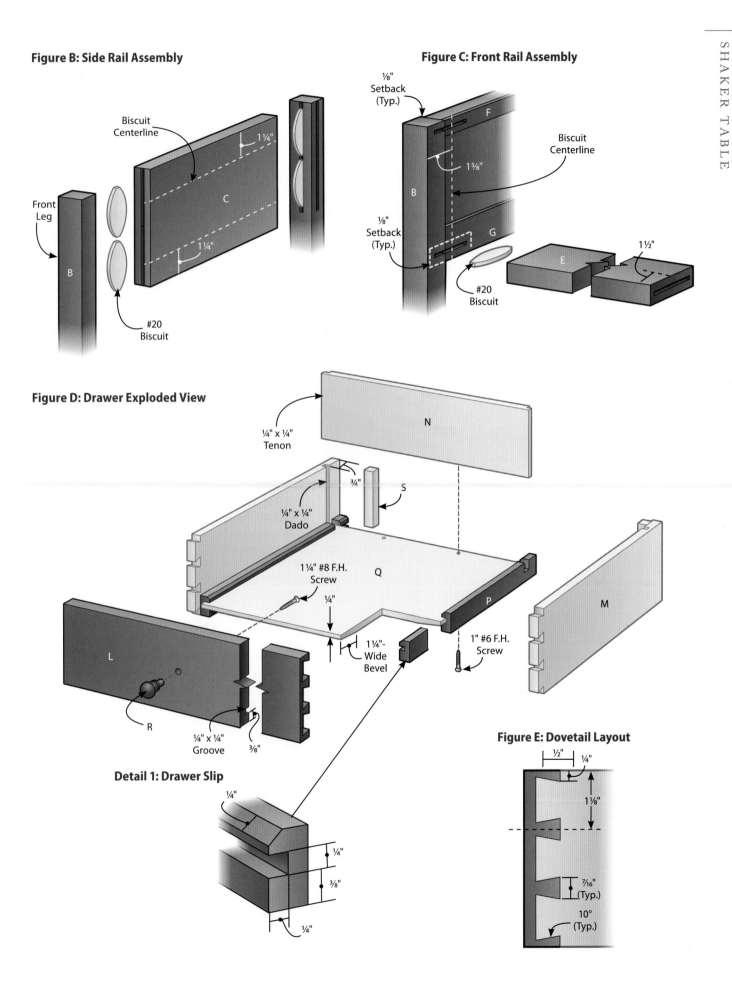

Figure B: Side Rail Assembly

Biscuit Centerline

1¼"

1¼"

Front Leg

B

C

#20 Biscuit

Figure C: Front Rail Assembly

⅛" Setback (Typ.)

F

1⅝"

Biscuit Centerline

B

⅛" Setback (Typ.)

G

#20 Biscuit

E

1½"

Figure D: Drawer Exploded View

N

¼" x ¼" Tenon

¾"

S

¼" x ¼" Dado

1¼" #8 F.H. Screw

Q

¼"

P

M

1" #6 F.H. Screw

L

R

¼" x ¼" Groove

⅜"

1¼"- Wide Bevel

Detail 1: Drawer Slip

¼"

¼"

⅜"

¼"

Figure E: Dovetail Layout

½"

¼"

1⅛"

⁷⁄₁₆" (Typ.)

10° (Typ.)

Glue drawer supports to the sides. Both supports have to be parallel so the drawer doesn't rock. Clamp a board to the front rail to make sure both supports are in the same plane.

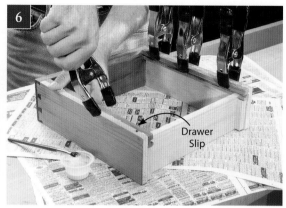

Add slips to widen and strengthen the drawer sides. The drawer sides are basswood, a soft wood that's easy to cut and pare for dovetailing. The slips, made from a hard wood, prevent the soft sides from wearing prematurely.

Plane the drawer to perfectly fit the case. The drawer should be about 1/32 in. narrower across the back than across the front, to make it easier to slide. Support the drawer with a board and a spacer.

Bevel the top's underside by hand or on the tablesaw. Planing goes quickly—about as fast as setting up a tablesaw—if you use a slightly curved iron set for a heavy cut. With a plane, you'll have no saw marks to remove.

Build the Drawer

12. Mill the drawer front (L). Crosscut it to exactly fit the opening from end to end. For successful dovetailing, all the drawer parts must be perfectly flat and straight. Machine these parts 1/8 in. larger than final thickness and let them sit for a few days, in case they bend or twist. Then rejoint the face sides and take the pieces down to their final thickness. Mill the drawer sides (M) and back (N). Rip the front, sides and back 1/32-in. narrower than the drawer opening. For now, cut the back to the same width and length as the sides.

13. Dovetail the sides to the front. Cut a groove in the front for the drawer bottom (Fig. D). Cut dados across the sides to receive the back. Assemble the sides and front without glue; then measure, crosscut and rip the back to fit. Cut rabbets in the back to fit the sides' dados. Drill the drawer front for the knob's tenon and screw.

14. Glue the drawer. Strengthen the rear joints with glue blocks (S).

15. Install the drawer slips (P) (Photo 6; Fig. D, Det. 1). Make them from a wide blank (see Cutting List). Groove the sides of the blank for the drawer

9

Attach the top with angled screws. Drill the pilot holes with an extender and a bit with a built-in countersink (see inset photo). Use the plate joiner to cut slots inside the table for tabletop fasteners. The fasteners allow the top to shrink and swell without cracking.

Tabletop Fastener

bottom. In addition, cut a groove of the same width in a scrap of wood to use as a test piece for fitting the drawer bottom. Plane a chamfer above each groove. Rip the slips from the blank. Notch the back of each slip to fit under the drawer's back; then glue the slips to the drawer.

16. Glue up the drawer bottom (Q) and cut it to fit. Use a hand plane to chamfer the underside to fit the drawer's grooves. As you're planing, test the chamfer's fit in the extra grooved piece. Stop planing when the bottom slides freely. Slide the bottom into the drawer and fasten it to the back.

17. Plane or sand the sides flush with the drawer's front. Install the knob (R) and test-fit the drawer in the case. It should be tight from side to side. Plane the sides so the drawer's rear fits loosely in the opening (Photo 7). Continue planing until the drawer's front is only a paper thickness narrower from side to side than the opening. Glue stops (K) to the back rail so the drawer front is flush with the rails.

Make the Top

18. Glue up the top (A) and cut it to final size. Mark the bevels under the top (Fig. A) and use a hand plane or tablesaw to trim to the lines (Photo 8).

19. Cut slots in the kickers and back rail for tabletop fasteners (Fig. A) using a plate joiner. Clamp the base to the top and drill angled holes in the top front rail (Photo 9).

Apply a Finish

20. Remove the top from the case and the bottom and knob from the drawer. Finish the top, the case and the drawer separately. On the drawer, only the front needs finish.

21. Assemble the table. Rub a few strokes of paraffin wax on the drawer sides to make the drawer slide easily.

Cutting List
Overall Dimensions: 27½" H x 18" W x 18" H

	Part	Name	Qty.	Dimensions	Material
Case	A	Top	1	¾" x 18" x 18"	4/4 walnut
	B	Leg	4	1⅛" x 1⅛" x 26¾"	5/4 walnut
	C	Side rail	2	¾" x 5" x 11¾"	4/4 walnut
	D	Back rail	1	¾" x 5" x 11¾"	4/4 walnut
	E	Front rail	2	¾" x 3" x 11¾"	4/4 walnut
	F	Top spacer	2	¼" x ¾" x 11¾" [1]	4/4 walnut
	G	Bottom spacer	2	¼" x 1½" x 11¾" [1]	4/4 walnut
	H	Drawer kicker	2	¾" x 1" x 10"	4/4 walnut
	J	Drawer support	2	¾" x 1" x 10"	4/4 walnut
	K	Drawer stop	2	¼" x 1½" x 3"	4/4 walnut
Drawer	L	Front	1	¾" x 3½" x 11¾"	4/4 walnut
	M	Side	2	½" x 3½" x 12½"	4/4 basswood
	N	Back	1	½" x 2⅞" x 11¼"	4/4 basswood
	P	Slip	2	½" x ⅞" x 12" [2]	4/4 maple
	Q	Bottom	1	5/16" x 11¾" x 11¼"	4/4 basswood
	R	Knob	1	13/16" diameter	Walnut
	S	Block	2	½" x ½" x 2½"	4/4 basswood

1 Mill pieces to 9/32 in., glue to side rails and then plane even with the legs.
2 Rip from a ½-in. x 3-in. x 12-in. blank.

by JOCK AND SUSAN HOLMEN

Tile-Topped Outdoor Table

THIS STURDY WHITE-OAK TABLE WILL LAST A LIFETIME AND WON'T BLOW OVER IN THE WIND

I f you love lounging on your deck and need a solid side table to hold your cool drink and snacks, here's the solution. We designed this stylish side table to be simple to build. It's made of white oak and finished with an outdoor stain, so it's sure to handle the weather. The ceramic-tile top provides a durable maintenance-free accent.

Project Requirements at a Glance

Tools:
Tablesaw, bandsaw, plate joiner, planer, jointer.

Materials:
4 bd. ft. of 8/4 (2-in.) white oak, 8 bd. ft. of 5/4 (1¼-in.) white oak, No. 20 biscuits, one 12 x 12-in. ceramic tile, exterior wood glue, exterior stain, silicone caulk.

Cost: About $50

Cutting List

Overall Dimensions: 18" x 18" x 19"

Part	Name	Qty.	Dimensions
A	Leg	4	1¾" x 1¾" x 19"
B	Apron	4	1" x 3" x 12¾"
C	Long frame	2	1" x 3" x (tile length + 6⅛")
D	Short frame	2	1" x 3" x (tile length + ⅛")
E	Tile supports	2	¾" x 3" x (tile length + ⅛")
F	Glue block	8	¾" x ¾" x 3"
G	Tile	1	¼" x 12" x 12"

Figure A: Exploded View

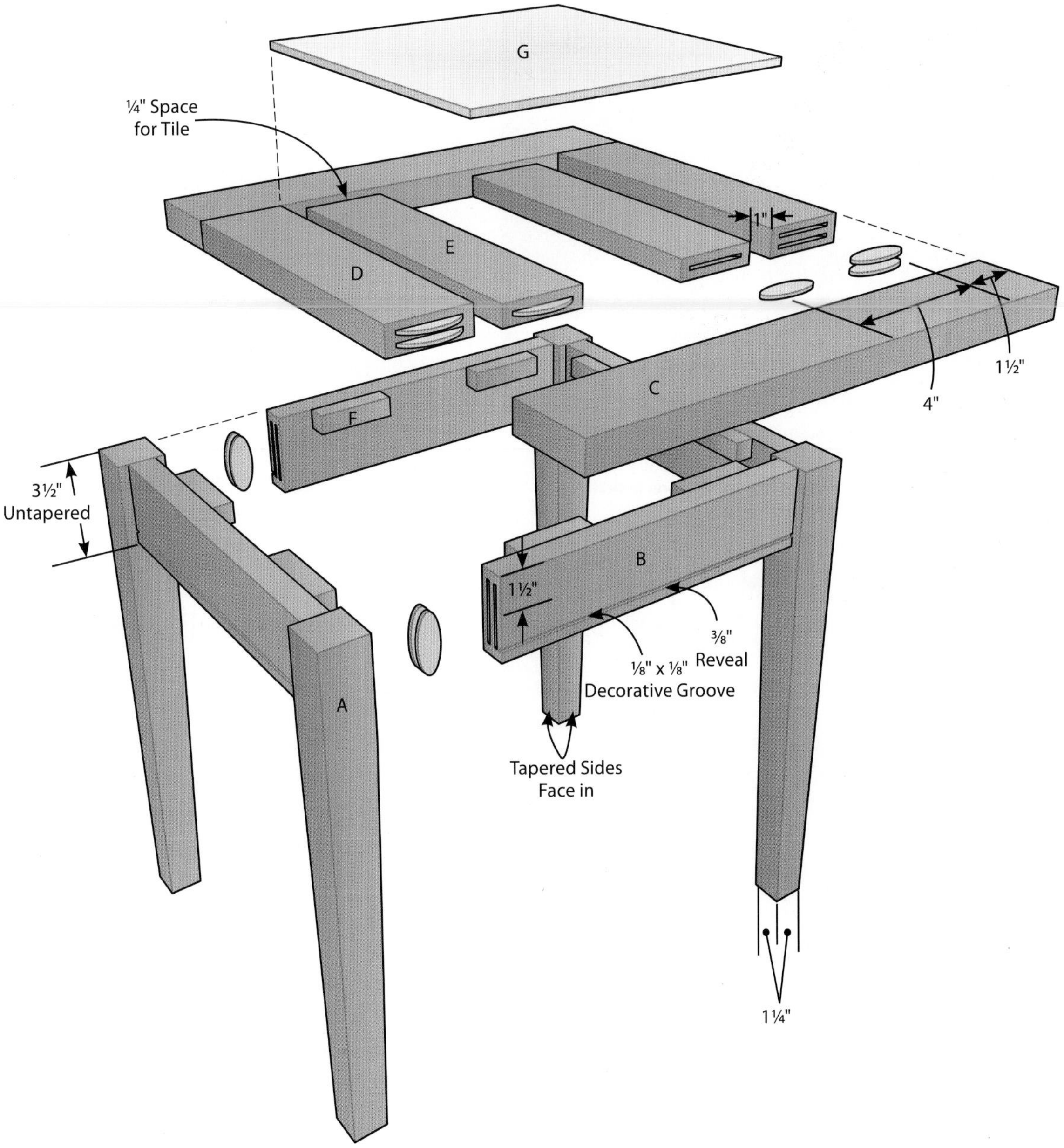
G
¼" Space for Tile
E
D
1"
C
4"
1½"
F
3½" Untapered
B
1½"
⅜" Reveal
⅛" x ⅛" Decorative Groove
A
Tapered Sides Face in
1¼"

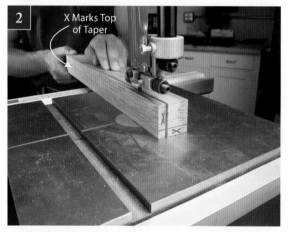

Rip thick lumber for the legs to rough size on the tablesaw. Always use a pushstick when cutting narrow boards. Joint, plane and crosscut the legs to final size.

Bandsaw two tapers on adjacent sides of each leg. Saw each taper about ¹⁄₁₆ in. oversize. The tapers are subtle, so mark an X at the top of each one to help you keep track of which surface is tapered.

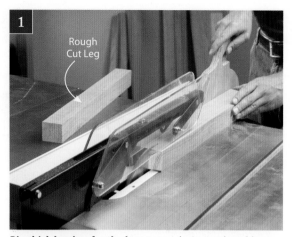

Smooth the tapered sides with your jointer. A freehand bandsaw cut can be fairly uneven, so smoothing might take two passes. Feed the legs top-end first. Use a push block and stick to guide the leg.

Before you Start

Buy your ceramic tile before you build this table, because the actual size of tiles can vary. We purchased a single 12-in.-square x ¼-in.-thick ceramic tile at our local home center. The actual size was closer to 11⅞-in. square. The tile is undersize to allow a grout joint in normal applications, but the amount can vary. We used white oak for its natural resistance to rot. Other wood, such as mahogany, teak, cedar, or ipe, will also withstand the elements.

Taper the Legs

Start by sawing the 8/4 lumber for the legs (A) ⅛-in. oversize (Photo 1). Then joint, plane and cut to the final size (see Cutting List).

Next, mark an X at the top of two adjacent sides on each leg. These two marked sides will be tapered. Use these Xs to help you keep track of the tapers. The tapers are subtle and it's possible to confuse them with the untapered outer sides (see "Oops!" page 207). Also, the legs are untapered where they join the aprons (B, Fig. A).

Mark lines for the tapers on each leg and saw the taper on the bandsaw (Photo 2). Stay about ¹⁄₁₆ in. away from your pencil line. After the first taper is cut, reattach scrap with masking tape and cut the second taper. Remove the bandsaw marks with a pass or two over your jointer (Photo 3).

Cutting the Double Biscuit Slots

Using spacers makes easy and accurate work out of cutting the double biscuit slots in the legs. This setup works with any biscuit joiner and the only measuring you need to do is to locate the center of the slot down from the top of the legs (Fig. A). Make sure to cut the biscuit slots in the legs with the adjacent taper down (Photos 4 and 5).

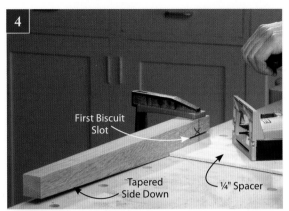

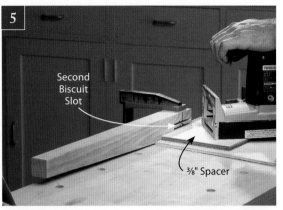

Cut a pair of biscuit slots in the legs. To center the apron on the leg, use a ¼-in. spacer for the first slot. To avoid a costly mistake, always clamp each leg with a tapered side down. Only cut the slots in faces marked with an X.

Cut the second biscuit slot in the legs. Add a ⅜-in. spacer on top of the ¼-in. spacer. Spacers are far easier to use than fiddling with the biscuit joiner's fence when you're making these double slots.

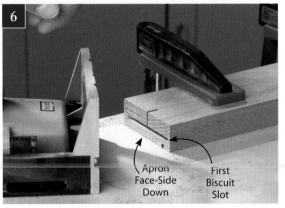

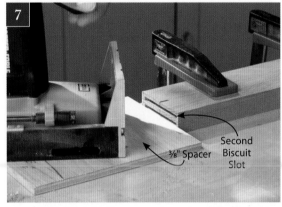

Cut biscuit slots in the aprons' ends. Clamp the apron face-side down. That's the side that has a decorative groove cut into it. This time, cut the first slot without the ¼-in. spacer.

Cut a second biscuit slot with the ⅜-in. spacer under the plate joiner. This is a foolproof system for making the slots in the legs and aprons exactly the same distance apart.

Make the Aprons

Cut the aprons (B) to final size. Cut the decorative groove on the bottom outside face (Fig. A) on your tablesaw using a standard ⅛-in. kerf saw blade. The groove is also a handy way to keep track of the outside face of the aprons during the upcoming biscuit-cutting steps. With the decorative groove facing down, cut the double biscuit slots in the ends of the aprons. Cut the first slot without any spacer and the second one with a ⅜-in. spacer (Photos 6 and 7).

Assemble the Base

First make two leg assemblies by gluing two legs and one apron together, then the other two legs and an apron (Photo 8). Make sure the decorative groove on the apron is facing out. Use an exterior glue for this project. After the glue has dried, complete the table base by adding the other two aprons (Photo 9).

Add the Tabletop

With your chosen tile in hand, use the information in the Cutting List's notes, to determine the correct lengths for the tabletop parts (C, D, and E). Make these parts and mark centerlines for the biscuit slots on their ends (Fig. A, page 203).

Cut the double biscuit slots in the outer frame boards (C and D) with their top sides facing up during slot cutting. Cut the bottom slot without using any spacer and the top slot using the ⅜-in. spacer. The tile support boards (E) are thinner and sit ¼-in. below the surface of the outer top frame boards. This offset provides room for the tile. The support boards are joined to the long tabletop frames (C) with only one biscuit at each end. Cut slots for these biscuits with the supports' top side facing up and without using a spacer.

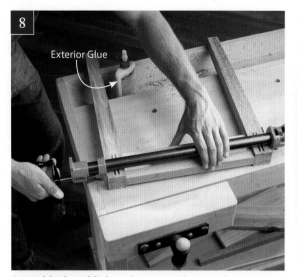

Assemble the table base in stages. Glue together two legs and one apron using exterior glue. Make sure both legs lie flat on your bench. Repeat this step with the other pair of legs and apron.

Assemble the entire table base. Work on a level surface, such as the top of your tablesaw. This will ensure the finished table won't wobble. Working upside down also prevents excess glue from dribbling down the legs.

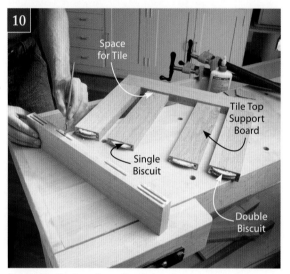

Assemble the top. A small paintbrush works great for applying glue to the biscuits and slots. The tile top of this table rests on support boards that are thinner than the rest of the frame. The tile top's support boards are connected with only a single biscuit.

Next, glue and clamp the top (Photo 10). After the base and top sections have thoroughly dried, give these assemblies a final sanding. Attach them to each other using glue blocks (F). Apply glue to each block and rub it back and forth several times until you feel the glue take hold slightly (Photo 11). Then put pressure on the block for about five seconds before letting go. Leave the table upside down until the glue is dry.

Use an Exterior Stain

We chose to apply exterior stain on our table. Exterior stain is very easy to apply with a brush or a rag (Photo 12). Be sure to work in a well-ventilated area and use the appropriate safety equipment. The exterior stain needs to be renewed every year or two, but it won't peel or crack like varnish.

When the stain is completely dry, glue the ceramic tile in place using silicone caulk (Photo 13). Center the tile so there is a 1/16-in. space between it and the wood frame. This space provides a place for rainwater to drain away. Now you're all set for a lazy afternoon on your deck.

Oops!

We were making such great progress, but we lost track of which side of this leg was tapered and cut a biscuit slot on the wrong side. Rather than make a whole new leg, we decided to repair the mistake. If you make a similar mistake, here's how to fix it.

Find a piece of wood that matches the color and grain of the leg you're repairing. Plane the piece of wood to fit the biscuit slot. Trace half the outline of a biscuit, making your outline about 1/16 in. larger than the biscuit's outline. Cut out this "half-biscuit" on your bandsaw or scrollsaw and test its fit. The half-biscuit should fill the slot from end to end and stand a little proud of the leg's surface. Glue the half-biscuit into the slot. When the glue is dry, sand the half-biscuit flush with the leg. If you do a good job of matching grain, the repair should be hardly noticeable—and it sure beats making a whole new leg.

Glue Block

Fasten the base to the top with glue blocks. This table doesn't use any metal screws or brackets that can rust out. You don't have to clamp these blocks. Just rub them hard back and forth to squeeze out the glue, and then hold them in place for a few seconds until the glue gets tacky.

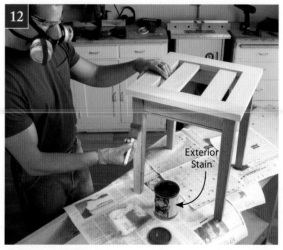

Exterior Stain

Finish the table with an exterior stain. Let it dry thoroughly before you install the tile top.

Silicone Caulk

Install the tile top using four spots of silicone caulk. Make sure the stain is completely dry before you install the tile, or the caulk may not stick to the support boards.

Quickies & Gifties

Sometimes you just want to make something that doesn't take too long or use too much material. The projects in this section are designed for just such a time. You'll find jewelry boxes, picture frames, puzzles, and more. Some of the projects are simple and uncomplicated, while others require more careful joinery. The keepsake box makes use of mitered corners with inset keys that require careful and accurate sawing. The pure and simple jewelry box is just that: pure and simple. Biscuits join the corners and the design lends itself to using scrap wood to create a one of a kind look. If you have young ones in your family or neighborhood and want to delight them with something from your shop, build a few of the Fiendish Knot Puzzles or Cube-in-a-Cube items. You'll probably enjoy making them as much as others enjoy playing with them. One final project not to overlook is the Pizza Paddle, a simple but surprisingly useful item—if you bake your own pizzas. If not, it makes a nice breadboard or wall decoration that shows off some of those unusual pieces of wood you've been hanging onto.

by MAC WENTZ

Keepsake Box

BUILD THEM IN BUNCHES AND AVOID GIFT SHOPPING THIS YEAR

As the holidays approach, my thoughts turn to how I can weasel out of gift shopping. And this year I have the perfect scheme: While the malls are jammed with poor saps, I'll be in my shop blissfully building these boxes for everyone on my list.

When they marvel at the elegant keyed joinery at the corners, I won't mention how fast and easy these boxes are to make. Making the jigs and resawing lumber takes a few hours, but once you're set up you can churn out three or four boxes in a day. There's no need to mention how cheap the materials are either. If you stick with common species like oak, cherry or maple, each box will cost only $10 to $15.

Tools and Materials

The box shown at left is made from ⅜-in.-thick wood, so I used a bandsaw for resawing and a planer to take the wood to final thickness.

If you don't have a bandsaw and planer you can also mail order ⅜-in. wood. You'll also

need a tablesaw, belt sander, router table, ⅛-in. and ¾-in. straight router bits and some 3-in. spring clamps.

Start With Grain Selection

Grain pattern has a big influence on the appearance of a small project like this box, so don't just rip up boards and leave it to chance. Begin by making paper windows that let you preview the look of the box parts (Photo 1). I generally use finer, straighter-grained material for the ends and sides and a more dramatic pattern for the top. This is not a hard and fast rule, so experiment until you get something you like. Grain pattern for the bottom isn't critical, since it doesn't show. For the keys I use a different color wood so they contrast with the box.

Cut the Sides

I strongly recommend you miter the box sides on a tablesaw using a tablesaw sled (Photo 2). The every-time accuracy of a well-made

Lay out the box parts exactly where you want them using a paper window. The window helps you see the grain patterns for each part before you cut them to final size.

Miter the box ends and sides on your tablesaw with the help of a tablesaw sled. Miter one end of all the pieces first. Then clamp a stop block to the sled when cutting the other ends.

tablesaw sled is hard to beat. In fact, I built a small one just for building these boxes. Cut the parts for the ends and sides and make an extra set to test your machine setups later on.

Next cut the dadoes in the ends and sides for the bottom (Fig. A). The dadoes should be wide enough to provide an easy fit for the bottom.

Now select two ends and two sides that have the least attractive grain and mark them "GP" for guinea pig. These GP parts are the first to go through each step in the machining process and hopefully the only ones to suffer from setup mistakes. Beginning with the GP parts, rout the relief in the bottom of the ends and sides to form the corner feet using a ¾-in. straight router bit in your router table (Photo 3).

The Bottom and Top

Cut the bottom for the box next. The bottom is about ¹⁄₁₆-in. undersize to give it some room for expansion. Next cut the top but don't cut the rabbets until the box is assembled. That way you can custom fit the top for a snug-but-not-too-snug fit.

Clamping Jigs Make Glue-up a Cinch

Assembling the box begins by making a set of clamping jigs. They are simply made from scraps of ¼-in. plywood that have 45-degree beveled blocks glued to them (Photo 4). Make them ¾-in. shorter than the outer dimensions of the box so they don't interfere with assembly. The advantage of these clamping jigs over other clamping methods is that you can deal with each joint independently, avoiding the frantic rush of trying to align, clamp and square all the corners at once.

Do a full dry assembly to make sure the jigs and box parts come together correctly. Then disassemble the box and sand the bottom and the inner surfaces of the ends and sides. Add the jigs, glue and spring clamps to the miters (Photo 5). Assemble a guinea pig box too, using the GP parts. Once the glue is dry you can level the feet (if they need it) on a piece of sandpaper (Photo 6).

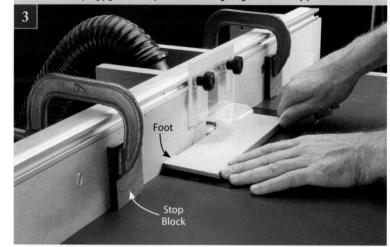

Clamping jigs take the panic out of the gluing and assembly process.

Create feet on the sides and end by using a ¾-in. straight bit in your router table. Set up a pair of stop blocks to limit the length of the cut. To prevent the grain from chipping out at the feet, make three passes, raising the bit about ⅛ in. after each pass.

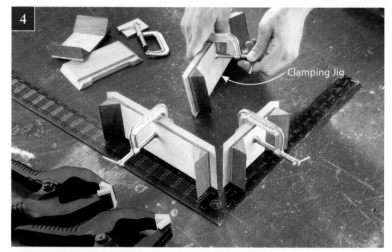

Attach clamping jigs to the ends and sides of the box. The jigs are a bit shorter than the parts so they don't interfere with the joint during assembly.

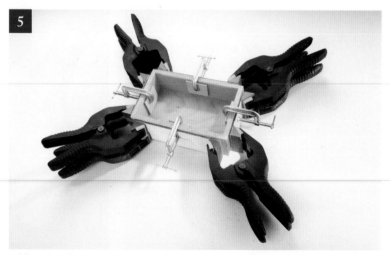

Add spring clamps to one corner at a time. Square the parts by adjusting the position of the spring clamps. Let the glue set for a few minutes before adding the bottom and the last side. Double-check that all the parts are square.

Figure A: Exploded View

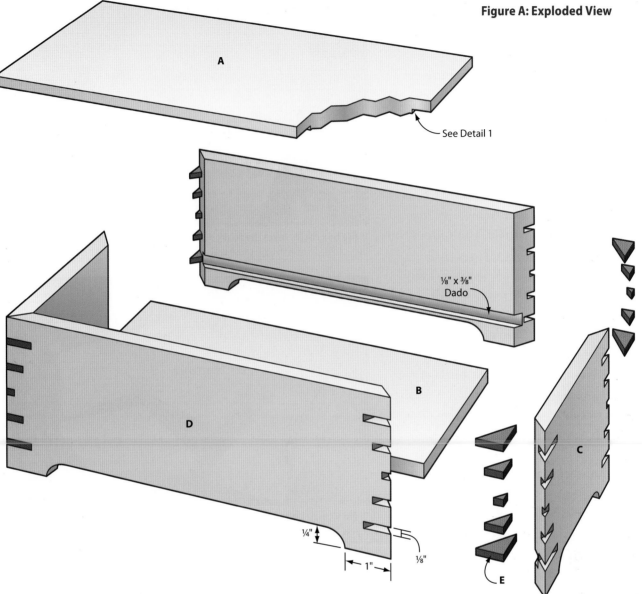

A

See Detail 1

⅛" x ⅜"
Dado

B

D

C

¼"

1"

⅛"

E

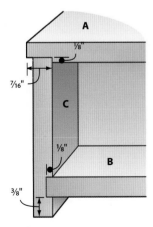

A

⅛"

⁷⁄₁₆"

C

⅛"

B

⅜"

Detail 1: Lid and Bottom Detail

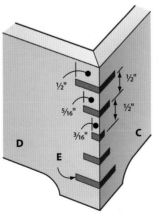

½"

½"

⁵⁄₁₆"

½"

³⁄₁₆"

C

D

E

Detail 2: Key Dimensions

Parts List
Overall Dimensions: 5⅝" W x 3¼" H x 9⅛" L

Parts	Name	Qty.	T"	W"	L"
A	Lid	1	⅜"	5⅝"	9⅛"
B	Bottom	1	⅜"	4¹⁵⁄₁₆"	8⁷⁄₁₆"
C	Ends	2	⅜"	3"	5½"
D	Sides	2	⅜"	3"	9"
E	Keys	20	⅛"	varies	varies
Carriage for routing keys					
Seat boards	2	¾"	6"	8"
Sides	2	¾"	5"	10"

Cutting Slots with a Carriage

To cut slots through the box corners, build a carriage that holds the box at a 45-degree angle as it passes over the ⅛-in. router bit. The carriage is just four pieces of plywood or MDF. See the Parts List, for dimensions. The two seat boards have a 45-degree bevel on the bottom edge (Photo 7). For stability and safety, I like a carriage that's wider than the box.

Assuming your carriage is made from ¾-in. material, set your router table fence 2¼-in. from the center of the ⅛-in. router bit. This will position a slot right in the middle of the box. Cut all four middle slots. Then use a ½-in. spacer board to reposition the box for the next set of slots (Photo 8). Use a second spacer board for the final set of slots. Using spacer boards eliminates the need to move the router table fence for each set of slots. You will, however, have to reset the height of your router bit for each set of slots and this may require some trial and error testing. This is where the guinea pig box comes in handy.

Cut, Glue, and Sand Keys

Rip the ⅛-in.-thick key material using a small-parts sled on your tablesaw (Photo 9). Cut scrap material first, readjusting the fence until you end up with key material that slips smoothly into the slots in the corners of the box. Make sure to use a zero-clearance insert to prevent the strips from falling down into the saw next to the blade.

Cut the key material into triangles with your bandsaw or a small handsaw (Photo 10). Cut the triangles about ⅛-in. oversize. When gluing the triangles in place, use glue sparingly and make sure you fully seat each key into its slot (Photo 11).

Sanding the keys flush with the box sides is fun because you finally see the decorative effect. It's also scary because it's easy to mess up a mitered corner or gouge a side of the box. My tool of choice for this operation is a belt sander mounted upside down on my bench and equipped with a 120-grit belt. To prevent gouging make sure to keep the box parallel with the sanding belt when sanding.

If the box rocks, level the feet on a sheet of 80-grit sandpaper. The top of the box can be leveled in the same way, if it needs it. Follow up with finer grits.

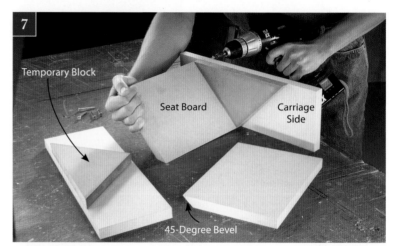

Build a carriage to support the box while cutting the corner slots for the keys. Screw temporary 90-degree blocks to the carriage sides and use the blocks to position the seat boards so their beveled ends just touch. Remove the 90-degree blocks before using the carriage.

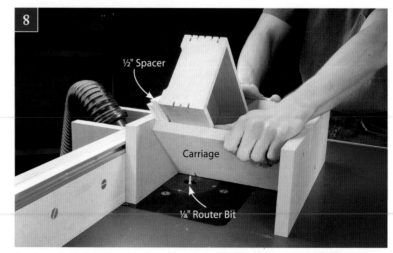

Rout the key slots through the mitered corners. Cut the center slots first. Then raise the bit for the slots next to the center slot and add a ½-in. spacer to position the box for these slots. Finally, add a second spacer and raise the bit for the top and bottom slots and cut them.

Finishing Touches

All the boxes shown in this article got a final sanding with 180-grit sandpaper followed by a couple coats of spray lacquer. Spray lacquer is available at hardware stores for about $7 per can. One can is enough for three or four boxes.

Oops!

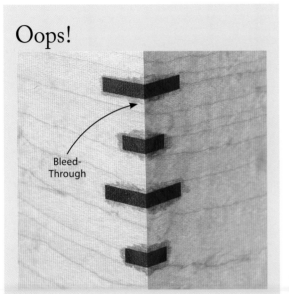

Bleed-Through

One of the things I love about making boxes is that I can experiment with exotic woods without spending a bundle. But unfamiliar woods can lead to unexpected problems. When I gave this box a coat of spray lacquer, the red padauk keys bled into the surrounding finish, making a pink mess. So I sanded off the lacquer and tried again. Two very light coats of lacquer, about 10 minutes apart, sealed the padauk and I was able to follow up with a normal coat about 20 minutes later. Lesson learned: When trying a new wood, I test the finish on my guinea pig box first.

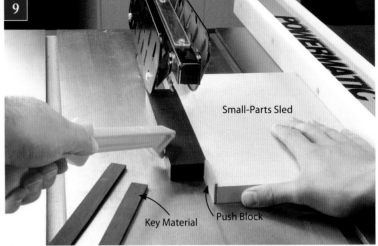

9

Small-Parts Sled

Key Material

Push Block

Saw wood strips for the keys using a small-parts sled; simply a rectangular scrap with a small block glued to one corner. Use a zero-clearance insert for this job to prevent the strips from falling down into the saw next to the blade.

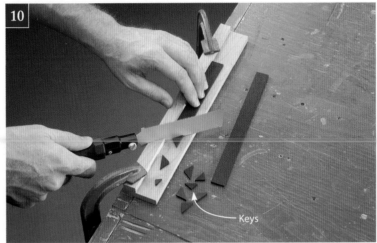

10

Keys

Cut the triangular keys with a bandsaw or small handsaw. Lay out the triangles on the wood strip as shown here. This way the grain will run in the same direction for all the keys.

11

Glue the keys into the slots. Be sure the keys completely seat to the bottom of the slots or you will end up with gaps. Keep a small block handy so you can push in any stubborn keys.

Framed Picture Frame

This frame consists of four pieces that are identical except for length (Fig. A). Each piece has two rabbets for the half-lap corner joints, one on each face. The pieces assemble "elephant" style (nose-to-tail). The framed edges are created prior to assembly, by routing away the center of each piece, using a custom-made jig (Fig. B).

You can make a simple version of this frame from a single piece of solid stock that's 2-in.-wide by 36-in.-long. Just plane it to final thickness and you're ready to cut the four pieces. To create the two-tone version shown here, start with three pieces of ¾-in. by 2-in. by 18-in. stock. Glue the pieces together with the contrasting piece in the middle. Resaw the blank in half (Photo 1). Then plane the resawn blanks to final thickness. Each blank contains two frame pieces, one long side and one short side. Cut the four pieces to final size. Then cut the rabbets on each piece (Photo 2).

Plane the center-routing jig's solid wood spacers to 9/16-in.—the same thickness as the frame pieces. During assembly, center one frame piece between the side spacers. The frame piece must fit snugly. Install the support block. Add the guide pieces, making sure they overhang the frame piece equally, by 3/16-in., the width of the framed edges. Slide each frame piece into the jig. After routing and squaring the corners (Photo 3), use the finger notch to grip the piece and remove it from the jig.

Dry-assemble the frame and mark the inside edges of each piece. Then use a straight bit to rout rabbets for the glass (Photo 4 and Fig. C). Fit one corner joint at a time when you glue the frame together (Photo 5). Clamping the frame between cauls assures a flat result (a good thing!).

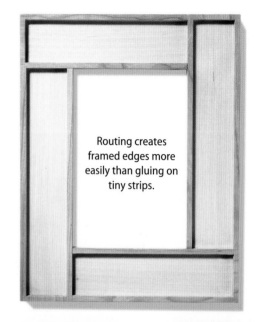

Routing creates framed edges more easily than gluing on tiny strips.

Saw rabbets for the half-lap joints on both ends of each piece. One rabbet goes on the top face; the other goes on the bottom face.

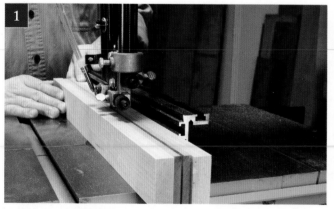

Create two-tone blanks for the frame pieces by resawing a lamination of ¾-in.-thick boards. Plane the cherry faces to 3/16-in. thickness. Then plane the maple faces until the stock reaches final thickness.

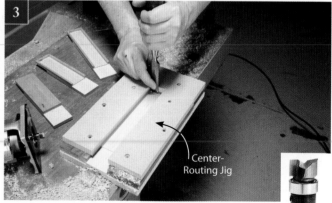

Create the framed edges by routing each piece, using the jig and a mortising bit (at right). Rout just deep enough to remove the top layer of wood. After routing, square the corners with a chisel.

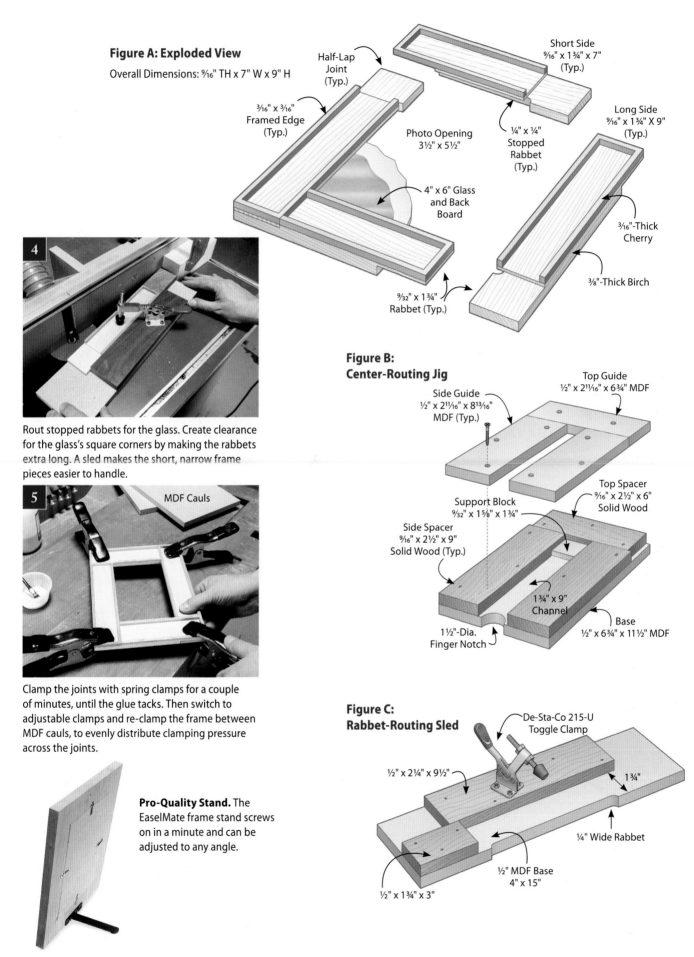

Figure A: Exploded View

Overall Dimensions: 9/16" TH x 7" W x 9" H

Half-Lap Joint (Typ.)

Short Side 9/16" x 1¾" x 7" (Typ.)

3/16" x 3/16" Framed Edge (Typ.)

Photo Opening 3½" x 5½"

¼" x ¼" Stopped Rabbet (Typ.)

Long Side 9/16" x 1¾" X 9" (Typ.)

4" x 6" Glass and Back Board

3/16"-Thick Cherry

9/32" x 1¾" Rabbet (Typ.)

⅜"-Thick Birch

4

Rout stopped rabbets for the glass. Create clearance for the glass's square corners by making the rabbets extra long. A sled makes the short, narrow frame pieces easier to handle.

5

MDF Cauls

Clamp the joints with spring clamps for a couple of minutes, until the glue tacks. Then switch to adjustable clamps and re-clamp the frame between MDF cauls, to evenly distribute clamping pressure across the joints.

Pro-Quality Stand. The EaselMate frame stand screws on in a minute and can be adjusted to any angle.

Figure B: Center-Routing Jig

Side Guide ½" x 2 11/16" x 8 13/16" MDF (Typ.)

Top Guide ½" x 2 11/16" x 6¾" MDF

Support Block 9/32" x 1⅝" x 1¾"

Top Spacer 9/16" x 2½" x 6" Solid Wood

Side Spacer 9/16" x 2½" x 9" Solid Wood (Typ.)

1¾" x 9" Channel

1½"-Dia. Finger Notch

Base ½" x 6¾" x 11½" MDF

Figure C: Rabbet-Routing Sled

De-Sta-Co 215-U Toggle Clamp

½" x 2¼" x 9½"

1¾"

¼" Wide Rabbet

½" x 1¾" x 3"

½" MDF Base 4" x 15"

Magnetic Picture Frame

This frame consists of four identical corner sections that assemble around the glass, photo and back board (Fig. D). Rare earth magnets hold the sections together. To make this frame, you'll need a routing jig (Fig. E), a pattern and two pieces of ¾-in. (or thicker) stock cut to 4¹⁄₁₆-in. by 4⁹⁄₁₆-in. rectangles.

Build the routing jig first. It's used to rout the inside edge of each piece as well as the grooves that house the photo assembly. Use the jig to make the pattern. Saw a 3¹⁄₁₆-in. by 4¹⁄₁₆-in. piece of ½-in. MDF into an L-shape. Install it in the jig and rout the inside edges with a 1-in.-dia. pattern bit (a flush-trim bit with the bearing mounted above the cutting flutes).

Use the pattern to lay out the frame pieces on the two blanks (Photo 1). Cut the short legs to length (Photo 2). Then cut the blanks apart on the bandsaw, install them in the jig and rout the inside edges (Photos 3 and 4). Install a ³⁄₁₆-in.-wide slot cutter and rout a ½-in. deep slot for the photo assembly (glass, photo and back board) in each piece (Photo 5). The photo assembly provides the frame's structure, so it must fit the slot snugly, but without binding. Size the slot's width to fit the thickness of your photo assembly (for single-strength glass and a ⅛-in. back board, the slot will be slightly less than ¼-in.-wide).

Fill the slots to fit the photo assembly (Photo 6). Before you glue in the strips, assemble the frame around the assembly to test the fit. After gluing, flush each strip with the end. Then drill centered holes for the rare-earth magnets (Photo 7) and install them flush with the ends—make sure to orient the magnets' poles correctly! Secure the magnets with epoxy.

Snaps together and pulls apart, so changing photos is easy.

Caution: The blade guard must be removed for this operation. ***Be careful!***

Cut the short legs to final length using the miter gauge with a fence and a stop.

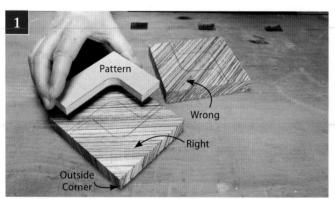

Lay out two corner sections on each blank. Make sure the grain runs across the outside corner. If it runs toward the corner, as on the blank in the background, the pieces will be impossible to rout.

Rout the inside edges with a 1-in.-dia. pattern bit. Because of the grain's direction, you can only rout one leg at a time. Stop before the bit touches the adjacent leg or disastrous tearout will occur.

Figure D: Exploded View

Overall Dimensions:
¾" TH x 6⅛" W x 8⅛" H

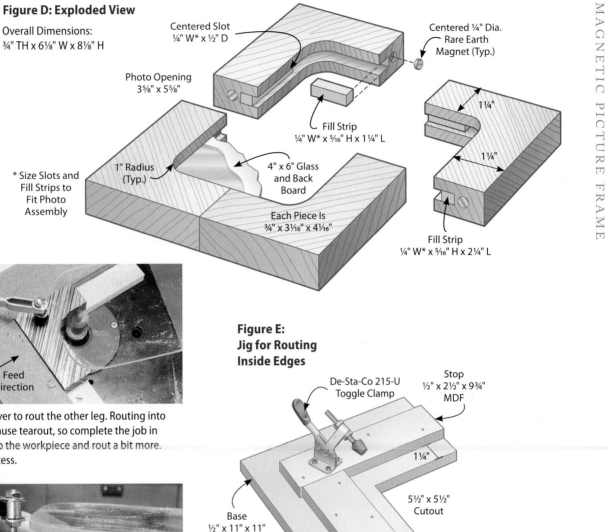

Centered Slot
¼" W* x ½" D

Centered ¼" Dia.
Rare Earth
Magnet (Typ.)

Photo Opening
3⅝" x 5⅝"

Fill Strip
¼" W* x ⁵⁄₁₆" H x 1¼" L

1¼"

1¼"

1" Radius
(Typ.)

4" x 6" Glass
and Back
Board

* Size Slots and
Fill Strips to
Fit Photo
Assembly

Each Piece Is
¾" x 3¹⁄₁₆" x 4¹⁄₁₆"

Fill Strip
¼" W* x ⁵⁄₁₆" H x 2¼" L

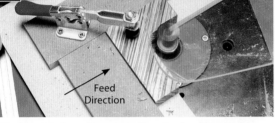

Feed
Direction

Flip the workpiece over to rout the other leg. Routing into the corner can still cause tearout, so complete the job in stages. Rout a bit, flip the workpiece and rout a bit more. Then repeat the process.

Figure E: Jig for Routing Inside Edges

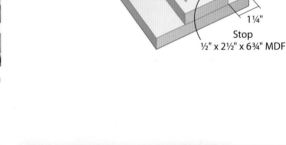

De-Sta-Co 215-U
Toggle Clamp

Stop
½" x 2½" x 9¾"
MDF

1¼"

5½" x 5½"
Cutout

Base
½" x 11" x 11"
MDF

1¼"

Stop
½" x 2½" x 6¾" MDF

Rout a centered slot in each piece. Center the bit by eye. Then make two passes, one on each face. Rout halfway, as before, then flip the workpiece. Once the slot is established, you can rout against the grain to widen it.

Reduce the slots' depth to ³⁄₁₆-in. by gluing in fill strips. Leave the inside corner ½-in. deep, to accommodate the square corners of the glass.

Drill holes for the rare earth magnets using a fence and a stop block. The fence centers the hole between the faces; the stop block centers it between the edges.

by TOM ADAIR

Pure & Simple Jewelry Box

GREAT-LOOKING WOOD AND BRIGHTLY-COLORED FELT ARE A HIT WITH MY CUSTOMERS

I'm hooked on making jewelry boxes—to sell. I sell my boxes at local craft shows. I use wood with strong character—locally-grown, when possible. I line all my boxes with felt and keep the design simple.

Make the Sides and Lid

1. I use lots of low-grade lumber from a variety of sources. What I'm looking for is bold figure.

2. I make boxes in a variety of sizes, depending on what the wood allows. These plans are for a relatively small box, but all my boxes have ⁷⁄₁₆-in. sides and ½-in. lids. Most lids (A, Fig. A) are glued from two or more pieces. I plane this wood to ⁹⁄₁₆ in., glue it together, then take the lid down to ½ in. using a drum sander.

3. The sides (B and C) must be straight and flat in order to make accurate miters. Mill this wood to ½-in. thick and ¼ in. over the final width. Let it sit for a few days, then joint the face sides again and plane and rip the pieces to final dimensions.

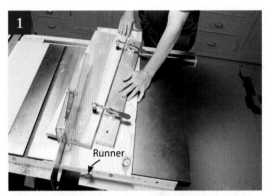

Runner

I use scrounged wood to make my boxes, so I don't mind wasting a bit to get the figure I want. I use a jig with a runner to rip boards so their grain patterns run parallel to the edge.

Subfence
Stop Block

Caution: You must remove your blade guard for this cut.

Miter the sides. Clamp the pieces to the subfence and use a stop block to cut them the same length. Fastening two miter gauges to the subfence eliminates wobble as you cut.

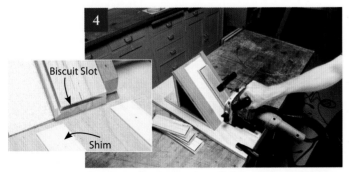

Biscuit Slot
Shim

Cut biscuit slots in the miters. Build a 45-degree fixture to hold the pieces. Locate the slots just below the miter's inside edge by raising the plate joiner on shims nailed to the fixture.

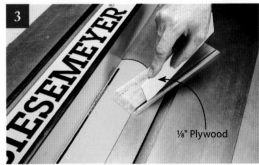

⅛" Plywood

Saw grooves to receive a ⅛-in. plywood bottom. The fit can't be tight, or the box will be too hard to assemble. Shift the fence about ¹⁄₆₄ in. to widen the groove until the fit is just right.

Figure A: Exploded View

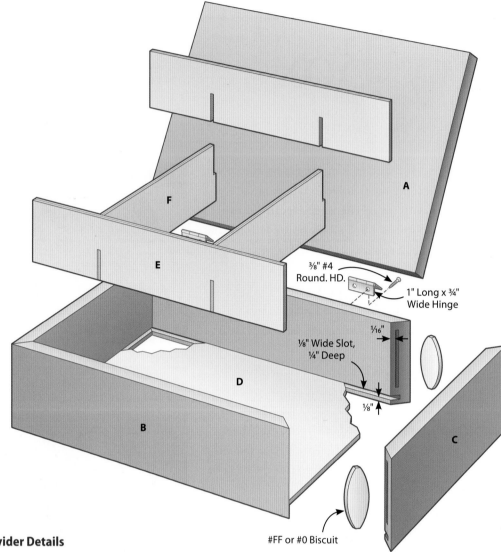

³⁄₈" #4 Round. HD.

1" Long x ¾" Wide Hinge

¹⁄₁₆"

⅛" Wide Slot, ¼" Deep

⅛"

#FF or #0 Biscuit

A

F

E

D

B

C

Figure B: Divider Details

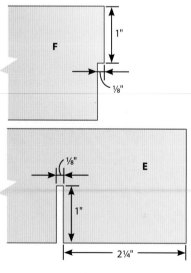

1"

⅛"

F

⅛"

E

1"

2¼"

Cutting List*			
Overall Dimensions: 3" H x 10¼" W x 7⅞" D			
Part	**Name**	**Qty.**	**Dimensions**
A	Lid	1	½" x 7⅞" x 10¼"
B	Front, back	2	⁷⁄₁₆" x 2½" x 10"
C	Side	2	⁷⁄₁₆" x 2½" x 7⅝"
D	Bottom	1	⅛" x 7³⁄₁₆" x 9⁹⁄₁₆"
E	Long divider	2	⅛" x 2" x 9"
F	Short divider	2	⅛" x 2" x 6½"

4. Cut miters using a crosscut blade (Photo 2).

5. Saw grooves for the bottom (D) (Photo 3 and Fig. A). Set the fence ⅛ in. from the blade and saw each piece once, then move the fence about ¼₄-in. farther from the blade and make a second pass. The plywood for the bottom should easily slip into the groove.

6. I use a fixture to cut biscuit slots (Photo 4). I use special FF biscuits, which are very small, because there's more leeway in locating the slots. Only a few plate joiners can make slots this size, however, so I've experimented with #0 biscuits. They work fine, but the slots have to be precisely located and the sides can't be less than ⁷⁄₁₆-in. thick. In fact, it would be better if they were about ⅟₃₂-in. thicker. For making #0 slots using my Porter-Cable plate joiner, I nail ⅟₁₆-in. thick shims to the jig. This places the slot ⅟₁₆-in. below the miter's inside corner.

Glue the Box

7. Cut the bottom to size. I use ⅛-in. thick plywood for making the bottom and dividers (E and F). This plywood is only available at craft and hobby stores, but ⅛ in. hardboard would be OK, too. When you figure out the bottom's exact size, leave ⅟₃₂ in. of play all the way around, so the miters are sure to draw up tight. I use my crosscut blade to saw this thin plywood for a smooth, vibration-free cut. Sand the plywood's edges to make them easier to insert into the grooves.

8. Apply glue to all the miters and slots and clamp the box together (Photo 5).

9. After the glue is dry, sand the outside faces and top edges. Round over the corners so they aren't sharp. Spray or brush a finish on the box and lid. Finish both sides of the lid, but only the outsides and top edges of the box.

Glue the box using rubber tubing or a band clamp to pull the miters tight. After the glue is dry, sand the sides and their top edges, then apply a finish. You don't have to sand or finish inside the box.

Spread a thin layer of glue over the bottom in order to attach a felt lining. Yellow glue works fine; liquid hide glue, as shown here, gives you a little more working time.

Place a piece of felt inside the box. Push down on the felt with a rounded wood stick to smooth it out. Then apply glue to the sides and smooth out each flap using the stick's point to get into the corners.

Trim off the excess felt using a double-sided razor blade held in a Vise-Grip.

Add Felt Lining

10. Cut a piece of felt, with notches, so its center section exactly fits inside the box. Dribble some glue on the box's bottom. Use a wooden spatula with a tapered end to spread the glue (Photo 6). Make sure the glue is spread thin, or it will soak through the felt.

11. Place the felt inside the box (Photo 7). Smooth it out on the bottom, making sure the cut corners line up correctly. Then glue the sides, one at a time.

12. Cut the excess felt flush (Photo 8). The cutting tool has to be extremely sharp, so I use a double-sided razor blade.

Make the Dividers

13. Cut the dividers to width and length. It's important that their lengths are just right to make a snug fit. Cut the notches on the short dividers first (Fig. B). Make these by placing a stop block right next to the blade. Move the stop block and cut notches in the long dividers (Photo 9).

14. Glue felt on the dividers, wrapping it around the dividers' top edges. Trim off the excess and cut around each notch (Photo 10). Assemble the dividers and insert them into the box. The assembly should fit tight, but not so tight that you'd have to hammer it in place.

Add the Lid

15. Screw hinges to the box. These hinges use delicate brass screws, so be sure to pre-drill the holes.

16. Install a chain. This screw should be 1¼ in. away from the lid's edge so the chain falls inside the box as it's closed.

17. Add self-adhesive round felt feet under each corner of the box.

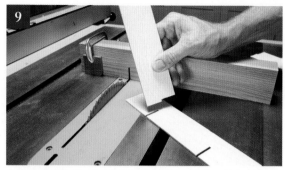

Cut notches in the dividers to make bridle joints. Using ⅛-in. plywood for the dividers, the notches are one saw-kerf wide. If that's too tight, insert a piece of paper next to the stop block in order to widen the notches.

Glue and wrap felt around the dividers. Cut around the notches so the dividers butt tight against each other.

Install hinges on the box, then mark screw holes for the lid. Place four pieces of paper between the box and lid so the lid won't bind as it closes.

Install a chain to hold open the lid. When I make a lid, I look for wood with beautiful figure on both sides.

Whittled Peg Rack

IT'S JUST YOU, YOUR KNIFE, AND THE WOOD

Have you ever had one of those days (or weeks) when everything went wrong and you wondered why you decided to take up woodworking in the first place? It's supposed to be fun, right?

Well, sometimes it helps to get back to basics. After all, the only things you really need to be a woodworker are: 1. wood; 2. something sharp. Whittling is just that. It's relaxing and enjoyable. You can do it anywhere, anytime. A young person or beginning woodworker would enjoy this project just as much as an old codger.

Historically, peg racks like this one were hidden. They were fastened to the back walls of wardrobes in the days before wire coat hangers were invented. But this one's too nice to hide!

You can adjust the length of your peg rack to fit any wall, and you can mount as many or as few pegs as you like. Plan on making a few extra ones. They don't all have to look alike, either. As your technique improves, the pegs will become more consistent.

Butternut is a good choice of wood. It's pretty and cuts easily. White pine and basswood work just as well, but need to be painted. Walnut and cherry are harder to cut, but stronger and more durable.

The only tool you need for whittling is a knife. Choose one that's comfortable. I prefer a big handle. Make sure the knife is sharp—you'll be able to make controlled cuts that are clean and smooth. A dull knife won't cut it.

Practice on an extra blank. Think of peeling a potato. Hold the piece of wood in your free hand, position the thumb of your whittling hand against the end of it, and draw the knife blade through the wood towards your thumb. Make deliberate, shallow cuts. Apply just enough pressure to let the knife do its job. Don't make too deep a cut and don't force the knife.

You'll be able to tell which way the grain runs by how the knife cuts. Cutting with the grain is smooth and easy. So is cutting across the grain, as long as you cut from the outer edges toward the center. However, cutting against the grain is likely to result in slips and tear-out. When this happens, just turn the piece around so you can cut with the grain. Whittling is so easy that with just a little practice it will become second nature.

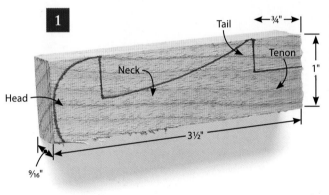

Transfer the peg's profile onto both sides of a blank. Orient the grain so it runs roughly parallel to the bottom of the blank.

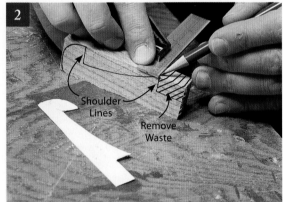

Extend the shoulder lines of the peg's head and tail across the top of the blank, then cut squarely along them to establish the shoulders. Remove the waste above the tenon.

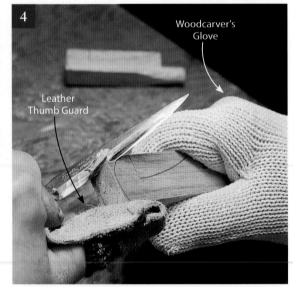

Round the back end of the tenon blank with short, paring cuts until it just starts to fit a ½-in. hole drilled in a scrap piece of butternut. Apply a little pressure and spin it to slightly crush the fibers of the unfinished part of the tenon. Remove the peg and pare the rest of the tenon to this mark. Test and pare as necessary for a snug fit.

Create the convex curve of the head by making shallow, flat cuts across the end grain. Work down from the top and up from the bottom towards the middle. That knife is sharp! I prefer a long-blade knife, but a shorter blade is safer. Always wear a woodcarver's glove and a leather thumb guard to protect yourself.

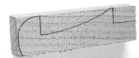

Cradle the blank in one hand and use a potato-peeling motion. Draw the knife through the wood to the stop cut at the shoulder. This is where a sharp, stiff blade is at its best. Work down by alternately chamfering the outer edges, then removing the center ridge until you reach the pattern lines. Finish the peg by chamfering all outer edges (see photo 6).

Chamfer the edges of a 2¾-in. wide backboard. Make it as long as you want. Drill ½-in. holes located 1⅝ in. from the top and spaced at least 5 in. apart. Drill holes between the outer two pegs on each end for attaching to a wall.

Apply glue around the insides of the holes with a wooden stick, then twist the pegs into place.

by ERIC SMITH AND RICHARD TENDICK

Tablesaw Picture Frame

SAFELY MAKE SHAPER-QUALITY MOLDING ON YOUR TABLESAW WITHOUT FANCY JIGS

This how-to story has a picture-perfect ending. In fact, you might want to round up some spectators for applause in the final steps. Richard Tendick has developed a safe, simple technique to help you make narrow, complex picture-frame stock using nothing more than a tablesaw. That's right, there are no routers or specialized jigs and sleds to make, either. With Richard's system, you actually glue the frame before the final cut. The fun comes when the frame is cut loose from the square stock.

Richard's molding also simplifies assembly. Mitering and gluing odd-shaped picture frame molding can be a struggle. With this technique, the frame is mitered and glued when the stock still has its square profile. That makes building a picture frame much easier.

Figure A: Picture Frame Profile Cuts

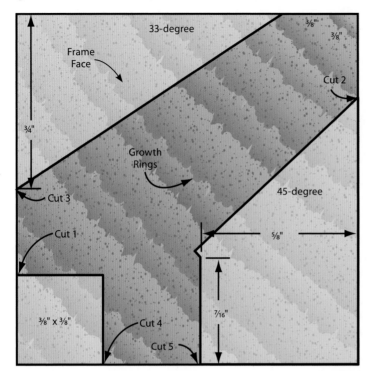

33-degree

Frame Face

3/4"

Growth Rings

Cut 3

Cut 1

3/8" x 3/8"

Cut 4

Cut 5

3/8"

3/8"

Cut 2

45-degree

5/8"

7/16"

Materials		
1½-in. square oak stair balusters		
Band clamp		
Tools		
Tablesaw		
Stock miter gauge		
Drill		
Sander		

Five rip cuts create the picture frame profile. The first four cuts are made with most of the 1½-in. square piece still intact. That means plenty of wood is riding against the tablesaw bed and fence—no rocking or pinching to worry about as you push the stock through.

When you plan your cuts, make sure the face of the frame is cut roughly perpendicular to the growth rings. This yields straight grain that flows smoothly from miter to miter.

Note: All profiles are shown from the outfeed end of the saw. For this project, we used a right-tilt tablesaw with the fence moved to the left of the blade. Reverse all diagrams for a left-tilt saw.

Grain and Color are Important

This technique requires 1½-in. square stock. For a frame to look good, the grain must flow smoothly around all four pieces (see "Oops," page 230), and the color must be consistent. Choose clear, straight-grained wood for your frame stock. It's best if you can cut the frame stock from a single length of wood. Buy extra wood for test cuts. We found 1½-in. square oak stair balusters sold at home centers to be an excellent source for frame stock.

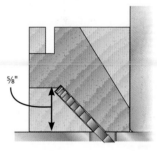

Fence

Cut 1

5/8"

Cut 2

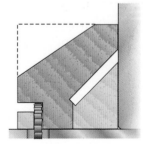

Cut 3

Cut 4

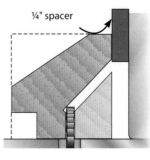

¼" spacer

Cut 5

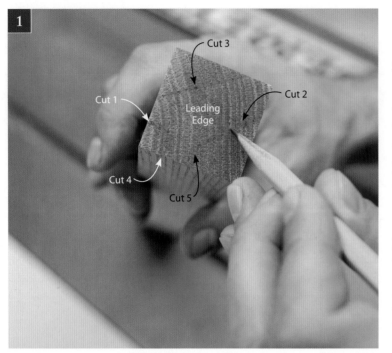

Sketch the saw cuts on the leading end (the end that goes into the saw blade first) of the frame stock before you start cutting.

Use spacer sticks to set the fence and blade height for Cut 2. With the blade at 45 degrees, use the ⅜-in. spacer to set the fence. When the teeth center on the ⅝-in. spacer's upper corner, you've reached the blade height.

Set up for the Cuts

1. Rough-cut the frame stock to a few inches over the finished dimensions for cutting on the tablesaw.

2. Sketch the cuts on the end of each piece for orientation (Photo 1; Fig. A). All cuts start at the same end, so if you find yourself reversing the piece, something is wrong. Pay attention to grain direction! (See Fig. A and "Oops.")

3. Cut spacer strips ⅜, ⅝ and ¾ in. wide by 18 in. long. You'll use these for setting the fence and saw blade height for some of the cuts.

Making the Saw Cuts

4. Set the blade to make a ⅜-in.-deep cut and make Cut 1 (Fig. A).

Oops!

At first we didn't pay attention to grain orientation. The result was mismatched grain and a bad-looking corner. Make sure the face of your frame is positioned so the growth rings run perpendicular to it. This will give you a straight-grained face, which will make the corners match better.

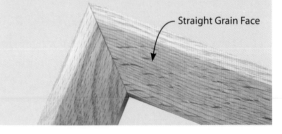

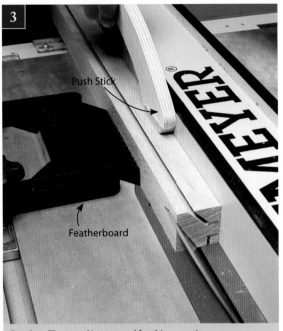

Caution: The guard is removed for this operation.

Caution: The guard is removed for this operation.

Tilt the blade 33 degrees to make Cut 3. Use a ¾-in. spacer to set the fence. A featherboard and a rubber-tipped push stick make the cut smooth and safe.

Make Cut 4 on the side of the blade away from the fence to prevent kickback. This also allows the stock's large sides to bear against the fence and table for greater stability.

5. Set the blade and fence for Cut 2 (Photo 2) and make the cut.

6. Make Cut 3 with the blade tilted to 33 degrees. Set the blade just high enough to poke through the wood about ¼ in. (Photo 3).

7. Make Cut 4 to create the rabbet that holds your picture, matte and glass (Photo 4). Set the fence and blade height using Cut 1 as a reference.

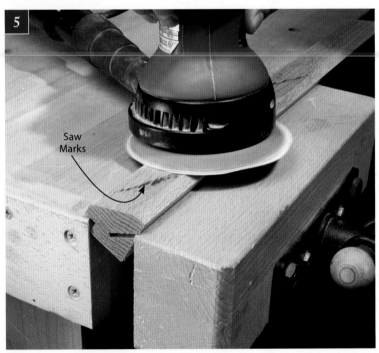

Sand off saw marks on the frame's face. The molding can be pinched in a vise to hold it steady.

Tip

Get a Better Grip

Hold small pieces of wood in the tablesaw with this rubber-tipped push stick. Just glue a standard eraser into the push stick notch.

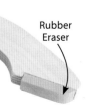

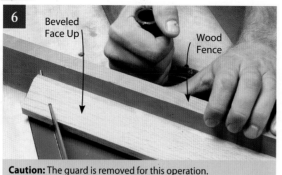

Caution: The guard is removed for this operation.

Make the first miter cuts to the left of the blade. Clamp the stock face up to a wooden fence attached to the gauge. The end being cut should angle toward you. Make this cut on all four pieces.

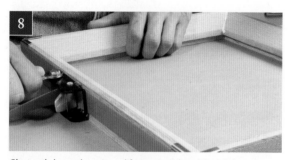

Caution: The guard is removed for this operation.

Make the second miter cut on the right side of the blade. Clamp a stop block to the fence so the frame's parallel sides will be exactly the same length.

Glue and clamp the mitered frame together. A band clamp is perfect for the job. The clamp's metal plates hang on each corner of the frame to help position the band and protect the wood.

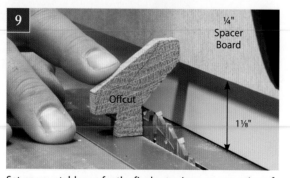

Set up your tablesaw for the final cut using a cross section of the frame stock as a guide. Clamp a ¼-in. spacer to the fence just above the offcut to create a gap between the offcut and the fence to prevent kickback.

Sanding, Mitering, and Gluing

8. Sand the frame before cutting the miters (Photo 5). It's a lot easier than sanding into the corners of an assembled frame.

9. Before you cut the miters, take a ½-in.-thick slice off your stock. Save the slice for setting up the last cut.

10. Attach a long subfence to the miter gauge. Use a drafting square to set the gauge at 45 degrees.

11. Cut the miters (Photos 6 and 7).

12. Test-fit the frame with a band clamp before gluing, to check for tight-fitting joints.

13. Glue the frame together, spreading a heavy coat of glue over the entire miter (Photo 8). Yes, that includes the part that will eventually be cut off. Wipe off excess glue with a damp rag.

The Final Cut (The Fun Part!)

14. Set up the tablesaw for Cut 5 (Photo 9).

15. Make the final cut on all four sides of the frame (Photo 10).

16. Lift the frame from its four-sided offcut (Photo 11). (You may want an audience for this step.)

17. If the inner frame doesn't fall away from the offcut immediately, don't panic. Ours didn't (and, of course, we panicked). It turned out that despite our best efforts, the blade was set a hair too shallow. All we had to do was push down gently on the frame to break that sliver of wood and release the offcut.

Caution: The guard is removed for this operation.

Make Cut 5 on all four sides of the frame. The offcut won't release from the frame until all the cuts are complete.

Lift the frame out of the offcut. If your last cut was a bit shallow, you may need to push down in spots to separate the frame from the offcut.

Drill pilot holes for a couple of 1-in. brads to reinforce each miter joint. Keep the brads on the back of the frame where they won't be seen.

Finishing Touches

18. Reinforce the corners with 1-in. wire brads (Photo 12). Predrill the holes with a No. 60 wire gauge bit or clip the head off a brad and use that as a bit. You may need to use a mini-chuck if your drill doesn't hold a bit that small. We don't recommend using a nail gun for this step—it's too easy to blow a nail out of the face of the frame. The nail would be hard to extract, and the resulting damage, difficult to repair. With a drill, if you accidentally drill a hole in the wrong spot, it's easy to hide with filler.

19. Sand the outside of the frame and fill the nail holes. Stain as desired and finish with at least two coats of varnish or polyurethane.

by RANDY JOHNSON

Table Hockey

IT'S FAST, IT'S WILD—GO FOR THE GOAL!

ART DIRECTION: EVANGELINE EKBERG ·PHOTOGRAPHY: RAMON MORENO · ILLUSTRATION: FRANK ROHRBACH

Looking for a great holiday gift project? This table hockey game is a blast to play, even for adults, and it's so simple, you can make it even if your gift-building time is running short. It's made from easy-to-get materials, and the finish is all water-based, so it goes on quickly.

It's basically a shallow box, made from ¾-in. hardwood (we used oak) with a playing surface of ½-in. birch plywood. Add some small pieces of mesh fabric (available from a fabric store) for the goals, a couple of strategically placed goalie blocks, a pair of sticks and a puck, and you're ready to play. Have fun!

PROJECT REQUIREMENTS AT A GLANCE

Power tools:

- Tablesaw
- Dado blade
- Jigsaw
- Drill
- Sander

Materials:

- ½-in. birch plywood
- ¾-in oak lumber
- Stain
- Paint
- Varnish
- Netting
- Screws
- Finish washers

Cost: About $75

Figure A: Exploded View

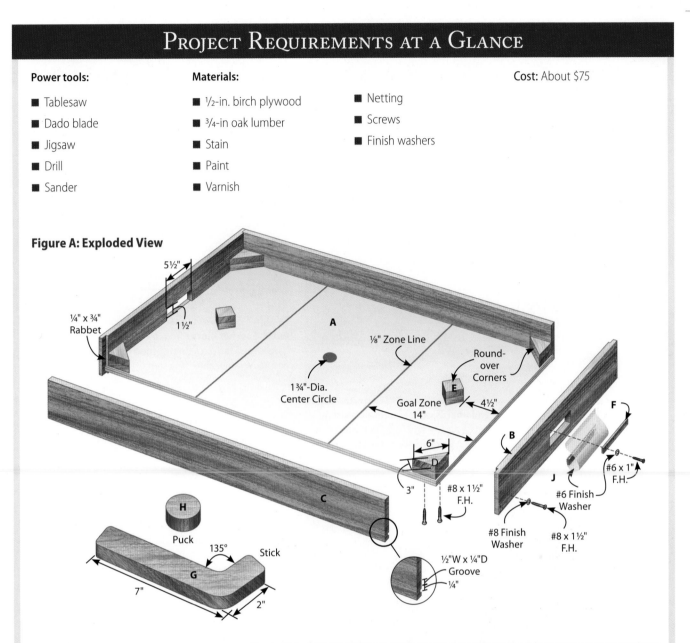

Cutting List

Overall Dimensions: 4¼" T x 32" W x 48" L

Part	Name	Qty.	Dimensions	Material	Notes
A	Bottom	1	½" x 31" x 47"	Birch plywood	
B	Ends	2	¾" x 4¼" x 32"	Oak	
C	Sides	2	¾" x 4¼" x 47"	Oak	
D	Corner blocks	4	1½" x 3" x 6"	Oak	Cut from two pieces of ¾" x 3½" x 24" lumber glued together.
E	Goalie blocks	2	1½" x 2" x 2"	Oak	Cut from two pieces of ¾" x 2½" x 18" lumber glued together.
F	Net boards	4	¼" x ¾" x 7½"	Oak	
G	Sticks	2	½" x 2" x 7"	Oak or birch plywood	
H	Pucks	2	½" T x 1¾" dia.	Oak or birch plywood	
J	Nets	2	7½" H x 7½" W	Mesh fabric	

Cut rabbets in the end boards, so the corners are strong enough to take abuse. Use an auxiliary fence to protect the main fence from damage. A ½-in. groove at the bottom edge houses the plywood playing surface.

Saw goal openings with a jigsaw. Holes near each corner make starting the cuts and turning the corners easy. Smooth the inside of the goal opening with a file or sanding block.

How to Build it

1. Mill the end and side boards (B, C) to final size and cut the grooves for the bottom panel (A, Fig. A).

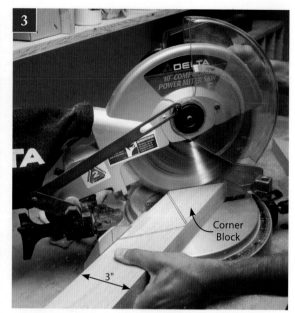

Cut the corner blocks from glued-up ¾-in. boards. These blocks keep the puck from getting trapped in the corners and allow interesting bank shots.

2. Cut the rabbets in the end boards (Photo 1). Use an auxiliary wood fence so you can run your dado blade right next to it. This setup also allows the auxiliary fence to serve as a guide when you cut the rabbets.

3. Cut out the opening for the goals using a jigsaw or scrollsaw (Photo 2).

4. Glue and clamp together two layers of ¾-in. lumber for the corner blocks (D). Wipe off any glue that squeezes out. When the glue is dry, rip the board to 3 in. wide for the corner blocks. Make the goalie blocks (E) the same way.

5. Cut the corner blocks and goalie blocks to final size (Photo 3) using your miter saw or tablesaw. You'll notice that the glued-up lumber stock is much longer than actually needed. This extra length gives you more to hold for safer mitering and crosscutting. Cut the net boards (F).

6. Use your bandsaw or scrollsaw to saw the sticks (G) and pucks (H) from either oak lumber or birch plywood. Make a couple extra pucks, so you won't have to take a time-out if a puck flies off the table and rolls under the couch.

Finish all the parts before you assemble them. After the blue stain on the bottom panel is dry, tape off and paint the zone lines and the center circle.

7. Sand and finish all the parts. We used water-based stain, paint, and finish. Water-based finishes tend to raise the grain after they are applied, which makes a rough finish. To prevent this, raise the grain first with a moist sponge. After the wood dries, do your final sanding. Then apply the stain to all the parts. When the blue stain on the bottom panel is dry, tape off and paint the zone lines and center circle (Photo 4). Finally, brush on the clear topcoat finish.

8. Assemble the hockey table with screws and finish washers (Photo 5). Drill shank and pilot holes in the sides to prevent splitting the wood or stripping the screw heads.

9. Attach the netting (J) over the goal openings with the net boards (F). The bottom net board goes inside the net and the top net board goes outside the net (Photo 6). Hold the netting in place with a bit of double-sided tape during assembly. You can substitute almost any kind of fabric for the netting, if you wish.

10. Attach corner and goalie blocks (D, E) with screws from the bottom. It's game time! Go for the goal!

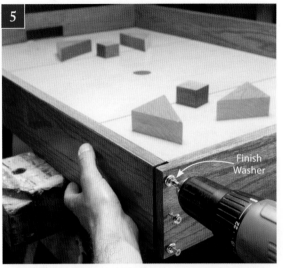

Assemble the parts with flat head screws and finish washers. Finish washers provide extra bearing surface for the screw heads and don't require countersinking.

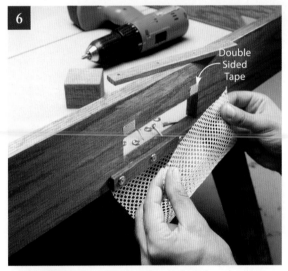

Attach the goal netting with the net boards and screws. Leave the net open on the sides to make it easy to retrieve the puck. You're ready to play!

Table Hockey Rules

You can play table hockey two ways. The first is free play. Players start with the puck on the center circle and both hit it around until a goal is scored. The only limit is that a player may not play the puck within the goal zone of the other player (see Fig. A). If the puck flies off the table during play, return it to the center circle and resume playing.

The second way to play is to take turns. Each player takes a predetermined number of shots. Two swings per player is common, but the exact number is up to you. You can handicap a better player by giving him or her fewer swings than a less experienced player. The entire rink area is open for play. If a puck is knocked off the table, it's turned over to the other player, who then gets to take one additional shot during his or her turn. Of course, it's also fun to make up your own rules!

Fiendish Knot Puzzle

Actual Size:
2½ in. square

Here's a puzzle that's devilishly difficult to solve but quite easy to make. All you need is some ¾-in. hardwood dowel rod, a ¾-in. Forstner bit, a tablesaw, and a drill press. At the end of one day in the shop you'll have a dozen of these inexpensive brainteasers to tantalize your friends.

Use dowels made from a hard wood. The kind of dowels you'd find at the local hardware store are probably too soft to cut cleanly, but birch is OK. You'll need about 24 inches of dowel to make one puzzle. A 36-in.-hardwood dowel costs from $3 to $5, depending on the species.

Follow steps 1 through 7 to make this puzzle. The last step is the hardest—that's where you have to put it together!

Left Offset Notch

Center
Notch

Piece #1

Pieces #2 and #3

Piece #6

Right Offset Notch

Pieces #4 and #5

Drilling Jig

Accurately aligned holes are the secret to making this puzzle work. Make a jig for drilling half-round notches, lock the jig in place on your drill press table and you're ready to go.

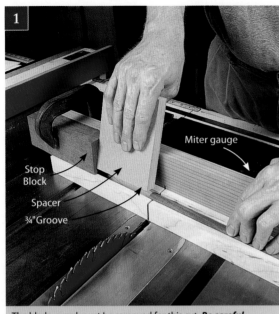

The blade guard must be removed for this cut. **Be careful.**

Cut the puzzle pieces to length safely and accurately with this jig. You'll need seven 2½-in.-long dowel pieces in all, six for the puzzle plus one extra to balance the drilling jig. Also, cut four ⅜-in.-long pieces to use as spacers in the drilling jig.

The trick in using this dowel-cutting jig is to avoid trapping the cut-off piece between the stop block and the blade. Instead, butt the dowel up to a removable spacer and withdraw the spacer before you make the cut.

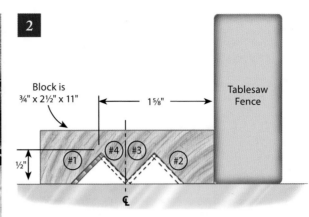

Make the drilling jig by cutting V-grooves into a hardwood block. First, draw the layout below on both ends of the block with a combination square.

Tilt your tablesaw blade 45 degree and raise it ½-in. above the table. Move the fence to align the blade with cut #1. Make the cut, turn the board end-for-end and make cut #2. Repeat the process for cuts #3 and #4. Caution: Use a push stick and stand to the right of your fence when cutting these pieces.

When you're done, check the jig for accuracy by nesting two dowels in the grooves. Their sides should touch.

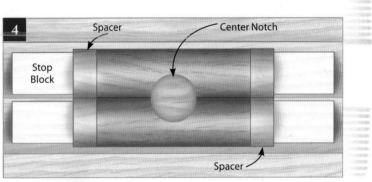

Drill center notches in three pairs of puzzle pieces by nesting them between spacers in the drilling jig (photo, page 238).

In this set-up, the spacers locate the puzzle piece in the exact center of the jig. In the next steps, the spacers will be shifted around so you can drill notches that are offset from the center by exactly one-half the diameter of the dowel.

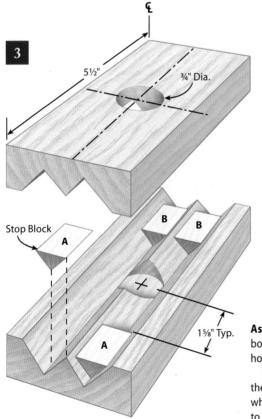

Assemble the drilling jig. Cut the V-groove block in half to make the top and bottom pieces of the drilling jig. Stack the pieces together and drill a ¾-in.-dia. hole exactly in the center.

Cut four stop blocks from the triangular waste pieces left over from ripping the grooves. The puzzle pieces and spacers are locked between the stop blocks when you set up the jig (see Step #4, above). For a tight fit, first glue block A to the jig. To position block B, place one of your puzzle pieces and both ⅜-in. spacers in the jig and butt them up to block A. Then butt block B to all three pieces and glue it to the jig.

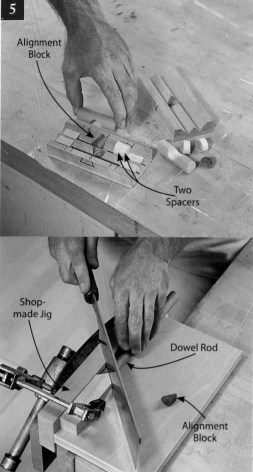

5

Alignment Block

Two Spacers

Shop-made Jig

Dowel Rod

Alignment Block

Insert alignment blocks into the jig for drilling the second set of offset notches. The alignment blocks turn the puzzle pieces 90 degrees to the center notch.

Cut these V-shaped blocks with a shop-made mitering jig. You'll need one block for each puzzle piece. Note: These blocks are too small to cut safely with a power tool.

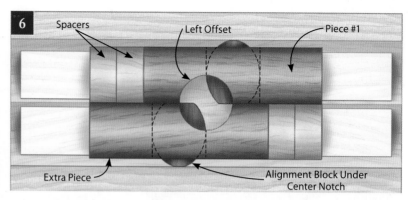

6

Spacers   Left Offset   Piece #1

Extra Piece   Alignment Block Under Center Notch

Arrange the drilling jig for offset notches. Drill piece #1 and the extra piece as shown above to make a left offset notch. Drill pieces #2 and #3 the same way.

Then, shift the spacers to the opposite ends and drill a second set of *right* offset notches in pieces #2 and #3. Drill pieces #4 and #5 with the spacers in their new positions (see top photo in Step 5).

7

Assemble the puzzle. The numbers used to identify the pieces also represent the order of assembly. This puzzle is so fiendish that we suggest you lightly write the number of each piece on the end to help you figure it out!

If the pieces fit too tightly, you can enlarge the notches with sandpaper wrapped around a dowel.

Magic Coin Bank

THE COIN SLOT IS LARGE ENOUGH TO FIT A SACAGAWEA GOLDEN DOLLAR!

Caution: Coins may present a choking hazard for children under three.

Kids love secrets—and so do adults! This small bank with its sneaky false drawer is a kick to make.

Making the Box

Cut the four sides of the bank box from ¼-in.-thick wood. Cut out the drawer opening with a dado set. You can join the sides of the box any way you want; dovetails, box joints, even a nailed and glued butt joint will do. Glue the box together and plane or sand all the edges and faces even.

Making the Drawer

Use a 12-in.-long, ¾-in.-thick piece of hardwood for the drawer. The finished drawer is actually much shorter, but the blank is easier to mill as a long piece. Cut the blank to width, drill the coin hole in the middle with a Forstner bit and then cut the dado that holds the false bottom. Cut a notch with a chisel for the bottom to pivot in. Then cut the blank to length.

Make the false bottom from the same wood as the drawer. Attach it to the drawer with small brads. Cut the drawer front to size and glue it to the end of the drawer.

Figure A: How It Works

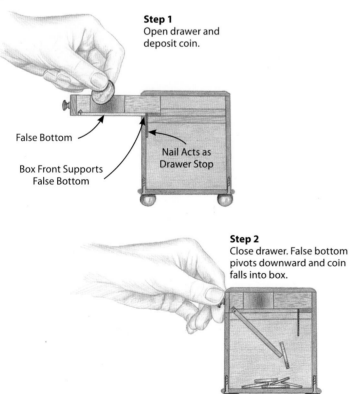

Step 1
Open drawer and deposit coin.

False Bottom

Box Front Supports False Bottom

Nail Acts as Drawer Stop

Step 2
Close drawer. False bottom pivots downward and coin falls into box.

Cutting List			
Overall Dimensions: 3⅞" H x 5⁵⁄₁₆" W x 3⁵⁄₁₆" D			
Part	**Name**	**Qty.**	**Dimensions**
A	Front and back	2	¼ x 3 x 5
B	Sides	2	¼ x 3 x 3
C	Drawer	1	¾ x 1⅝ x 2½
D	False Bottom	1	⅛ x 1¼ x 2
E	Drawer front	1	¼ x ¾ x 1⅝
F	Runners	2	1½ x 1½ x 2½
G	Top	1	¼ x 3 x 5
H	Bottom	1	¼ x 3⁵⁄₁₆ x 5⁵⁄₁₆
Hardware:			
1 knob and eight #4, ⅝" L F.H. screws.			

Hanging the Drawer

Make the two drawer runners as one piece about 12-in. long. Cut the rabbet, then crosscut the runner into two pieces to fit your box. Apply glue to the ends of one of the runners and position the runner in the box.

After the glue is dry, use the drawer as a guide to position the second runner. Then, wrap the drawer in a piece of paper to act as a shim, and insert it and the runner into the box. Squeeze the runner tight to the drawer, and remove the drawer and paper. The paper shim ensures a smooth sliding drawer.

Pre-drill a small hole and tap a small finish nail into the underside of the drawer to act as a drawer stop. Hold the nail with a pair of pliers.

Attaching the Top and Bottom

Once you're sure the drawer works, glue the top on the box. Drill pilot holes and screw the bottom in place. To empty the bank, unscrew the bottom.

Epoxy the brass feet and drawer knob so a child can't unscrew them.

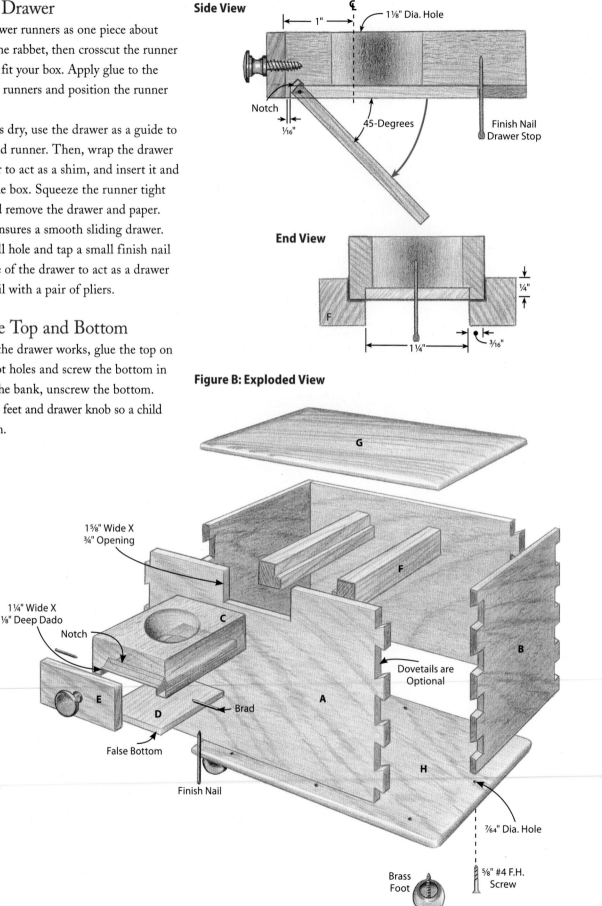

Side View

1"

¢

1⅛" Dia. Hole

Notch

1/16"

45-Degrees

Finish Nail
Drawer Stop

End View

¼"

F

1¼"

3/16"

Figure B: Exploded View

G

1⅝" Wide X
¾" Opening

1¼" Wide X
⅛" Deep Dado

Notch

F

C

Dovetails are
Optional

B

E

D

Brad

A

False Bottom

H

Finish Nail

⁷/64" Dia. Hole

Brass
Foot

⅝" #4 F.H.
Screw

Hefty Bookends

RESAW YOUR OWN VENEER TO HIDE THE LEAD SHOT INSIDE

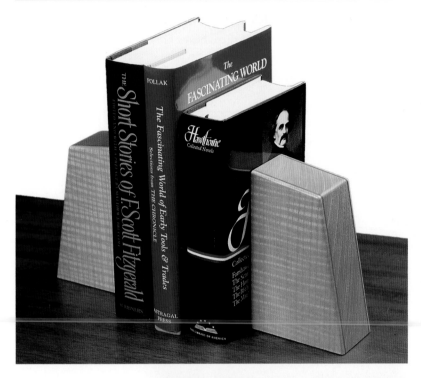

You'll need a bandsaw to cut your wood, a large-diameter Forstner bit to drill the holes for the lead shot and a router with a flush-trim bit.

Making the Laminations

Each face of these bookends has two layers of laminations. The outer layer is resawn from a piece of solid, figured wood. The inner layer is a contrasting color composed of thin sheets of dyed veneer glued one on top of another.

To make the outer layer, smooth the faces of a ¾-in. thick, 4-in. wide and 13-in.-long figured hardwood block. Set the fence of your bandsaw ⅛-in. away from the blade and resaw both faces of the block, making two pieces of ⅛-in.-thick veneer. Sand the rough side and cut the pieces in half to make four pieces.

Make the inner layer by building up two or three thicknesses of dyed veneer. Use a veneer saw to cut the veneer into 4-in. wide by 6½-in.-long pieces. Make two cauls, the same sizes as the pieces of veneer, from ¾-in. plywood or MDF. Glue the veneer between the cauls. To keep the veneer layers from sticking to the cauls, separate them with newspaper.

Making the Core

For the core, select a piece of solid wood that's close in color to the figured wood you used for the outer layer. Saw the wood into two matching pieces (Fig. A). Then drill a large hole in each side of both pieces with a 2-in.-dia. Forstner bit (Fig. B).

Fill the holes with a mixture of lead shot and epoxy to add weight to the bookends. Pre-measure your lead shot by pouring it into the cavity. (Lead shot is available at gun shops.) Then mix the lead with two-part epoxy glue and spoon it into the hole. Be sure not to overfill the hole.

Fill the holes in both sides of the core pieces with a mixture of lead shot and two-part epoxy resin. Be careful not to overfill the holes.

Got a small chunk of figured wood that you'd like to show off? Resaw it into thick veneers and make a pair of matching bookends. They're laminated to conceal holes filled with lead shot. Although these blocks look light, they're actually heavy enough to support a row of large books.

Laminating the Core

Cut the figured wood and colored-veneer laminations so they're slightly larger than the core pieces. An overhang of about ⅛-in. all around will allow for the laminations to slip a bit when you glue them to the core.

Use the cauls you made for gluing the colored veneer together to laminate one outer layer and one inner layer to each face of the core blocks. After each face is glued, trim the overhanging laminations with a bottom-bearing flush trim bit in your router.

Round the edges with a small-diameter round-over bit or a block plane and apply a finish. Finally, add felt circles to the bottoms to protect the surface on which these heavy bookends will sit.

Figure A: Bookmatched Figure

Create mirror images on the top of your bookends by cutting both core pieces from a single piece of wood. Lay out the angled sides of the blocks with a compass.

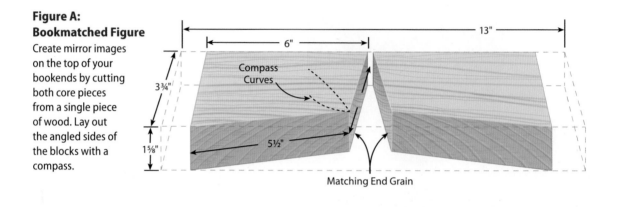

13"

6"

3¾"

1⅝"

5½"

Compass Curves

Matching End Grain

Figure B: Exploded View

Cover the lead-filled core with two layers of veneer. Resaw your own figured wood to make the outer layer. Laminate two to three sheets of dyed veneer to make the inner layer.

Side View of Core

Drill holes from both sides, leaving a small section of solid wood in between.

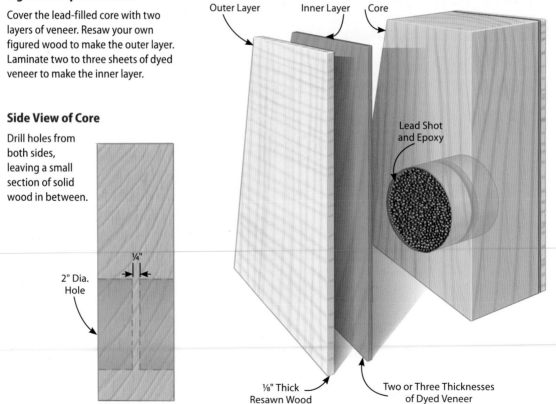

Outer Layer   Inner Layer   Core

Lead Shot and Epoxy

¼"

2" Dia. Hole

⅛" Thick Resawn Wood

Two or Three Thicknesses of Dyed Veneer

by JOCK HOLMEN

Cube in a Cube

"KIDS PLAY WITH IT LIKE A TOY, BUT IT DRIVES ADULTS NUTS. THEY THINK IT'S A PUZZLE. THEY'RE SURE THERE'S SOME WAY TO GET THE LITTLE CUBE OUT OF THE BIG CUBE. YOU CAN'T"

Crosscut a 3x3x14-in. blank into four cubes. Solid wood is best, so it doesn't look like you put the little cube in the big cube by gluing parts together. Three-in. table-leg stock works well, but you can make the cubes from 2½ in. or smaller stock if you want.

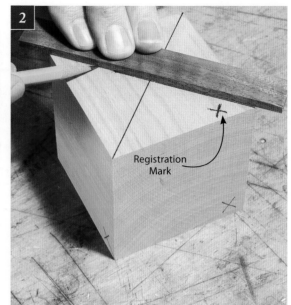

Mark centerlines on one face. Mark one corner of every face with a small X. You'll be drilling each hole more than one time. The X's will help register the cube in the same orientation on the drill press.

Set your drill press to run at its slowest speed. Arrange the belts so the smallest diameter drive pulley turns the idler pulley. Connect the idler to the largest diameter spindle pulley.

Set up your drill press with a 2 in. Forstner bit. (Use a smaller bit with a smaller block.) Position a fence and stop block so the bit drills exactly in the cube's center. Drill one hole about ¹⁄₁₆-in. deep.

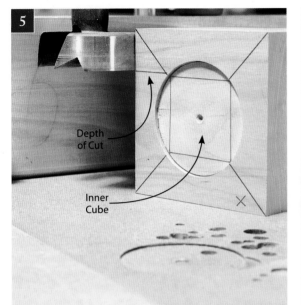

Set the bit's depth of cut. Draw a line from the point where a diagonal intersects the hole you made. Adjust the drill press so the bit stops about ⅟₁₆ in. above this line. This method works for any size cube and any size hole. (I've drawn the inner cube so you can see how this works.)

Drill holes in the end-grain sides first. Then drill the other four faces. Always place the X's in the same corner relative to the fence and stop block.

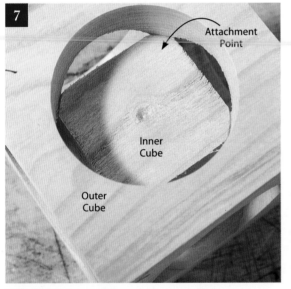

Drilling all six faces produces a cube in a cube. The inner cube is attached to the outer cube by a thin section of wood. The reason for drilling the end-grain faces first is to avoid breaking these weak attachment points. End-grain drilling requires more downward pressure than face-grain drilling.

Set the drill bit ⅟₃₂-in. deeper and repeat drilling all the holes. Again, drill the end-grain faces first. Use light pressure to avoid breaking the attachment points.

9

As you drill, check the thickness of the attachment points. Your goal is to make them as small as possible, to the point where the inner cube almost releases itself. This may require drilling some holes a tiny bit deeper. Draw check marks to show how many times you've drilled each hole.

10

Release the inner cube by cutting the attachment points with a thin knife, going with the grain. After cutting all eight corners, the inner cube will drop free. But it won't come out!

11

Wedge

Sand the corners of the inner cube. Raise the inner cube above the hole by positioning it at a diagonal. Prop up the cube with a wedge or your fingers.

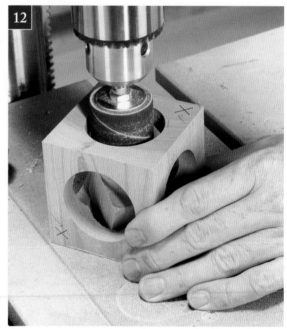

12

Sand burn marks or rough grain with a fine-grit drum-sanding attachment. Rub the drum with a crepe-rubber belt cleaner now and then to keep the drum working efficiently.

13

Smoothing the faces of the inner cube is tough, because they're hard to get to. I usually just leave them alone, but if you must do some clean-up work, use a file to start, then switch to sandpaper.

Dip the cube in oil to finish it. Rub thoroughly with a rag to remove the excess oil, and you're ready to play!

14

by FRITZ SCHROEDER

Pizza Paddle

HANDLE HOMEMADE PIZZA LIKE A PRO

Wednesday is homemade pizza night at our house. Everybody likes different toppings, so we each make our own personal size pizza. My favorite is hot Italian sausage with tomatoes, mushrooms and mozzarella. Making pizza is especially easy with ready-made crusts, and you can bake them right on the oven rack.

As a home pizza specialist/woodworker, I decided to create my own paddle. Restaurant chefs use similar paddles (called "peels" in the trade) to efficiently slide pizzas in and out of their ovens. Making my own paddle was fun and easy, and using it makes me feel like a proper pizza chef. Now I just need the proper chef's hat!

All you need to make your own paddle is a board for the handle and wide blade, a couple thin strips for accents, a 12" planer, and a simple shop-made tapering sled. The completed paddle measures 11⅜" × 24", the perfect size to handle 12" pizzas.

Build the paddle

Starting with a ¾" × 6" × 24" board, rip a 1⅜" strip from one side to create the handle (Photo 1). Then use the wide offcut to make the blade pieces. Mark the centerline and draw a small radius at each end, on opposite sides. Then make a single S-shaped bandsaw cut to create a pair of pieces with one rounded (outside) shoulder and one transitional (inside) shoulder.

Rip a pair of ¾" × ½" × 14" maple strips to accent the walnut blade. Position all the parts for assembly. You can't use biscuits or dowels to help with alignment, because the blade is going to be tapered, so make sure the parts are flat. Joint all the edges and then glue and clamp the assembly (Photo 2). Before tapering, plane the paddle to 9⁄16" thick.

Make the Tapering Sled

The sled is simply a base with a tapered platform that holds the paddle at an angle as it passes through the planer (see Fig. A). The platform consists of three long rails that taper from ¾" to 0". To make consistently tapered rails, tack together three ¾" × ¾" × 24" blanks, using double sided tape. Bandsaw the long taper and smooth the cut edge by sanding. Then pull the rails apart.

Glue the front stop to the leading edge of the base. Glue the tapered rails to the sled's base with the tall ends butted up against the stop. Glue the front support strips between the tall ends of the tapered strips. These strips support the front edge of the paddle while planing. Lay the paddle on the sled and frame the handle by gluing blocks on both sides and behind. This frame correctly positions the paddle on the sled.

Taper the paddle

Drill and countersink a hole in the end of the handle. When the paddle is finished, you can use this hole to hang it on the wall, but for now, use it to screw the paddle to the sled for added security (Photo 3).

Start planing (Photo 4), feeding the blade end first. Take light passes to avoid tear-out. Continue until the tip of the blade is ⅛" thick. Round the corners on the leading edge of the blade. At the top end of each accent strip, extend and fair the transitional curve from the blade piece to the handle. Round over the sharp edges and make the handle comfortable to hold (Photo 5). Use a sander or block plane to bevel the leading edge of the blade to ¹⁄₁₆" thick, or slightly less, so it's easy to get under the pizza (Photo 6). Finish sand and add a coat of food-safe mineral oil to beautify and protect the wood.

Figure A: Tapering Sled

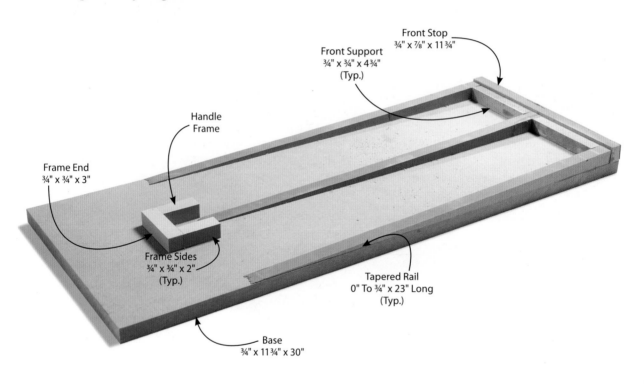

Front Stop
¾" x ⅞" x 11¾"

Front Support
¾" x ¾" x 4¾"
(Typ.)

Handle
Frame

Frame End
¾" x ¾" x 3"

Frame Sides
¾" x ¾" x 2"
(Typ.)

Tapered Rail
0" To ¾" x 23" Long
(Typ.)

Base
¾" x 11¾" x 30"

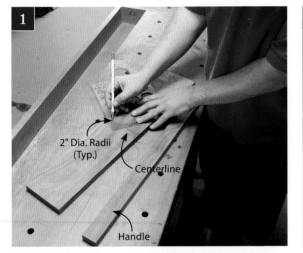

Cut the paddle's three main pieces from a single board. First, rip the handle. Then band saw the remaining section into the two side pieces, after marking radii on opposite sides of the centerline.

Add accent strips between the handle and the sides and glue the paddle together. The wide part that holds the pizza is called the "blade."

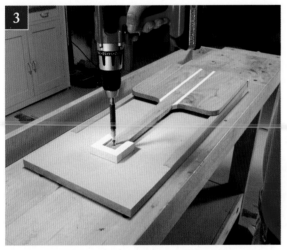

Install the paddle in the tapering sled. Secure it by driving a screw through a hanging hole drilled in the end of the handle.

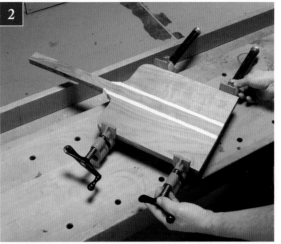

Taper the paddle using the planer. Take light passes until the blade's leading edge is ⅛" thick.

Ease the handle's sharp edges to create a comfortable grip.

Round the front corners of the blade and bevel its edge to slightly less than ¹⁄₁₆".

Index

Note: Page numbers in **bold** indicate projects.